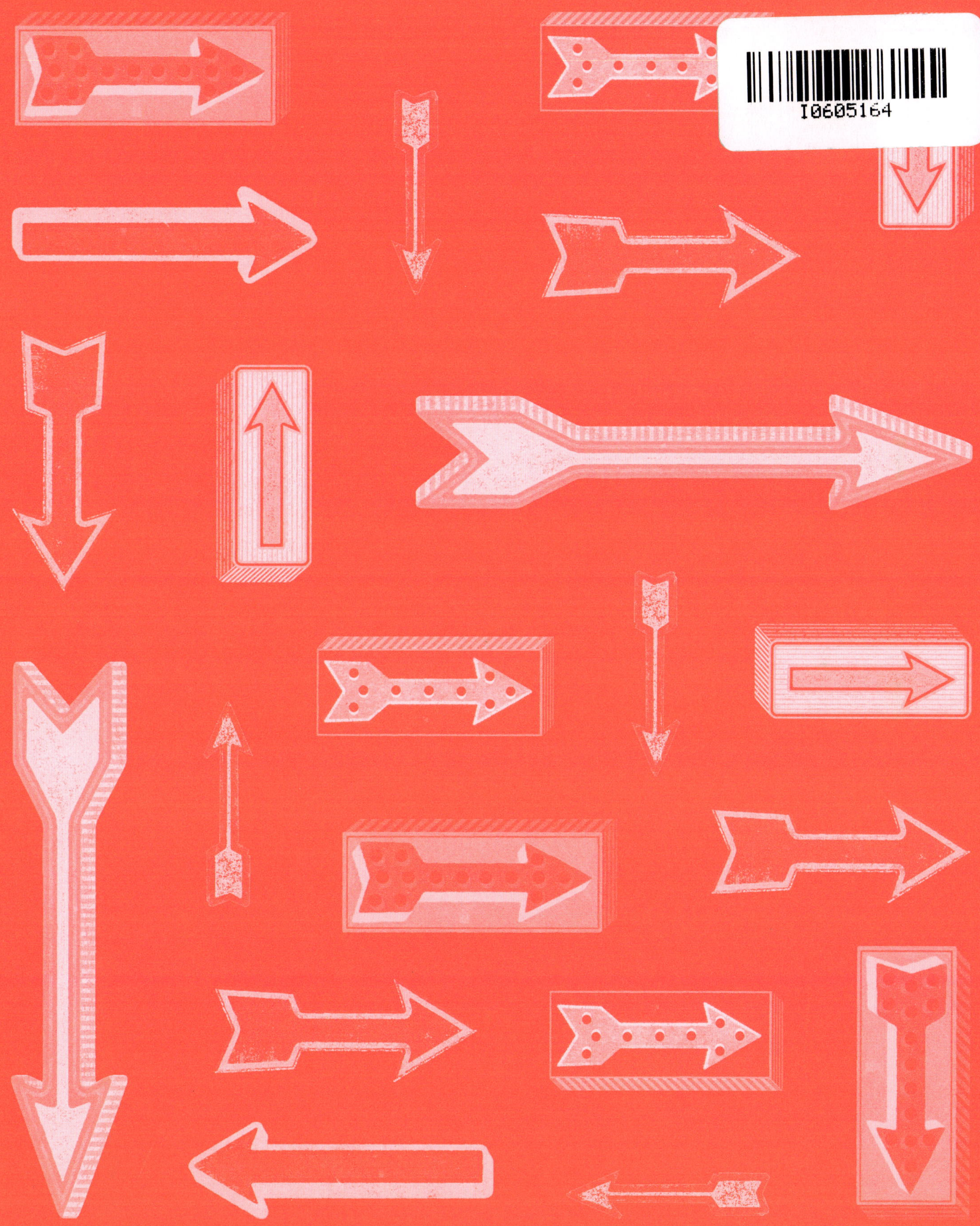

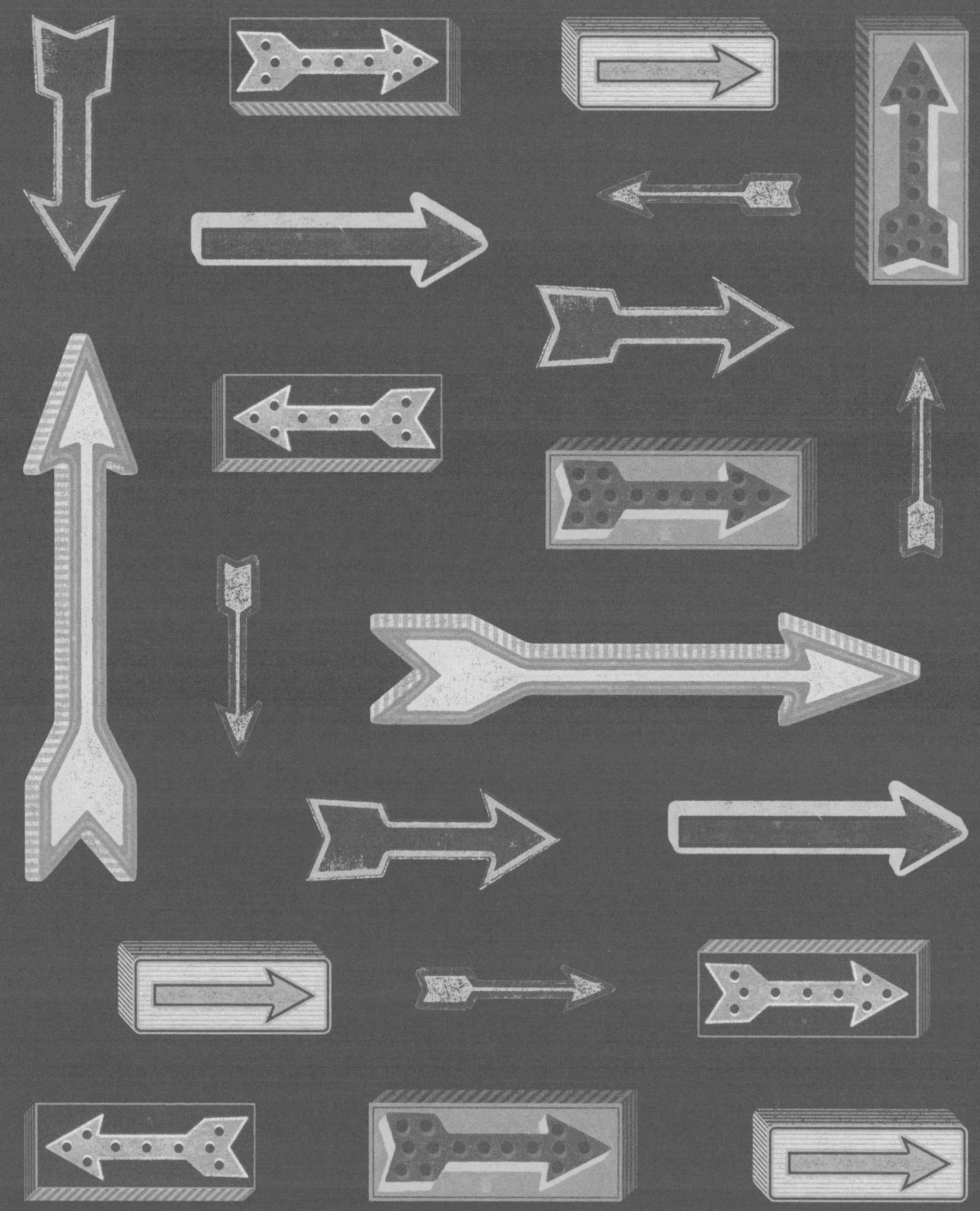

# ROUTE 66

## A TRIBUTE TO AN AMERICAN ICON

ROUTE
66
CONTAINS
LEAD

# ROUTE 66

## A TRIBUTE TO AN AMERICAN ICON

## INTRODUCTION
6

## THE ROUTE
10

## THE LOWDOWN
12

## 100 YEARS OF ROUTE 66
16

## PREPARING FOR YOUR ROAD TRIP
248

## INDEX
250

## ACKNOWLEDGMENTS
254


**PREVIOUS PAGE**
Vintage gas pumps sitting by the historic highway in Illinois

◆ ◆ ◆ ◆ ◆ ◆ ◆ ◆ ◆

ILLINOIS 18
MISSOURI 54
KANSAS 84
OKLAHOMA 100
TEXAS 136
NEW MEXICO 156
ARIZONA 188
CALIFORNIA 220

# INTRODUCTION

Route 66 might be one road, but its stories are truly endless. Buckle up as we hit the highway to celebrate a century of diners and drive-ins, motels and muffler men, not to mention the people who've worked tirelessly to preserve the Mother Road for generations to come.

When the Route 66 highway was established in 1926, no one, not even its visionary founders, Cyrus Avery and John T. Woodruff, could have imagined what it would become. Nor could they have foreseen the hold it would maintain on the popular imagination 100 years later.

Route 66 began, like all roads, as nothing more than a way to get people from Point A to Point B. And yet this simple stretch of highway eventually grew into America's greatest road trip, a 2,400-mile (3,862-km) thread stitching cities, towns, and open countryside together, all the way from the Great Lakes to the Pacific Ocean. Today, it passes through farming communities, old mining settlements, and ranchlands, through thick forests, open plains, and vast deserts. In short, it introduces America to itself. It's also seen as a place where the country's most prized values manifest. Setting off on the open road, just you and your motor, feels like the ultimate act of independence. There's also a certain sense of equality attached to traveling Route 66—destitute farmers escaping the Dust Bowl drove along this road, but so did Elvis. All this has made the highway an irresistible muse, inspiring movies, music, and literature that further burnished its reputation. Eight decades later, we're still humming the King Cole Trio's "(Get Your Kicks on) Route 66;" we still know exactly what John Steinbeck's coinage "the Mother Road" refers to.

Of course, as with anything so mythologized, some actual myth clings to the highway. For starters, there is no such thing as "Route 66," so to speak. From its very beginning, the highway was a half-paved hodgepodge of preexisting national, state, and local roads, and it was in constant flux during its lifetime, forever changing course as new pavement was laid or bridges were built. Nor did the highway's notions of freedom and equality always apply. In Route 66's heyday, many businesses refused to serve Black motorists, while Indigenous culture was typically seen as something to hawk to tourists, with little concern for accuracy.

**RIGHT**
Route 66 stretching through the desert as far as the eye can see in California

ROY'S
NO VACANCY
MOTEL
CAFE
ROUTE
US
66

**"Route 66 has endured through the ages, thanks to the people who have refused to let it disappear. Its story is their story, a tale of resilience."**

Times have changed, though, and today Route 66 road-trippers will find not just classic drive-ins, roadside motels, and offbeat attractions but also vibrant immigrant neighborhoods, thriving LGBTQ+ scenes, and museums dedicated to Indigenous histories and the Black experience. In fact, for all the 1950s nostalgia attached to the highway, there's probably never been a better time to drive it than right now, as renewed interest in the road (particularly thanks to its 2026 centenary) means that numerous historic sites have been restored and new attractions are poised to carry the country's most storied road into its second century.

Route 66 has endured through the ages, thanks to the people who have refused to let it disappear. Its story is their story, a tale of resilience, reinvention, and pride. Shuttered diners have been revived, ghost towns reawakened, and communities united to keep the spirit of the road alive. In essence, the Mother Road lives on because of those—past and present—who continue to preserve, protect, and pass on its legacy.

Trips on Route 66 are frequently envisioned as journeys west, following the country's expansion, and that's how we've structured this book. But to suggest that Chicago to Los Angeles is the only way to experience the highway wouldn't be in keeping with its spirit of going where you want, when you want. Route 66 is, in a literal sense, a two-way street, and driving west to east offers up an entirely different experience. Nor is driving the highway from start to finish in one go a prerequisite for Route 66 road trips. Tackling the journey in smaller chunks allows you to slow down and, ultimately, make your road trip last longer.

This is more than just a book about Route 66 history and its most iconic sites. It's a tribute to the Mother Road, its legacy, and all those who have shaped it. So come on, it's time to go get your own kicks on Route 66.

**ABOVE RIGHT**
A mural by artists from Diaz Sign Art adorning the Route 66 Hall of Fame & Museum in Pontiac, Illinois

**LEFT**
The iconic Roy's Motel and Café sign, dating from the 1930s, in the largely abandoned town of Amboy, California

# THE ROUTE

**TOTAL DISTANCE**
2,400 miles (3,862 km)

**TOTAL DRIVE TIME (NONSTOP)**
Approx. 35 hours

IDAHO

WYOMING

NEVADA

UTAH

COLORADO

CALIFORNIA

LOS ANGELES

FLAGSTAFF

SANTA FE

ALBUQUERQUE

ARIZONA

NEW MEXICO

PACIFIC
OCEAN

MEXICO

0 miles 200
0 km 200

NORTH

NORTH DAKOTA
SOUTH DAKOTA
MINNESOTA
WISCONSIN
Lake Michigan
IOWA
NEBRASKA
CHICAGO
ILLINOIS
MISSOURI
ST. LOUIS
KANSAS
TULSA
OKLAHOMA
OKLAHOMA CITY
AMARILLO
TENNESSEE
ARKANSAS
MISSISSIPPI
LOUISIANA
TEXAS
CANADA
USA
MEXICO
AREA OF MAP

# THE PLAYLISTS

 SOUNDS OF ROUTE 66 

As you prepare to drive Route 66 and discover its iconic sights, don't forget its equally iconic sounds.

All eight states along the Mother Road have inspired and produced artists across numerous genres, from jazz and art rock in Chicago to hip-hop and surf sounds on the California coast. America, in many ways, is mapped out in music.

For each state, we've selected a handful of songs that capture its unique musical heritage and connection to Route 66. Simply scan each code you see, and our playlist will transport you to the sounds of America's most influential road.

LISTEN ON 

# THE LOWDOWN

A Route 66 road trip is the perfect reminder that it's the journey—not the destination—that truly matters. Along this legendary highway, you'll encounter breathtaking scenery, historic towns and cities, and a whole host of weird and wonderful attractions. Here's just a taste of what awaits along the Mother Road.

## CITIES OF 66

From Chicago to Los Angeles, Route 66 links iconic cities shaped by migration, industry, and diverse cultures, each offering a unique snapshot of America's evolving identity.

## MUFFLER MEN

These friendly roadside giants are the ultimate roadside attraction. Some still advertise businesses, as they were first intended; others are simply reminders of 66's playful past.

## MUST-VISIT MUSEUMS

Sure, many highway towns have a museum dedicated to all-things Route 66, but you'll also discover collections devoted to cowboys, RVs, fast food, and even barbed wire.

## HERITAGE SITES

A road trip on Route 66 is a journey through history. Expect to encounter trapped-in-time 1940s villages, Civil War battlefields, and a former president's family home.

## DINERS AND DINING SPOTS

Stopping off at a diner is an essential road trip experience, but Route 66 plates up more than corn dogs and grilled cheese. Expect farm-to-table fare and home-cooked Indian specialties.

## SHOPS AND STORES

From handmade crafts to oddball antiques, Route 66 has plenty of places to browse, buy, and bring home a little piece of the Mother Road.

## ODDITIES AND AMERICANA

A giant ketchup bottle, half-buried Cadillacs, countless "trees" made from salvaged steel and glass bottles—spotting roadside curiosities is a highlight of any Route 66 road trip.

## INDIGENOUS HERITAGE

Route 66 passes through more than a dozen Indigenous nations, giving visitors a chance to discover the histories and cultures of those who first traversed these lands.

## NATURAL WONDERS

Some of America's most enchanting natural wonders cross the Mother Road's path. Make time to explore national parks, sinkholes, desert preserves, and cavern systems.

## HOTELS AND MOTELS

Is there anything more Route 66 than the flickering buzz of a neon "Vacancy" sign? Stop for the night in one of Route 66's classic hotels or kitsch motels.

# 100 YEARS OF ROUTE 66

**1921**

Congress passes the Federal-Aid Highway Act to create a national road network, leading to miles and miles of new highway and improved safety.

**1926**

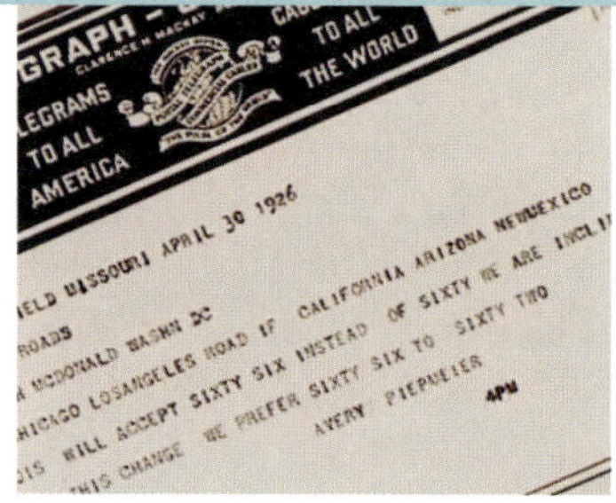


The Federal Highway System is launched, creating a nationwide road numbering system. Route 66 is officially born on November 11.

**1946**

Bobby Troup composes "(Get Your Kicks on) Route 66," and the King Cole Trio, led by Nat King Cole, releases its iconic rendition of the song.

**1949**

Three years after first inventing the corn dog, Ed Waldmire opens the Cozy Dog Drive In *(p36)* on Route 66 in Springfield, Illinois.

**1956**

President Eisenhower signs another Federal-Aid Highway Act to support the interstate highway system, sounding the death knell of Route 66.

**1960–1964**

The TV series *Route 66* follows two men traversing the country in a Chevrolet Corvette convertible, bringing the road into American living rooms.

**1962**

The first muffler man, a lumberjack holding an axe, is erected at the Paul Bunyan Cafe on Route 66 in Flagstaff, Arizona *(p209)*.

**1984**

The last stretch of Route 66 to be unaffected by the Interstate finally succumbs when it's bypassed by I-40 in Williams, Arizona.

**1929**

The landmark Chain of Rocks Bridge is constructed over the Mississippi River. Seven years later, Route 66 is rerouted over the bridge.

**1931–1940**

Hundreds of thousands of people fleeing the Dust Bowl migrate to California along Route 66, cementing the highway in the national consciousness.

**1937**

New Mexico's portion of Route 66 is rerouted to bypass Santa Fe and head straight to Albuquerque via a more direct route.

**1938**

In Oldham County, Texas, the last section of Route 66 is paved, making it the first highway in the U.S. to be completely paved.

**1939**

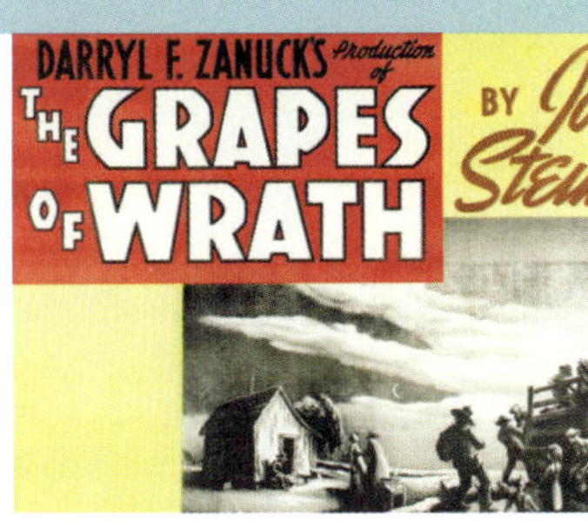


John Steinbeck proclaims Route 66 "the Mother Road" in his novel *The Grapes of Wrath*, giving the highway its most indelible nickname.

**1941**

Truck traffic between Chicago and St. Louis quintuples compared to a decade earlier, a sign of Route 66's economic and commercial importance.

**1985**

Route 66 is officially decommissioned. Motorists driving from Chicago to Santa Monica are instead served by I-55, I-44, I-40, I-15, and I-10.

**1999**

The National Park Service establishes the Route 66 Corridor Preservation Program, helping those who want to preserve the highway's historic sites.

**2026**

Route 66 celebrates its 100th birthday in the same year that the U.S. marks the 250th anniversary of the Declaration of Independence.

# ILLINOIS

It all starts in Illinois. Start your engine amid the skyscrapers of downtown Chicago, the traditional departure point for a Route 66 road trip, before shooting through the suburbs and southwest across the heart of the state. This portion of 66 roughly follows an old Indigenous route that once linked Lake Michigan and the Mississippi River. As you make your way toward St. Louis, the highway serves up history in abundance, especially in the state capital of Springfield, where Black history and the legacy of Abraham Lincoln abound. Between cities, the highway rolls through the Midwest's agricultural heartland, traversing small farming communities and fields of corn and soybeans. Scattered amid these rural scenes are some of 66's most kitschy curiosities, including a giant spaceman and the world's largest bottle of ketchup.

CATSUP
GREEN-BOOK
A Classified
MOTORIST'S & TOURIST'S GUIDE

# ILLINOIS

**DISTANCE**
303 miles (488 km)

**DRIVE TIME (NONSTOP)**
Approx. 7½ hours

**LANDSCAPE**
Chicago's vast urban sprawl gradually gives way to mile upon mile of flat farmland punctuated by small towns.

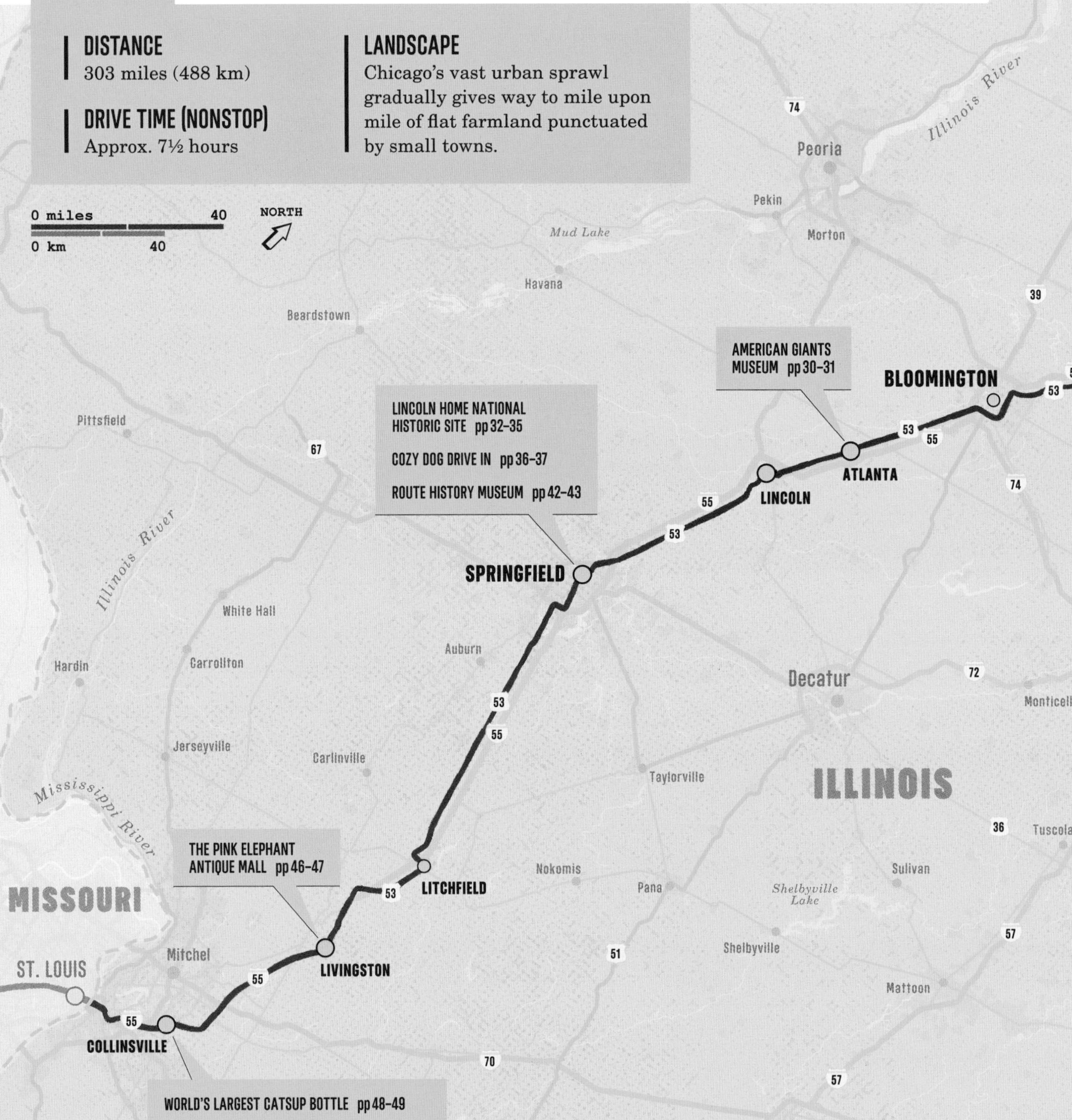

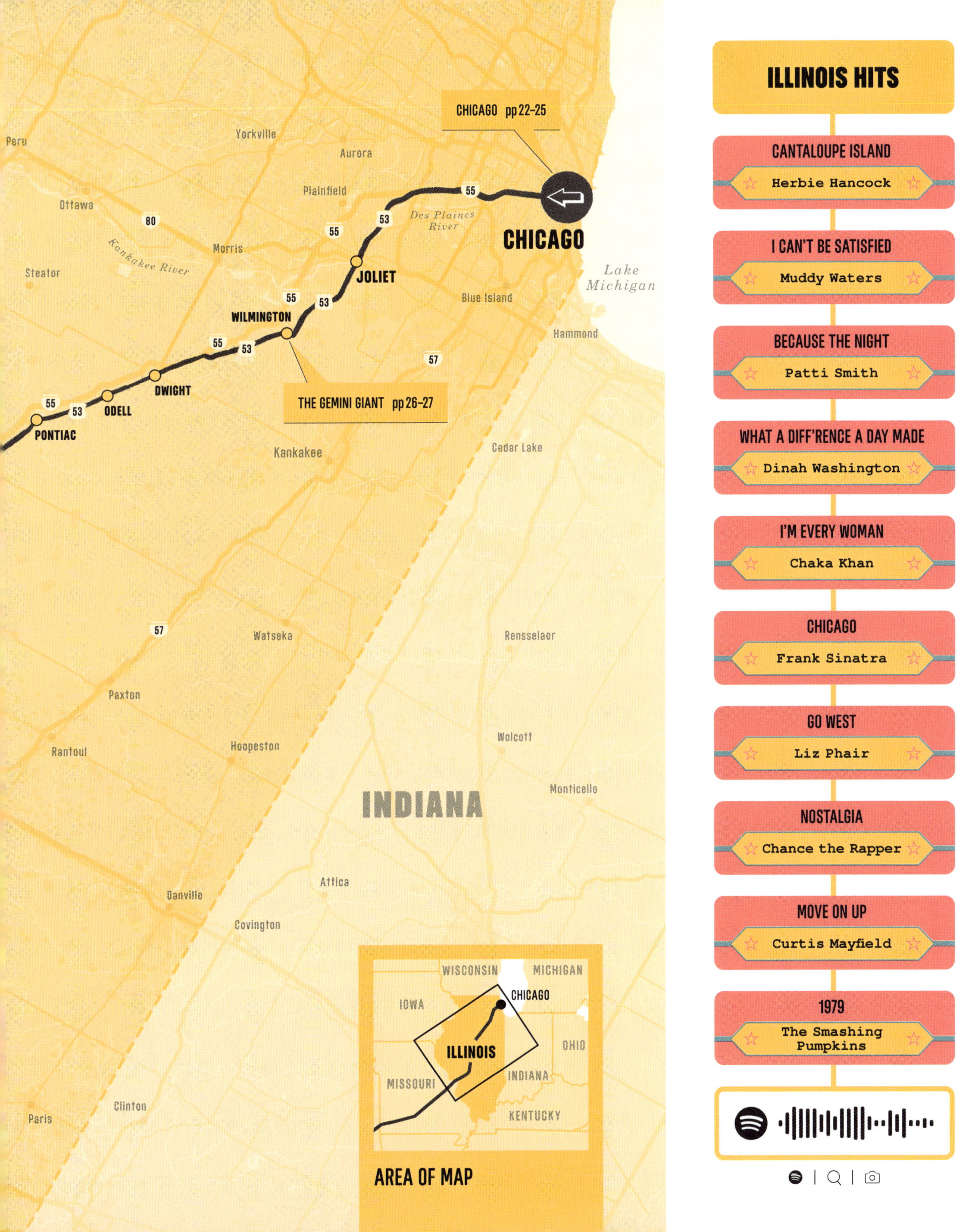

CHICAGO pp 22–25
Peru
Yorkville
Aurora
Plainfield
Ottawa
80
55
53
Des Plaines River
CHICAGO
Kankakee River
Morris
Steator
JOLIET
Lake Michigan
Blue Island
WILMINGTON
Hammond
57
DWIGHT
ODELL
PONTIAC
THE GEMINI GIANT pp 26–27
Kankakee
Cedar Lake
Watseka
Rensselaer
Paxton
Wolcott
Rantoul
Hoopeston
Monticello
INDIANA
Attica
Danville
Covington
Clinton
Paris
WISCONSIN
MICHIGAN
IOWA
CHICAGO
ILLINOIS
OHIO
MISSOURI
INDIANA
KENTUCKY
AREA OF MAP
ILLINOIS HITS
CANTALOUPE ISLAND
Herbie Hancock
I CAN'T BE SATISFIED
Muddy Waters
BECAUSE THE NIGHT
Patti Smith
WHAT A DIFF'RENCE A DAY MADE
Dinah Washington
I'M EVERY WOMAN
Chaka Khan
CHICAGO
Frank Sinatra
GO WEST
Liz Phair
NOSTALGIA
Chance the Rapper
MOVE ON UP
Curtis Mayfield
1979
The Smashing Pumpkins

# CHICAGO

CITIES OF 66

Before it becomes the legendary open road, Route 66 begins with an urban cruise through the heart of Chicago. Combining ambitious architecture and blue-collar roots, immigrant enclaves and historic eateries, the city is the ideal introduction to a road trip across America.

It's fitting that Route 66, the great American road, starts in what the writer and journalist Norman Mailer deemed "the great American city." Both a city of beauty and industry, Chicago is at once home to the country's most magnificent architecture and to the railyards and factories that saw another literary luminary, the poet Carl Sandburg, anoint it the "City of the Big Shoulders." Anchoring the Midwest, Chicago is rooted in the American interior, but it has long rivaled its coastal peers as a kaleidoscopic tapestry of nations, attracting immigrants from the likes of Poland, Mexico, and all points in between. In short, if you want to find America, you can find it here, which makes Chicago the perfect place to kick off a drive across the country.

**ABOVE**
Begin here: a road sign at the start of Route 66

**RIGHT**
The heart of industrious downtown Chicago

## THE START OF 66

Route 66 begins downtown, at the corner of Michigan and Adams. It ends, for anyone driving the route from west to east, a block south, a quirk that owes itself to Chicago's maze of one-way streets. Until those traffic patterns were fixed in the 1950s, however, Route 66's end was also its beginning, with cars setting off on the long drive to L.A. from the corner of Michigan and Jackson.

Those first few blocks couldn't be more different from the Route 66 of popular imagination. Instead of open highway and open sky, the beginning of 66 is a claustrophobic drive through a canyon of towering skyscrapers that cast the pavement in nearly perpetual shadow. The buildings themselves, however, are beacons of design. Along Adams alone are several structures that show off inventive Chicago's architectural style and diversity. There's the architect Ludwig Mies van der Rohe's elegant

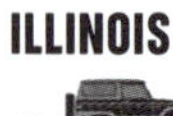

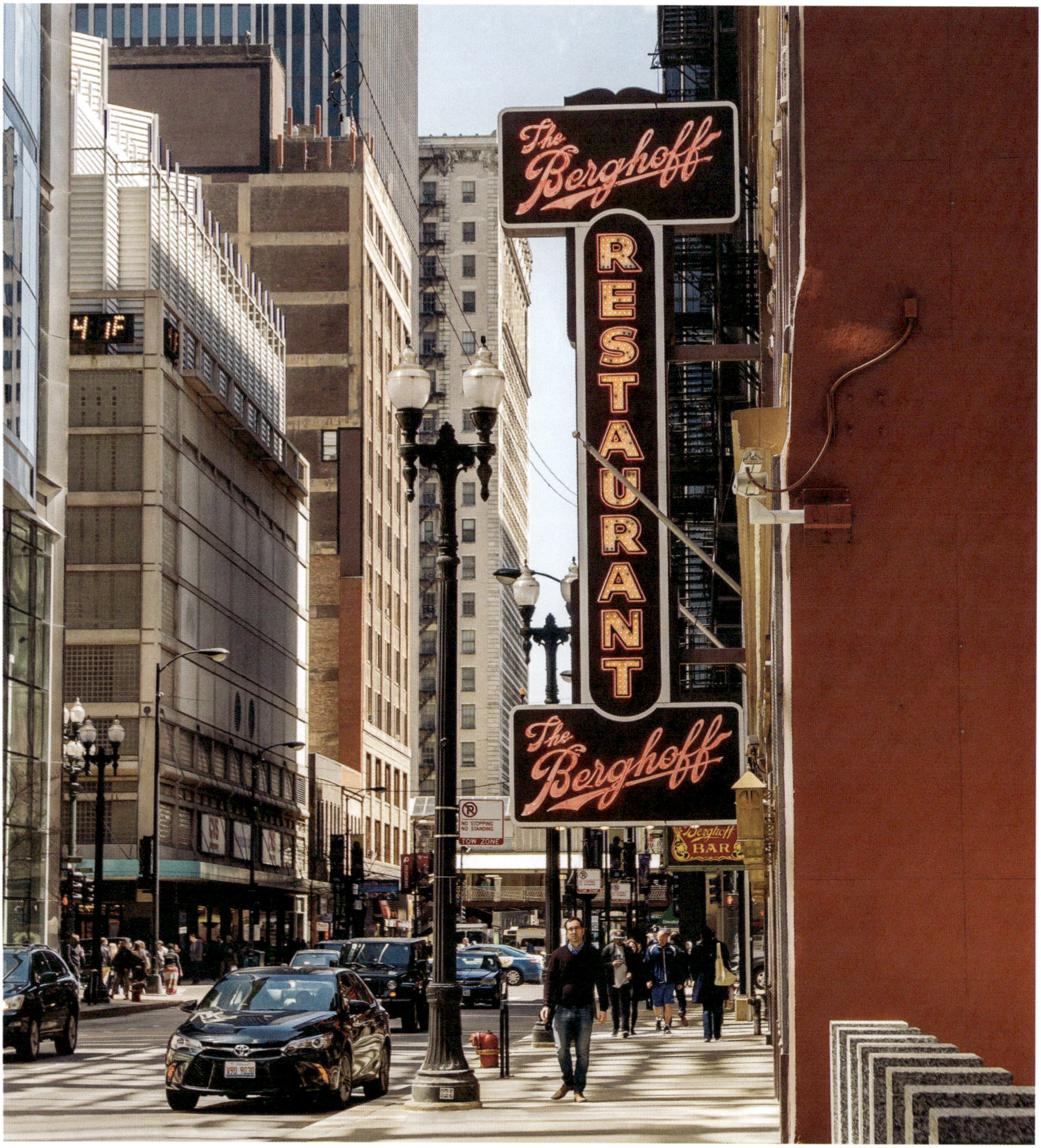
The Berghoff
RESTAURANT
The Berghoff
41F
NO STOPPING NO STANDING
TOW ZONE
Berghoff BAR

and efficient Federal Center, an exemplar of the sleek International Style. It stands in stark contrast with the Rookery, on the very next block. Stately and sturdy, the Rookery's redbrick and terracotta exterior conceals an airy atrium designed by the great American architect Frank Lloyd Wright. When the 11-story building opened in 1888, it was one of the tallest in the world. Of course, it was eventually dwarfed by Chicago's most famous building and skyscraper, the Willis Tower, just a couple of blocks farther along. When the 110-story, black behemoth was completed (and first named the Sears Tower) in 1974, it was the tallest building in the world, reaching 1,451 ft (442 m). It was knocked off the top spot in 1998, when the Petronas Towers in Kuala Lumpur snatched the title, but remains the third-tallest building in the western hemisphere.

**LEFT**
Vintage signage for the Berghoff beer hall

**BELOW**
Locals kicking back on Peoria Street, Fulton Market District

## LOU MITCHELL'S AND THE BERGHOFF

In downtown Chicago, instances of Route 66's more typical attractions appear. Fronting Jackson Boulevard on the "inbound" 66 is Lou Mitchell's. Established in 1923, three years before the highway, it's as fine an example of the all-American diner as any you'll find on the route. A big red neon sign scrawls the restaurant's name above the door, usually with a letter or two burnt out, while inside, hungry customers receive complimentary donut holes, and eggs are served in skillets.

Up on Adams, the Berghoff is even older. A German immigrant and onetime performer in Buffalo Bill's Wild West Show named Herman Berghoff opened the historic beer hall in 1898, selling taps for a nickel. The Berghoff pivoted to German staples like schnitzel and sauerbraten during Prohibition, but when the ban on alcohol was lifted in 1933, it was the first in line to get a liquor license from the city. The Berghoff's promptness has become a local tradition, with city hall awarding the venue Chicago's first license each year.

## OPPORTUNITY'S PROMISE

Exiting downtown, Route 66 runs through Chicago's trendy West Loop neighborhood. Once a meatpacking district, the area and its warehouses have been transformed into boutique hotels, stylish shops, and many of the city's best restaurants. It's also the site of one of Chicago's historic immigrant enclaves, Greektown, where Greek restaurants and the National Hellenic Museum remind travelers of the population's impact on American culture.

When 66 leaves the West Loop, it makes a beeline southwest on Ogden Avenue. In 66's heyday, this was a major artery in and out of the city, and the surrounding neighborhoods became home to a number of immigrant communities over the years—Italian, Russian Jewish, Czechoslovakian, Polish, Mexican—each searching for the opportunity that the country, the city, and, in microcosm, the highway promised.

# THE GEMINI GIANT

MUFFLER MEN

WILMINGTON

## The Space Age never quite ended in Wilmington. Whether he's a visitor from another world or just a supersized spaceman from ours, the Gemini Giant possesses serious star power as one of the Mother Road's most recognizable muffler men.

Standing on an island in the Kankakee River, miles from the nearest spaceport, and 60 miles (97 km) southwest of Chicago, the Gemini Giant looks more than a little lost. Dressed in an emerald green jumpsuit, wearing a space helmet resembling a welder's mask, and holding a silver rocket in his outstretched hands, he forever seems to be waiting for someone to come beam him up.

Until that happens, though, he'll remain one of the most iconic and out-of-this-world muffler men on Route 66. These giant fiberglass statues were popular marketing tools in the 1960s and early 70s, used to promote everything from hot dog stands to the muffler shops that eventually gave them their name. They largely disappeared with the rise of the Interstates, but some still stand along smaller highways.

The Gemini Giant was built in 1965 for the Launching Pad, a casual restaurant that used to sit where Route 66 enters Wilmington. A local elementary school ran a competition to officially name the 23-ft (7-m) fellow, with winner Cathy Thomas taking inspiration from the NASA Gemini space program, which sought to land astronauts on the moon. The Giant tempted motorists to stop for a Launching Pad burger until 2023, when the restaurant closed and he was put up for sale. It wasn't long before the Joliet Area Historical Museum used a state grant to purchase the much-loved spaceman for $275,000 in 2024. After a thorough restoration, he was donated by the museum to the city of Wilmington and installed in his current location, less than a mile down the road from where he first touched down.

**RIGHT**
Wilmington's space-inspired muffler man, standing at 23 ft (7 m)

5422

# JOEL BAKER

Founder of the American Giants Museum

No bit of Route 66 Americana looms larger than muffler men, and no one has done more to preserve the legacy of these giants than Joel Baker. An audio tech and videographer, Baker lives in Colorado but spends a good portion of his time traveling the country, tracking down and restoring muffler men that have disappeared or fallen into disrepair.

Muffler men, like Wilmington's Gemini Giant *(p26)*, were once a common sight on Route 66, but the advent of the Interstate rendered them obsolete as advertising tools, and most were taken down. Some were destroyed or discarded, but the fates of many have remained a mystery. Since 2011, Baker has spent thousands of hours poring over newspaper archives and social media, fielding tips, and driving across the U.S. to find them. Rarely is it a straightforward process. "From hearing about a muffler man to finding it can be 10 years in some cases," Baker says.

Through his efforts, Baker has become arguably the world's foremost authority on muffler men. He documents his work and the history of muffler men on his website, American Giants, and a YouTube channel of the same name. In 2024, he helped found the American Giants Museum *(p30)* in Atlanta, Illinois, which displays muffler men and artifacts from his own personal collection. "I think the value of muffler men is the difference they make to our road trips," he says. "They just add a special spark and joy to your adventures."

# AMERICAN GIANTS MUSEUM

MUST-VISIT MUSEUMS

ATLANTA

**ABOVE**
Muffler man resembling the mascot of satirical magazine, *Mad*

**RIGHT**
The museum forecourt, designed to look like a Texaco gas station

Bigger is always better at the American Giants Museum in the tiny town of Atlanta. The brainchild of muffler man researcher Joel Baker, it celebrates the legacy of these giant, mid-century icons of Americana with displays and refurbished statues.

Nowhere has as many muffler men as the elfin town of Atlanta. Two hours from Wilmington, along a stretch of the old highway, past cornfields and small farming communities, this former railroad town feels like a Route 66 film set, with nostalgic gift shops and fast-fading murals painted on brick facades. Running right through downtown, Arch Street formed part of 66's original layout, and it's where travelers will find the largest collection of muffler men on the route.

Along with Joel Baker *(p29),* the American Giants Museum was established by the Atlanta Betterment Fund (ABF), a local small business organization. "Baker had giants, he had body parts, he had artifacts, but what he didn't have was a museum," says Bill Thomas of the ABF. "So I said, 'OK, Joel, one day, we'll work on it for you.'" Designed to look like a vintage Texaco station, the museum houses information boards with photographs, muffler men parts, and documents from International Fiberglass, the California company that built the prominent statues. Installed on the grounds outside are the museum's marquee attractions: a gap-toothed Happy Halfwit-style muffler man, resembling the old *Mad* magazine mascot Alfred E. Neuman, and a Texaco Big Friend. The latter is especially notable. Of the 300 Big Friends that International Fiberglass produced for the service station chain, only six are left. The museum plans to install more muffler men, but its giants aren't the only ones here in Atlanta, Illinois. Across the street is a muffler man holding an enormous hot dog, and just down the road, the Country-Aire Restaurant is home to a 19-ft (5.8-m) waitress who tempts passing drivers with a gigantic apple pie.

AMERICAN GIANTS
Museum
TEXACO
OPEN
ENTRANCE

# LINCOLN HOME NATIONAL HISTORIC SITE

HERITAGE SITES

SPRINGFIELD

Less than an hour's drive from the American Giants Museum, Springfield is a major stop on Route 66. It was here that Abraham Lincoln lived for more than two decades before becoming president, and it's where travelers can encounter the life and legacy of the country's greatest statesman.

When Abraham Lincoln moved to Springfield on April 15, 1837, he was 28 years old, a lawyer, and a second-term legislator in the Illinois General Assembly. Yet despite the distinction of his profession, he arrived in town with his belongings packed into just two saddlebags. It was in Springfield that Lincoln truly came of age. The year after his arrival, he won his third Assembly term, and a year after that, he met Mary Todd, the daughter of a wealthy Kentucky family. The two were married by the Reverend Charles Dresser in 1842, and in 1844, they bought a home—the Reverend Dresser's, in fact—on the corner of Eighth and Jackson for $1,500. It was the only home Lincoln ever owned. He lived there until 1861, when he left to take up residence in the White House as the United States's 16th president.

When Route 66 was laid out, some six decades after Lincoln's election, its course ran just west of his former home. Today, the house and the surrounding four blocks have been restored to appear as they did in 1860, and together they form the Lincoln Home National Historic Site, one of the most historically significant places on the highway.

The Lincoln home was one-and-a-half stories tall and had five rooms when it was built in 1839. Over the course of the 17 years he lived there,

LEFT
Visitors meandering around outside Abraham Lincoln's picturesque home, Springfield

## "Lincoln's exalted place in American history can make it hard to imagine him as Abe from down the block."

Lincoln remodeled and expanded it, adding a full second story and a master bedroom suite. A handsome tan structure with dark green shutters, the home mixes Greek Revival and Italianate designs. Inside, it reveals not only how life was lived in the mid-19th century but also particulars of Lincoln's political rise. A top hat hangs on a coat rack in the entryway. Off the hall, a wood-burning stove and candelabras accent the parlor, where Lincoln met with fellow politicians and, on May 19, 1860, received the Republican Party's formal offer to be its presidential candidate. Presumably, his young sons missed the historic moment, as they weren't allowed in the room, lest they damage the expensive furniture. Upstairs, the master suite was divided into separate bedrooms for Lincoln and Mary, a common practice among the era's upper-middle-class households. Lincoln's room contains a four-poster bed, a wardrobe, a dresser, and a small desk, where he likely composed his famed "House Divided" speech. Delivered at the 1858 Republican State Convention, it warned of the danger inherent in a country split between free states and slave states.

Lincoln's exalted place in American history can make it hard to imagine him as Abe from down the block, but the National Historic Site makes it

**ABOVE LEFT**
The cozy parlor, where Lincoln met politicians

**ABOVE RIGHT**
Lincoln's writing desk in his bedroom

apparent that, in Springfield at least, he was just that. The Lincoln home isn't particularly grander than any of the other dozen houses around it, and the neighbors represented a cross section of American life: farmers, schoolteachers, bricklayers, and geologists. The monumentality of Lincoln's life is easier to perceive at several other Springfield sites. A few blocks away, there's the reconstructed Old State Capitol, where 75,000 mourners gathered as Lincoln's body lay in state after his 1865 assassination. Then there's the Abraham Lincoln Presidential Museum, which displays an original handwritten copy of Lincoln's Gettysburg Address and the pen he used to sign the Emancipation Proclamation. Finally, there's the grand Lincoln Tomb, where Lincoln's body rests alongside those of his wife and three of their sons.

Lincoln may never have made it back to Springfield after leaving for Washington, but his imprint on the city is so pronounced and he looms so large in the American imagination that it can feel as if something of him—his spirit, his ideals, his agonies—is still here. It's the inescapable presence the poet Vachel Lindsay, a Springfield native, channeled in the poem "Abraham Lincoln Walks at Midnight," penned 50 years after Lincoln's death and still relevant a century later:

*He cannot sleep upon his hillside now.*
*He is among us:—as in times before!*

**BELOW LEFT**
Abraham Lincoln with devoted followers outside his home, 1860

**BELOW RIGHT**
The Lincoln Tomb, the final resting place of Abraham Lincoln

# COZY DOG DRIVE IN

DINERS AND DINING SPOTS

SPRINGFIELD

**ABOVE**
The Cozy Dog's two mascot corn dogs hugging atop a road sign; the diner's simple exterior

**RIGHT**
Route 66 paraphernalia and more hugging corn dogs inside the diner

It's not all presidential heritage here in Springfield—take the Cozy Dog Drive In on the southern side of the city. Plenty of Route 66 diners can claim a long history, nostalgic retro decor, or even a list of celebrity guests. But only one can claim to have invented the corn dog.

The sign on the roof of the nondescript diner just says "FOOD." Inside, the walls are plastered with Route 66 memorabilia, and Formica-topped tables hold red and yellow bottles of ketchup and mustard. Close to the door is a large wooden cutout of two embracing frankfurters, clearly in love—a motif that reoccurs around the diner.

Welcome to the Cozy Dog Drive In, a storied locale in the history of American cuisine. To understand why, you have to go back more than eight decades, to when a young man named Ed Waldmire came across a hot dog baked in corn bread at a roadside diner in Muskogee, Oklahoma. It was good, but, as Waldmire complained to his friend Don Strand, it took too long to make. Fast-forward a few years to 1946, and Waldmire is serving in the Air Force at Amarillo Airfield when he gets a call from Strand saying that he's solved their hot dog problem. Strand sends Waldmire some of the mix he's engineered to stick to a dog while it's deep-fried, and Waldmire, using cocktail forks for sticks, the military kitchen for a lab, and the ample spare time afforded by the Pax Americana, perfects the recipe. Thus, to the long list of U.S. military inventions—duct tape, the microwave oven, the internet—we can add the corn dog.

Waldmire and Strand initially called their invention a "crusty cur" (cur meaning a mongrel), but Waldmire's wife, having more marketing sense than her husband, suggested a more tempting name was in order. They settled on "cozy dogs." Waldmire began selling them at the Lake Springfield Beach House in 1946 and opened the Cozy Dog Drive In on Route 66 three years later. The beloved diner has been in the family ever since, and while it did move to a new location on S. 6th Street on Springfield's south side in 1996, it's still serving travelers the same sausages on a stick just as it first did 80 years ago.

COZY DOG
ICE COLD
Pepsi-Cola
5¢
MOTOR OIL
GOODYEAR
BELTS & HOSE
BAN SEMI-AUTOMATICS
Make the Streets Safe For Criminals
BL8ANT 2
ROUTE
66
75TH ANNIVERSARY
LAND OF LINCOLN
COZY
DOGS
66
USA 200
104
65
LINCOLNFEST
Phillips
66

PEOPLE OF THE ROAD

PEOPLE OF THE ROAD

# BOB WALDMIRE

Artist and Cartographer

No one lived a life more deeply connected to Route 66 than Bob Waldmire. Born in St. Louis in 1945, he grew up in Springfield, where his parents ran the famed Cozy Dog Drive In *(p36)*. After college, Waldmire hit the road, traveling the country in an orange Volkswagen van and selling his pen-and-ink drawings and maps to anyone who'd buy them. His love affair with Route 66 began in 1987 when, stuck in traffic on the Interstate, he took an exit and set off on the Mother Road. He'd spend the next four years traveling the highway, drawing, creating a Route 66 map, and encouraging efforts to preserve the recently decommissioned road.

Waldmire divided his later years between Illinois and Arizona, where he reopened a general store in the Route 66 ghost town of Hackberry. Whether he was in the Midwest, the Southwest, or on the road somewhere in between, he continued to make artwork and to champion Route 66 preservation efforts. Appropriately, the inveterate traveler's vehicles grew as famous as his drawings. His VW van became the inspiration for the character Fillmore in the Pixar film *Cars (p90)*, while his other vehicle was one of the most recognizable on American highways: a 1966 school bus that Waldmire converted into a mobile home and that resembled a cabin on wheels. Both are on display at the Route 66 Association of Illinois Hall of Fame and Museum in Pontiac.

Waldmire continues to remain a part of Route 66. After he died, of cancer, in 2009, his ashes were divided between the family burial plot, his home in Arizona's Chiricahua Mountains, and Route 66's endpoints in Chicago and Santa Monica.

DO NOT PULL ON
DUCK!

HISTORY

# THE GREEN BOOK

A car, the open road, half of the country to explore—Route 66 road trips have often stood as shorthand for freedom. But not everyone experienced the highway the same way.

When Route 66 was inaugurated, many states and localities enforced segregationist Jim Crow laws, often forbidding Black American people from using the same train cars, drinking fountains, or textbooks as white people. Even in places without explicit Jim Crow laws, it was frequently made clear that Black travelers were not welcome. In the route's early years, roughly half of the communities along 66 were all-white. Many destinations along the route were so-called sundown towns, where Black citizens were expected to leave by dark or risk being subjected to intimidation or violence. Such towns weren't limited to the South, either. More than 100 existed in Illinois alone.

To aid his fellow Black travelers, Victor Hugo Green, a postal employee in Harlem, began publishing a guidebook listing hotels, restaurants, salons, gas stations, and other businesses that were either owned by Black individuals or provided service to Black travelers. The first edition, published in 1936 as *The Negro Motorist Green Book*, only ran across ten pages and was limited to Green's native New York City. But by soliciting input from Black colleagues in the postal service, Green expanded the guide to include thousands of listings across the entire country.

**1** Citizens protesting Jim Crow laws outside a bus depot

**2** El Rey Court in Santa Fe, one of the few businesses listed in the Green Book that's still in operation today

**3** The 1940 edition of the Green Book, which featured an updated list of lodgings and other amenities for Black motorists

**4** Postal employee Victor Hugo Green, creator and author of the Green Book

**5** A train passenger waiting outside a segregated railroad station waiting room

At its peak, the guide sold some 15,000 copies per year. While it underwent several name changes, it was most often known to travelers simply as the Green Book.

In Route 66's early decades, no travel companion was as essential to Black motorists as the Green Book—the importance of having a copy in the glove compartment is hard to overstate. Without it, Black travelers risked finding themselves in dangerous situations or having to go without food or lodging while on the road. To give an idea of the difficulty of simply finding a place to stay, in 1955, just six out of 100 motels in Albuquerque, New Mexico, admitted Black guests. In some smaller towns, that number was zero. In those places, the Green Book listed private homes where the owner could instead rent out rooms.

Jim Crow laws finally came to an end in 1964, when Congress passed the Civil Rights Act, outlawing racial discrimination. The last edition of the Green Book was published two years later. Most of the businesses the guidebook listed have since disappeared, but a handful still operate along Route 66, including El Rey Court in Santa Fe *(p171)*; La Posada Hotel in Winslow, Arizona *(p200)*; and Clifton's Restaurant in Los Angeles *(p243)*.

# ROUTE HISTORY MUSEUM

MUST-VISIT MUSEUMS

**SPRINGFIELD**

Springfield's Route History Museum is dedicated to the Black experience on Route 66, exploring the difficulties Black American motorists faced on the road, but also the joys and opportunities that could be found on the highway.

There is a wealth of museums along Route 66 that explore the highway's story, but Springfield's Route History Museum is particularly unique and significant. Owned by Drs. Gina Lathan and Stacy Grundy *(p45)*, the museum is dedicated to the often-overlooked experience of Black travelers.

Route History opened just a block from 66 in downtown Springfield in 2019. The building was originally an Esso gas station, which is appropriate, as the company (now ExxonMobil) was one of the era's most Black-friendly businesses, welcoming Black motorists, allowing Black entrepreneurs to own franchises, and selling copies of the Green Book *(p40)*. More generally, Springfield was the first reliably safe spot for Black travelers setting out on Route 66 from Chicago, as many of the towns in between were sundown towns, where Black citizens were not welcome after dark. As the museum explains, once in Springfield, Black motorists could find lodging, food, and entertainment at places like Cansler's Lounge, a jazz club that hosted the likes of Ella Fitzgerald. A virtual reality setup allows visitors to experience Route 66 as various Black travelers might have, including a Negro League baseball team and a family joining the Great Migration (the 20th-century movement of Black American people from the South to northern cities).

Displays about Springfield's Black history give context to the story of Black citizens and travelers on Route 66 in Illinois. Take William Donnegan, who made shoes for Abraham Lincoln and helped enslaved people escape on the Underground Railroad. And then there's Eva Carroll Monroe, founder of the Lincoln Colored Home, the first orphanage in Illinois that cared for Black children. Ample space is also devoted to the 1908 Springfield Race Riot, when a white mob destroyed the homes of two Black citizens and lynched two Black men. The tragedy helped spur the creation of the National Association for the Advancement of Colored People (NAACP), the country's oldest civil rights organization.

**ABOVE**
A detailed mural and informative road signs outside the museum

**LEFT**
Black-and-white photographs illustrating the Black experience

## "The museum is dedicated to the often-overlooked experience of Black travelers."

1947
GREEN-BOOK
ESTABLISHED 1936
A Classified
MOTORIST'S & TOURIST'S GUIDE
Covering the United States

PEOPLE OF THE ROAD

# ☆ DR. STACY GRUNDY & DR. GINA LATHAN ☆

Co-owners of the Route History Museum

When Dr. Gina Lathan approached her cousin Dr. Stacy Grundy about opening a Route 66 museum, she said she wanted to focus it on the Black experience. Co-owners and co-CEOs of the Route History Museum, Lathan and Grundy are both Illinois natives, both have backgrounds in public health and advocacy, and both grew up hearing about Black history from their parents and grandparents. “It wasn’t until we started Route History that I started making the connections between Black history and Route 66,” says Grundy. “I never saw my story in that road.” Though, ironically, both Lathan’s and Grundy’s families were part of that story, having made some of their journey from Mississippi to Illinois during the Great Migration on Route 66. They’d also experienced many of the era’s hardships, having lived in the era of segregation and sundown towns.

Telling the stories of families like theirs, and filling in the too-often forgotten gap in Route 66’s history, has become Lathan’s and Grundy’s mission. “With Route 66, usually you just hear about things like muscle cars and road trips, but the Black experience was very different,” Grundy says. “It was about strategy and getting to where you needed to go, even though it was still a road of opportunity for those families that drove it. Through Route History, we’ve been able to tell a fuller story.”

# THE PINK ELEPHANT ANTIQUE MALL

SHOPS AND STORES

LIVINGSTON

Yes, that is a pink elephant, and no, you're not hallucinating. This gigantic antique mall is Route 66's best place to shop for the weird and wonderful, or just to snap a cheesy photo with its outsize collection of oddball objects.

**ABOVE**
The kitsch ice-cream cone exterior of the delectably named Twistee Treats Diner

A word of advice: clear some space in your trunk before you visit the Pink Elephant Antique Mall. Enter this high church of tchotchkes, this Taj Mahal of trinkets, and you're liable to leave with a weathervane, some Elvis art, a few old Coca-Cola signs, and who knows what else. After an hour spent driving through southern Illinois's hypnotically unending cornfields, the Pink Elephant appears like a mirage on the roadside. Open only since 2005, it has established itself as one of Route 66's newest can't-miss stops by following a familiar formula: larger-than-life attractions, lots of stuff to buy, and classic eats.

In the grounds outside the mall, visitors encounter a muscular muffler man in a Harley-Davidson shirt and his slimmer (but still 20-ft/6-m) buddy, dressed in white shorts and a pink T-shirt, seemingly on his way to Miami Beach. There's the titular pink elephant statue, too, of course, plus a giraffe, a dinosaur, and a mascot for the Big Boy restaurant chain, because why not? Most unusually, there's what looks like a flying saucer, which is actually a Futuro Pod, one of fewer than 100 prefabricated homes designed by the Finnish architect Matti Suuronen in the 1960s and 70s.

Inside, the antique mall covers 30,000 sq ft (2,787 sq m) of a former high school. (Many who work at the mall have claimed the school is haunted and that you can hear the sound of fingernails creepily scraping down a chalkboard at night.) Most of the mall's vendors can be found in the school's gym, which is filled wall-to-wall with stalls selling everything from antique furniture and lamps to washboards and souvenir beer mugs. Trips down memory lane work up an appetite, and to that end, the mall serves up decadent burgers and gigantic portions of ice cream from its Twistee Treats Diner, a 50s-themed

**"The Pink Elephant appears like a mirage."**

diner with a hot-pink-and-white checkered floor that's housed, appropriately enough, inside a giant ice-cream cone. And speaking of sweet treats, next door is the mall's sweetshop, which sells all manner of tasty goodies, including candied nuts, saltwater taffy, and homemade fudge. In short, the Pink Elephant Antique Mall is delightfully sentimental and kitsch in the extreme, but isn't nostalgia central to Route 66's cultural identity, after all?

**CLOCKWISE FROM TOP**
Era-inspired details inside the Twistee Treats Diner; the mall's pink elephant mascot; a muffler man welcoming visitors into the mall

GSS
Brooks
MAKES EVERYTHING TASTE BETTER
OLD ORIGINAL
CATSUP

# WORLD'S LARGEST CATSUP BOTTLE

ODDITIES AND AMERICANA

COLLINSVILLE

Do you want fries with that? You're gonna need them. Towering over the city of Collinsville, the world's biggest bottle of ketchup (or catsup, as originally spelled) is the sauciest example of roadside marketing on Route 66.

About 40 minutes from the Pink Elephant Antique Mall *(p46)*, and deserving of a quick detour off the highway, is what's billed as the world's largest bottle of catsup (or ketchup, if you prefer). Dressed in natty white pinstripes, the king-size condiment claims to be the "tangy-est"—the slogan of Brooks Old Original Catsup, which was produced by the G.S. Suppiger Company of St. Louis. The company no longer exists, but in the mid-1900s, sales were sufficiently brisk (G.S. Suppiger crowed about Brooks being the country's fourth-most popular ketchup) that a bit of a boast seemed in order. So, in 1949, the company had this giant bottle constructed next to its Collinsville plant. Standing atop a 100-ft (30.5-m) tower, the 70-ft-(21-m-) tall bottle is visible from nearly a mile away. Its cap is 8 ft (2.4 m) wide. All told, the bottle could hold 100,000 gallons (378,541 liters) of ketchup. At one tablespoon per serving, that would provide two servings for every last person in the state of Illinois.

Alas, the bottle never actually held any ketchup. It functioned as a water tower for the plant, providing 25,000 gallons (94,635 liters) for production and holding the rest in reserve in case of fire. The water tower didn't function all that long, either. By the early 60s, the plant had closed and the bottle was emptied. Over time, the water tower fell into ruin and was in danger of being torn down, but in 1995, a preservation group raised $100,000 to save it, and in 2002, it was added to the National Register of Historic Places. Today, it has its own fan club, having earned a namecheck in the 2010 movie *The Twilight Saga: Eclipse*, and a dedicated festival in July, complete with obligatory ketchup taste testing.

**LEFT**
The towering roadside bottle, once an advertisement, then a water tower, now an icon

# CAHOKIA MOUNDS STATE HISTORIC SITE

INDIGENOUS HERITAGE

COLLINSVILLE

**ABOVE**
Visitors climbing the stairs of Monks Mound to take in the view

Cahokia may be the biggest city you've never heard of. At its height in the early 12th century, it had a population larger than London's. Then, by the 15th century, it was abandoned, leaving behind giant earthen mounds and unsolved mysteries.

On the final leg of Route 66 in Illinois, and on the other side of the Mississippi River from St. Louis, lies the remains of Cahokia, the largest pre-Columbian Indigenous site north of Mexico. The area was first settled around 700 CE, and over the ensuing centuries a city took shape, gradually developing into a major political, religious, and economic center. Cahokia's denizens were part of the Mississippian culture, which stretched from the Great Lakes to the Gulf of Mexico and the Atlantic coast; archaeological excavations have uncovered pottery, copper, seashells, and shark teeth, indicating extensive trade networks. The city reached the height of its success in the 12th century, when it was home to 20,000 people, a population bigger than that of London, England, at the time.

In its heyday, Cahokia's most notable feature was its estimated 120 earthen mounds, with Monks Mound at its heart. Roughly 100 ft (30.5 m) high, and with four terraces, it's one of the largest such structures in eastern North America, and it was here that the city's leader resided. (The mound is known now for a group of 19th-century Trappist monks who cultivated a garden here.) Today, 80 mounds remain, of which 72 are protected within the State Historic Site. Trails wind between them, and a set of stairs allows visitors to ascend central Monks Mound. There are also

**"Cahokia's most notable feature was its estimated 120 earthen mounds, with Monks Mound at its heart."**

partial reconstructions of other major structures: a 2-mile- (3.2-km-) long palisade wall that encircled the city's core, and as many as five "Woodhenges," enormous circular calendars of sacred cedar logs that aligned with the sunrise at certain times of the year.

Despite its accomplishments, by the late 1300s Cahokia had been abandoned. Drought, disease, invasions, and deforestation have all been suggested as the reason, but the definitive cause of its demise remains unknown, making Cahokia not only one of the country's most important Indigenous sites but also one of its most mysterious.

**ABOVE**
Cahokia's impressive Monks Mound, standing 100 ft (30.5 m) high and 955 ft (291 m) long

ROUTE

The Old Chain of Rocks Bridge, connecting Illinois with Missouri

# MISSOURI

From the banks of the Mississippi River, where the state of Missouri awaits, Route 66 winds its way through St. Louis, the point of departure for countless westward journeys throughout American history. After drivers have waved goodbye to the city's much-loved Gateway Arch, the highway escorts them across the lower half of the state. On the way, it encounters natural wonders, like the marvelous Meramec Caverns and lush national forest, and plenty of human-made attractions, too. These include both earnest tributes to mid-20th-century life, like a lovingly restored gas station and an entire salvaged town, and a fair share of oddball attractions, including a giant rocking chair. The highway also makes an appropriate stop in Springfield, Route 66's official birthplace.

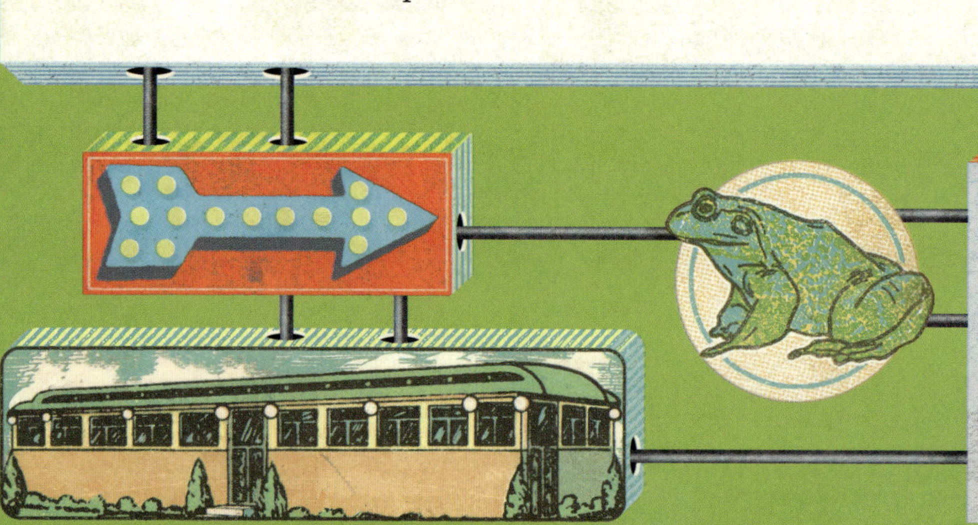

# MISSOURI

**DISTANCE**
330 miles (531 km)

**DRIVE TIME (NONSTOP)**
Approx. 8 hours

**LANDSCAPE**
Missouri's portion of Route 66 runs through the heart of the Ozarks, an upland region of rolling hills and rocky ridges.

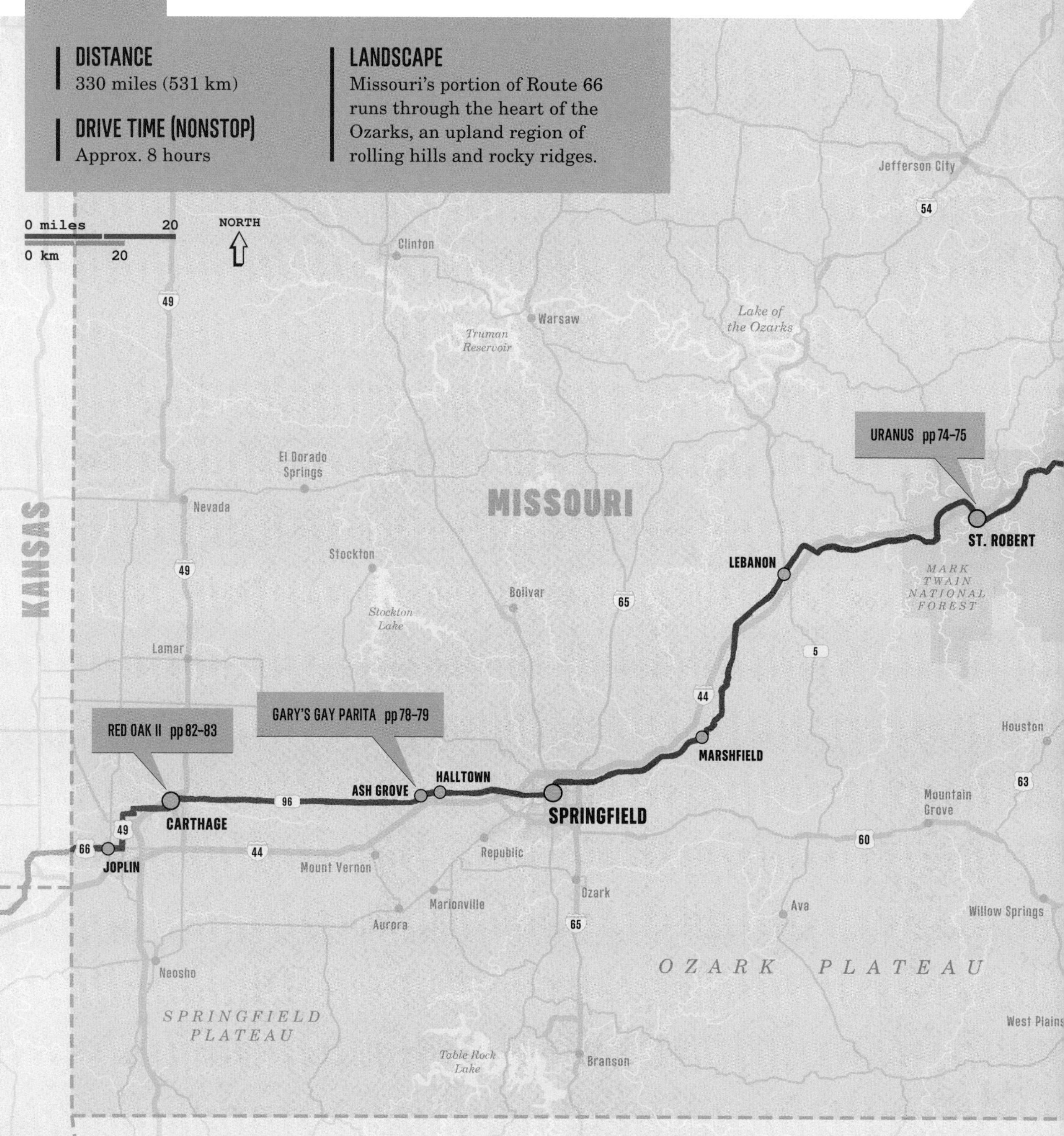

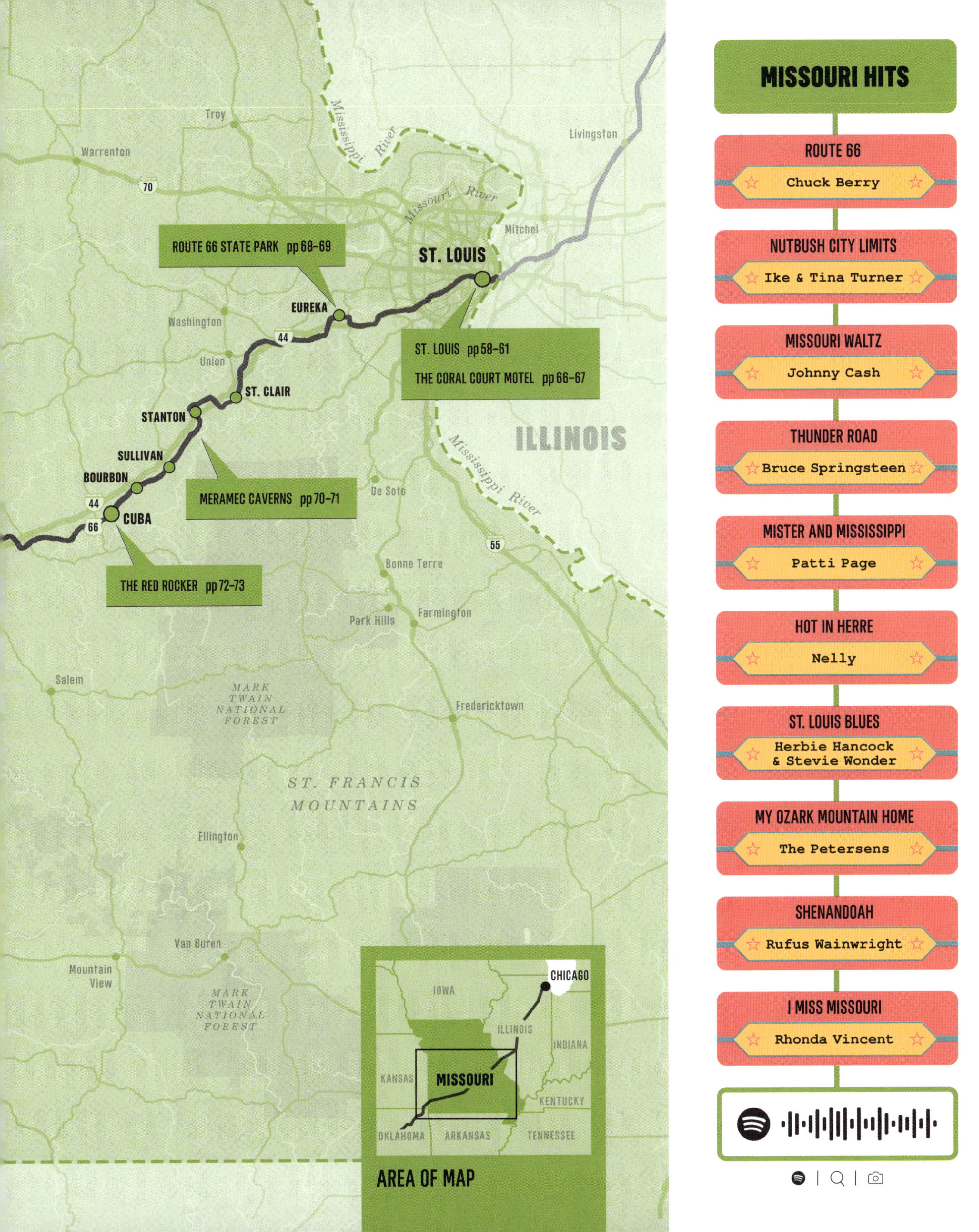

Troy
Warrenton
Livingston
70
Mississippi River
Missouri River
Mitchel
ROUTE 66 STATE PARK pp 68–69
ST. LOUIS
EUREKA
Washington
44
ST. LOUIS pp 58–61
THE CORAL COURT MOTEL pp 66–67
Union
ST. CLAIR
STANTON
ILLINOIS
SULLIVAN
BOURBON
MERAMEC CAVERNS pp 70–71
De Soto
44
CUBA
66
55
THE RED ROCKER pp 72–73
Bonne Terre
Park Hills
Farmington
Salem
MARK TWAIN NATIONAL FOREST
Fredericktown
ST. FRANCIS MOUNTAINS
Ellington
Van Buren
Mountain View
MARK TWAIN NATIONAL FOREST
CHICAGO
IOWA
ILLINOIS
INDIANA
KANSAS
MISSOURI
KENTUCKY
OKLAHOMA
ARKANSAS
TENNESSEE
AREA OF MAP
MISSOURI HITS
ROUTE 66
Chuck Berry
NUTBUSH CITY LIMITS
Ike & Tina Turner
MISSOURI WALTZ
Johnny Cash
THUNDER ROAD
Bruce Springsteen
MISTER AND MISSISSIPPI
Patti Page
HOT IN HERRE
Nelly
ST. LOUIS BLUES
Herbie Hancock & Stevie Wonder
MY OZARK MOUNTAIN HOME
The Petersens
SHENANDOAH
Rufus Wainwright
I MISS MISSOURI
Rhonda Vincent

# ST. LOUIS

CITIES OF 66

Perched on the banks of the Mississippi, St. Louis has long been a gateway for travelers journeying West, everyone from Lewis and Clark and 19th-century pioneers to contemporary road-trippers driving down the ever-changing Route 66.

As drivers exit Illinois, they encounter one of Route 66's major geographical milestones: the Mississippi River. Where to cross it has depended on when they traveled, as changes to Route 66's official alignment have, over the years, seen at least five different bridges carry motorists over the river and into neighboring Missouri. The most interesting of these is the old Chain of Rocks Bridge *(p52)*. Opened in 1929, it has an unusual 30-degree kink halfway through, a concession to riverboat pilots who complained that the original straight design would complicate navigation in a stretch where they already had to deal with a tricky underwater shoal.

## WELCOME TO ST. LOUIS

It feels like Route 66 was destined to pass through the city of St. Louis. From the time it was founded as a fur trading post in 1764, St. Louis has been a staging ground for Westward journeys. In 1804, that was the Lewis and Clark expedition, when explorers Meriwether Lewis and William Clark led an expeditionary party—including enslaved people and Sacagawea, a Shoshone interpreter—to establish a presence in the west of the country. In the ensuing decades, it was pioneers in covered wagons heading for Utah or the coast. At the turn of the century, it was train passengers pouring through Union Station, then one of the world's largest and busiest rail hubs. Road-trippers on America's greatest highway were the obvious next step.

St. Louis's legacy of movement is celebrated in the city's most unmissable monument, the Gateway Arch, also known as the Gateway to the West. Soaring 630 ft (192 m) above the Mississippi, the elegant silver structure was designed by the Finnish American architect Eero Saarinen and constructed from 1963 to 1965 using a shell of stainless steel over layers of carbon steel and concrete.

**LEFT**
The skyline of St. Louis, with its much-loved Gateway Arch rising above the Mississippi River

**CLOCKWISE FROM TOP LEFT**
The Chase Park Plaza Hotel overlooking leafy Forest Park; signage pointing to the Donut Drive-In; hungry hopefuls lining up outside Ted Drewes Frozen Custard

## SWEET DREAMS ON ROUTE 66

Early Route 66 alignments took travelers west from the Mississippi to St. Louis's lovely Forest Park, the site of the 1904 World's Fair. Opposite its northeast corner is the Royal Sonesta Chase Park Plaza St. Louis. When one thinks of nights on Route 66, novelty inns and motels with flickering neon signs usually spring to mind. But travelers with a bit of cash were more likely to bed down somewhere like this Italian Renaissance-style haven, which has hosted everyone from Elvis to U.S. presidents. Opened in 1922 as the Chase Park Plaza Hotel, it later added a 27-story Art Deco tower and just about every service a motorist of means could ask for, including gas pumps, a telegraph office, a drugstore, a salon, and even a chocolate shop.

Later, Route 66 ran farther south, skipping the Chase Park Plaza but guiding drivers with a sweet tooth straight to a pair of classic St. Louis stops, just blocks away from each other on Chippewa Street. Opened in 1953, the Donut Drive-In has one of the highway's best neon signs, advertising "Fresh Do-Nuts" and displaying little red donuts falling down the side. Many of its recipes have never changed. A minute away is Ted Drewes Frozen Custard, open here since 1941, though the fourth-generation family business has been in operation since 1929. Famously, their shakes are thick enough to be served upside down.

## NATIONAL MUSEUM OF TRANSPORTATION

On the way out of town is the National Museum of Transportation. Some of its inventory predates Route 66, like a 1915 Ford Model T, while other pieces, like a 1957 Chevrolet Bel Air convertible, are highway icons. Then there's the "Dream Car," a custom automobile hand-built in 1960 by four Detroit mechanics and covered in 30 coats of ruby red paint mixed with diamond dust, for sparkle. It resembles a best mid-century guess at what might make its way through St. Louis next, after the covered wagons and Studebakers, a vision for Route 66's future that never quite came to pass.

**BELOW**
A 1963 Chrysler Turbine, made in Italy and painted in "turbine bronze"

**"Early Route 66 alignments took travelers west from the Mississippi to St. Louis's lovely Forest Park."**

EAST
100

HISTORI
MISSOURI
U S
66
BYWAY

HISTORIC
MISSOURI
U S
66
BYWAY

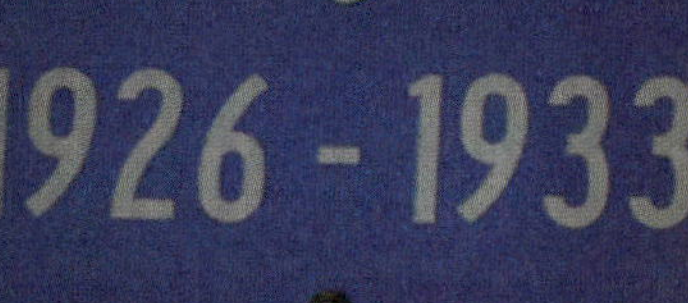
1926 - 1933

A web of road signs on the highway in St. Louis, Missouri

HISTORY

# ROUTE 66'S CHANGING COURSE

Route 66 was never static. From the very start, its path was always shifting, adapting to new roads and driving habits, though it would eventually succumb to the Interstate Highway System.

1

America's most famous highway wasn't created so much as it was assembled—pieced together from a mishmash of preexisting roads—its course changing as new roads were added or old ones were improved. The result was a highway that often seemed more like a river than a road, constantly seeking out the most efficient course across the land.

The highway's shifting paths around St. Louis are a case in point. When Route 66 was inaugurated, it entered the city's north side via the McKinley Bridge (which is still open to traffic). Once drivers had crossed the Mississippi River, they'd head downtown to Locust Boulevard, which they'd take west and along the northern edge of the city's sprawling Forest Park. From there, the route headed south to Manchester Road—one of 66's earliest paved sections—and exited the city.

St. Louis's first major Route 66 realignment came in 1929, when changes to the Illinois portion of the route sent motorists into Missouri via the Municipal (now the MacArthur) Bridge, on the south side of downtown. Instead of taking Locust, drivers motored west on Chouteau Avenue and skirted Forest Park's southern edge.

That route predominated only until 1936, when further changes on the Illinois side saw Route 66 redirected

**1** Locals kicking back and enjoying the scenery in the Chain of Rocks Park

**2** A photograph, dating from 1951, showing the view looking north along 3rd Street from atop MacArthur Bridge

**3** St. Louis's Market Street, with the Gateway Arch curving across the skyline

**4** A postcard showing the McKinley Bridge, at the time the largest electric bridge in the world

some 12 miles (19 km) north, over the Chain of Rocks Bridge, notable for its dogleg in the middle. From the bridge, the new route paralleled the Mississippi as it headed into St. Louis. It eventually ended up on Tucker Boulevard, where drivers who looked east as they crossed Market Street were treated to a clear view of the Old Courthouse and Gateway Arch before Chippewa Street took them west.

Within years, motorists were presented with yet another option, one that permitted them to avoid the city altogether. Instead of heading south after crossing the Chain of Rocks Bridge, they could continue west on the new Bypass 66, part of the Interstate Highway System. Though there would be other changes to the route in the coming years, this one was a sign of things to come. As Jack D. Rittenhouse wrote in his 1946 tome, *A Guide Book to Highway 66*, "This 'belt line' is a wide, high-speed route, with plenty of gas stations… It avoids city traffic completely." You can almost hear something ominous in those lines. A cursory glance at an old map shows just how closely the Bypass traced today's I-270, the last great realignment. It was this that would finally doom Route 66, as motorists favored the Interstate's faster through-travel and clearer road markings.

**"The Coral Court opened in 1942 and it was among St. Louis's most striking motels."**

# THE CORAL COURT MOTEL

HOTELS AND MOTELS

ST. LOUIS

In its heyday, the Coral Court was one of the most famous—and infamous—motels on Route 66, having hosted countless illicit affairs and even playing a role in one of Missouri's most talked about crimes.

As Route 66 exits St. Louis along its 1936 alignment, now Watson Road, it passes a long white subdivision fence. Midway through, the fence is interrupted by a low stone wall, which once formed the exterior wall of one of the highway's most notorious motels.

The Coral Court opened in 1942, and was among St. Louis's most striking motels, with 10 bungalows of marigold-yellow, glazed ceramic brick as well as glass blocks, and designed in the era's popular Streamline Moderne style. The postwar years saw the motel expand to 77 rooms, each complete with amenities like free TV and air-conditioning, while out front a coral pink-and-chrome neon sign advertised moderate rates and a swimming pool. A favorite of road-trippers, the Coral Court also gained a reputation as a venue for illicit affairs, thanks to the private garages attached to each room, the four-hour rates it offered (ostensibly for the convenience of truck drivers), and its famously discreet staff.

The most sordid bit of Coral Court history, however, is its connection to one of Missouri's most nefarious murders. In September 1953, Carl Hall and Bonnie Heady kidnapped Bobby Greenlease Jr., the six-year-old son of a wealthy Kansas City car dealer. Bobby's parents paid a $600,000 ransom, unaware that Hall and Heady had already murdered their son. After getting the money, the pair traveled to St. Louis, where Hall deserted his partner and hid out at the Coral Court for two days. A tip from a cab driver soon led to his arrest at a different St. Louis motel, after which Hall led the cops to Heady. Somewhere along the way, half of the ransom money disappeared. Two of the arresting police officers were indicted on suspicion of making off with the cash, but some believe it was hidden somewhere on the Coral Court grounds. If so, it will likely never be found. The motel was demolished in 1995, though one bungalow is preserved at the National Museum of Transportation in St. Louis.

**TOP LEFT**
The motel's entrance, as seen before the place was demolished; today the wall alone remains

**BOTTOM LEFT**
A postcard showing the Coral Court's tempting swimming pool, a big draw for motel guests

# ROUTE 66 STATE PARK

HERITAGE SITES

**EUREKA**

A ghost road, a ghost town, a 1930s roadhouse. Just outside St. Louis, in Eureka, on the Meramec River, Route 66 State Park is the site of several spectral remnants that offer a glimpse into the highway's much-storied past.

In 1925, the *St. Louis Times* ran an offer where anyone who purchased a six-month subscription and also paid an additional $67.50 would receive a plot of land in the new resort development of Times Beach on the Meramec River, outside St. Louis. As newspaper promotions go, it sure beats a tote bag. For the first four and a half decades, Times Beach was a great place to live. But it turned into a nightmare. In 1971, the town began spraying oil on its dirt roads to reduce dust, a common practice at the time. The oil it used had been contaminated with dioxin, a by-product in the making of Agent Orange, which was used by the military in the Vietnam War. Animals started dying, children became sick. In 1983, the government evacuated the entire town.

Cleanup was finally completed in 1997, and what used to be Times Beach is now Route 66 State Park. Housed in a former 1935 roadhouse, its visitor center has displays on Times Beach and Route 66's history. In front of the visitor center, travelers will find an original strip of 66 that they can drive, but only as far as the skeletel, and impassable, Meramec Bridge.

The bridge is one of Route 66's many ghost roads, sections that still exist but lead nowhere. They pop up along the length of the route, providing a window into the highway's demise: a weed-pocked stretch alongside a rock quarry in McCook, Illinois; two forlorn lanes running through the plains outside Erick, Oklahoma. Occasionally, they offer a more optimistic tale, of how the old route has found new life, as in Williams, Arizona, where a stretch of decomposing pavement has been turned into a hiking trail. There are hopes that the Meramec Bridge can one day be similarly reincarnated, but for now, it's impossible to cross the river via Route 66. The only way to reach the other side is on the very thing responsible for so many of those ghost roads: the Interstate.

**"The bridge is one of Route 66's many ghost roads, sections of pavement that still exist but lead nowhere."**

**ABOVE**
The abandoned Meramec Bridge running alongside the busy Interstate

**LEFT**
Studying the display boards in the park's visitor center

# MERAMEC CAVERNS

NATURAL WONDERS

**SULLIVAN**

**ABOVE**
A roadside barn advertising the caverns, attracting motorists on the highway

**RIGHT**
The theatrically named Stage Curtain, standing at 70 ft (21 m)

While Route 66 passes through the verdant, rolling hills of Missouri, another world lies hidden underground. Missouri is, in fact, known as the "Cave State" for the more than 7,500 caverns found beneath its surface, though none quite match Meramec for size, splendor, or stories.

Found halfway between the community of Stanton and city of Sullivan, Meramec Caverns is one of the largest cave systems west of the Mississippi, with 4.6 miles (7.4 km) of passages sprawling across seven different levels. The complex is so deep that a seven-story building could stand inside it. Within it, colonies of bats roost in an unchanging temperature of 58°F (14°C), and visitors encounter bizarre features like the "Wine Table," a 6-ft- (1.8-m-) tall onyx formation seemingly adorned with clusters of grapes.

The cave has been a popular tourist attraction since Route 66's early days, but its colorful history goes back much further. During the Civil War, Union troops took advantage of its ample saltpeter deposits to set up a secret gunpowder production facility. Local lore says it was a stop on the Underground Railroad. Perhaps most famously, some claim that the famed Missouri outlaw Jesse James used it as a hideout, pointing to rifles and strongboxes found in the cave as proof. In the late 19th and early 20th centuries, local Missourians escaping the summer heat hosted social events here, often in what came to be known as the Ballroom, a section of the cave that could accommodate a 2,500-sq-ft (232-sq-m) dance floor.

The party really got started in 1933, though, when the entrepreneur Lester Dill bought the cave and started offering tours. A tireless promoter of his admittedly impressive hole in the ground, Dill plastered roadways with signs for the cave and had advertisements painted on the sides of barns in no fewer than 14 states. His most ingenious stunt, however, was to hire local boys to roam the parking lot and, while people were busy touring the cave, tie small signs promoting the caverns to the bumpers of their cars, thus getting free mobile advertising and, in the process, pioneering the concept of the bumper sticker.

ROUTE 66 ROCKER
FANNING
US
66
OUTPOST
WORLD FAMOUS

# THE RED ROCKER

ODDITIES AND AMERICANA

CUBA

**Route 66 is peppered with big, weird things: muffler men, a giant condiment bottle, sedans planted headlights-first in the ground. Central Missouri's claim to outsize fame is a giant rocking chair. Why? Well, why not?**

Believe it or not, the U.S. has a thing for giant rocking chairs. In 2002, a 26-ft (7.9-m) rocking chair appeared in Texas, followed by another standing at 34 ft (10.3 m) in Indiana, in 2004. Then, in 2008, chairs reaching 34 ft (10.3 m) and 35 ft (10.7 m) were erected in South Dakota and Mississippi, respectively. Besting them all? That'll be the towering 42-ft (12.8-m) Red Rocker in Cuba, Missouri.

This curious oddity was the passion project of Dan Sanazaro, a local business owner who envisioned it as the perfect way to attract customers to his archery and feed store. Sanazaro enlisted a couple of friends, John Bland and Joe Medwick, to design and build the chair using steel pipes, and they installed it on April Fool's Day, 2008. More than 20 ft (6.1 m) wide, and weighing in at 27,500 lb (12,474 kg), it was the world's new largest rocking chair. For Guinness World Records to certify it, though, it had to actually rock, so that fall, Medwick cut some of its welds, and Sanazaro and company got it moving back and forth. Sanazaro grew concerned that someone might injure themselves (or worse) and soon had it rewelded and immobilized. Although the chair no longer rocked, for a while tourists could be hoisted onto its seat to have their pictures taken. Perhaps unsurprisingly, insurance concerns put an end to the fun in 2015.

Once a giant rocking chair arms race gets started, it's nearly impossible to stop. Sure enough, in that same year a 56.5-ft (17.2-m) rocker appeared in Casey, Illinois, snatching the title of the world's largest. Perhaps it was simply a coincidence, but Sanazaro soon closed his business. Today, the Red Rocker in Cuba advertises its replacement, the Fanning 66 Outpost General Store, while the chair's rockers and legs—the parts that folks can reach—have become an informal Route 66 guest book, covered in stickers slapped on by passing road-trippers looking to leave their own mark on the Mother Road.

**LEFT**
Missouri's Red Rocker, a roadside advertisement turned local legend

# URANUS

ODDITIES AND AMERICANA

ST. ROBERT

Come for the fudge, stay for the cheesy photo ops, questionable "museum" exhibits, and boatloads of off-color jokes. It's all in good fun, and bad taste, at this temple of American roadside kitsch. There's nowhere quite like Uranus.

Halfway between St. Louis and Springfield, Missouri, Uranus isn't an actual town. It's more a state of mind. And that state of mind is squarely in the gutter. Business owner Louie Keen founded Uranus in 2015 with the purest intention of making it a tourist trap, and in that regard, it may be unrivaled on all of Route 66. There's a homemade fudge shop, giant dinosaur statues, the world's largest belt buckle, and the Uranus Sideshow Museum, where everything—from shrunken heads and a resident sword swallower to a creature that's half fish, half monkey—is "either really real

**RIGHT**
Windows into the weird world of Uranus, outside the venue's fudge factory

or really fake." Lording over it all is Louie Keen himself, the self-proclaimed Mayor of Uranus, who insists he was elected because he's very handsome but with a bit of prodding might admit that only one person in Uranus has voting rights, and it's him. This being Route 66, Keen also lords over everything in muffler-man form. His 20-ft (6-m) likeness is done up in his traditional mayor's garb: American flag suit, American flag shades, and American flag cowboy hat.

Uranus's foremost attraction, though, is simple: butt jokes, which are found everywhere. Visitors are reminded that "the best fudge comes from Uranus!" On the miniature golf course, players are encouraged to "sink some balls into our putt-holes." In the escape rooms, participants try to flee the Uranus Dental and Proctology Clinic. Photo-takers stick their heads into cutouts not where the zebra or giraffe's face would be but where... well, you get the picture.

Is it tasteful? Absolutely not. Is it a tacky good time? Let's just put it this way—you could have chosen to stop anywhere, but if you can get your own mind in the gutter for a while, you'll be glad you picked Uranus.

**"Halfway between St. Louis and Springfield, Missouri, Uranus isn't an actual town. It's more a state of mind."**

**CLOCKWISE FROM TOP LEFT**
The local jailhouse and neighboring tattoo parlor in the wacky world of Uranus; the Mega Mayor Muffler Man, built in the image of the town's creator; Fudge Factory signage

The story of the Mother Road begins in Springfield, Missouri. It was here that a telegram was sent to Washington, D.C., officially giving birth to the iconic highway and its legendary number.

HISTORY

# THE BIRTHPLACE OF ROUTE 66

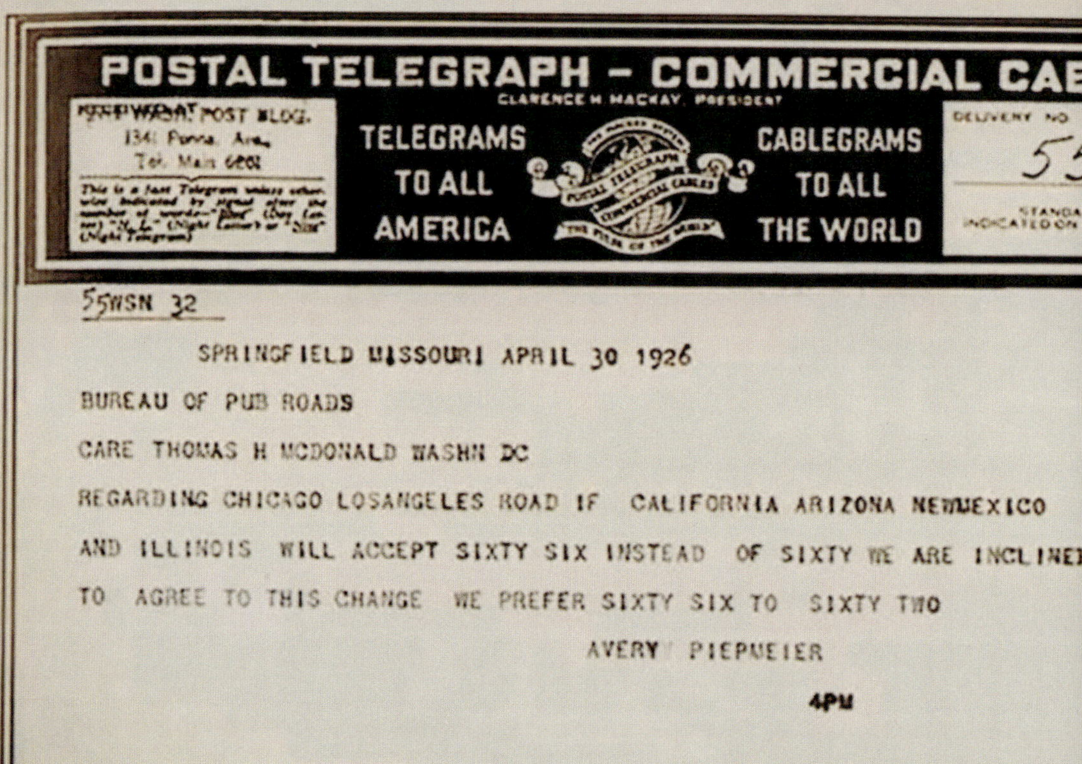

POSTAL TELEGRAPH - COMMERCIAL CAB

CLARENCE H. MACKAY, PRESIDENT

TELEGRAMS TO ALL AMERICA

CABLEGRAMS TO ALL THE WORLD

55WSN 32

SPRINGFIELD MISSOURI APRIL 30 1926

BUREAU OF PUB ROADS

CARE THOMAS H MCDONALD WASHN DC

REGARDING CHICAGO LOSANGELES ROAD IF CALIFORNIA ARIZONA NEWMEXICO AND ILLINOIS WILL ACCEPT SIXTY SIX INSTEAD OF SIXTY WE ARE INCLINE[D] TO AGREE TO THIS CHANGE WE PREFER SIXTY SIX TO SIXTY TWO

AVERY PIEPMEIER

4PM

While Springfield, Illinois, is better-known for its presidential roots *(p33)*, Springfield, Missouri, has its own place in U.S. history books. In 1925, the U.S. highway system was just starting to take shape. Routes were being planned, and the American Association of State Highway Officials was busy approving a new system for naming interstate highways. North-south routes were to be given odd numbers, with the most important ending in either 1 or 5, while east-west routes were to be given even numbers, with the most important ending in 0. The highway running from Chicago to Los Angeles was to be Route 60.

Kentucky governor William Jason Fields had a problem with this, however. Miffed that no routes ending in 0 passed through his beloved Kentucky, Fields lobbied federal officials to instead give the number 60 to the highway running from Newport News, Virginia, to Springfield, Missouri. The Chicago to L.A. highway would have to find a different number. Initially, this was to be 62, but Cyrus Avery *(p114)*, the then Oklahoma Department of Highways chairman, felt that 66 had a nicer ring to it, and on April 30, 1926, he and John T. Woodruff *(p81)* sent a telegram from Springfield's Colonial Hotel notifying officials in

1 The famous telegram sent to Washington, D.C. by Cyrus Avery from Springfield, on April 30, 1926, suggesting the route be numbered 66

2 Cars passing a Greyhound bus depot and Texaco gas station in increasingly busy Springfield, 1953

3 This way to Springfield, the birthplace of the country's most famous and beloved highway

4 Driving along the Mother Road into Springfield, where Route 66 was given its iconic number

5 Springfield's History Museum on the Square, where eight galleries explore how the Missouri town has made its mark on American history

Washington, D.C., of their pick. After a few months of deliberation, federal officials telegraphed back on November 11 with their approval, making Springfield, Missouri, the official birthplace of U.S. Highway 66.

Route 66 would soon become one of the country's most popular highways, transporting people from east to west, and it was the first to be paved from start to finish. It also transformed its birthplace, helping make Springfield an important regional transportation hub. Drivers passed right through the heart of the city, cruising down St. Louis and College streets and through Park Central Square, where a small plaque now commemorates Springfield's status as the official hometown of Route 66.

Today, Springfield celebrates its singular role in highway history each August with the Birthplace of Route 66 Festival. The event's centerpiece is—naturally—a car and motorcycle show, where vehicle enthusiasts exhibit antique, classic, and modified vehicles; many also take part in the festival's parade. In addition to the auto displays, the event includes concerts, Route 66–themed art shows, lectures by historians and authors, and displays of Route 66 memorabilia, making it one of the country's biggest Route 66–related events.

# GARY'S GAY PARITA

MUST-VISIT MUSEUMS

**ASH GROVE**

Nowhere exemplifies Route 66's appeal across the eras like Gary's Gay Parita. Built in 1930, the gas station burned down during the highway's golden era, only for a local family to resurrect it for a new generation half a century later.

Half an hour from downtown Springfield, past a few small creeks and farms spread out on the rolling Ozark hills, an old Sinclair gas station seemingly teleported from the 1930s comes into view. Alongside original gas pumps are small statues of Sinclair's dinosaur mascot and antique signs advertising Wonder Bread, Lee Tires, and Opaline Motor Oil. A classic car is parked alongside the pumps, and others dot the grounds, including a 1928 International Six Speed Special.

Fred Mason opened a gas station here in 1930, giving it the unusual moniker Gay Parita. Gay was his wife's name, but where Parita came from is a bit fuzzier. It may have been an old place name for this little corner of rural Missouri, or it could have been a well-intentioned but misguided attempt at the Spanish word for "equality" (it's almost, if not quite, the Italian equivalent). In any case, the station was a Route 66 fixture in the highway's early years, serving travelers with fuel and cabins to rent.

Sadly, Gay Parita burned down in 1955, though its memory lived on. Half a century later, in 2005, relatives of Gary Turner built a replica of the gas station, and Gary and his wife, Lena, took over its management, turning it into something between a museum and visitor center. The main attraction, though, was Gary himself, a gregarious Missourian whose free watermelon slices and seemingly endless stories soon made him a Route 66 celebrity. Not only that, but what was now named Gary's Gay Parita became a must-stop destination on the Mother Road. When Gary and Lena both passed in 2015, the station threatened to disappear for a second time, but, in 2016, their daughter Barb reopened it and has carried on her dad's legacy in the years since. She's even had a bit of help bringing Gary's Gay Parita to a new generation of travelers: pop star and Springfield native Chappell Roan filmed much of the video for her hit song "Hot to Go!" at the beloved Springfield station.

**ABOVE**
Vintage signage and a classic car outside Gary's Gay Parita

**RIGHT**
Unmissable Route 66 road markings across the way from the gas station

Sinclair
OPALINE
Motor Oil
PENNZOIL
GAS
66
ROUTE
US
66

# ☆ JOHN T. WOODRUFF ☆

Lawyer and transportation advocate

Perhaps no one is as responsible for the success of Route 66 as John T. Woodruff. Born to teenage parents in a Missouri log cabin in 1868, Woodruff grew up in poverty. He left home at 16, and though he had no formal law education, he passed the state bar exam in 1889. Eventually, he was hired as an attorney for the St. Louis–San Francisco Railway, a job that took him to Springfield, where he quickly became a major figure, developing a hospital, golf course, fairgrounds, and the city's first "skyscraper," the 10-story Woodruff Building (now Sky Eleven).

Woodruff's job with the railroad impressed upon him the importance of efficient transportation, and he became a prominent supporter not just of rail but of improving the country's generally poor road system. This brought him into contact with Cyrus Avery *(p114)*, chairman of the Oklahoma Highway Commission, and together they conceived of a highway that would stretch from Chicago to Los Angeles, linking both urban and rural areas.

Inaugurating Route 66 was only the beginning, though. Most rural travel at the time was done by train, and travelers had to be convinced of the new highway's merits. The year after the route's founding, delegates from across the Southwest formed the U.S. Highway 66 Association, electing Woodruff to be its president. Under his leadership, the association advocated for paving the highway and worked to encourage tourism along the route. It didn't take long for Route 66 to become America's favorite highway, but even Woodruff may have been surprised at how celebrated his creation remains a century later.

# RED OAK II

HERITAGE SITES

CARTHAGE

When Lowell Davis returned to his childhood hometown after many years away, only to find it nearly abandoned, he set about trying to find a way to save it. His solution is a testament both to his vision and to the enduring pull of the past.

**ABOVE**
A tiny wooden cottage surrounded by scrubland in Red Oak II

**RIGHT**
Gas pumps outside a Phillips 66 Station, dating back to the 1920s

Every trip down Route 66 is an exercise in nostalgia. It's a choice to not take the Interstate, to instead travel a highway that had its heyday decades ago, where so many attractions—rusting gas stations, retro diners, aging motels—are appeals to a bygone era. That impulse to idealize the past is natural. We all possess it, though some more than others. Take Lowell Davis…

Davis grew up in Red Oak, Missouri, a hamlet not much more than the meeting of two country roads. He went to school here in the 1940s, in a one-room schoolhouse, and helped out at his dad's general store. Eventually, he moved away to Dallas, Texas. When he returned years later, he found that Red Oak had emptied out and all but become a ghost town. Davis was something of a Renaissance man—he painted and made prints, crafted figurines and bronzes, made music boxes and wrote books; he also had a strong sentimental streak for his rural upbringing, and he decided to make Red Oak his next project.

By that point, Davis owned a farm outside Carthage, about an hour from the Kansas border, and he began buying up Red Oak's structures and relocating them to his property 23 miles (37 km) away, recreating his hometown one building at a time. Among the structures he rescued were the general store, the schoolhouse, a blacksmith shop, a Phillips 66 gas station, and several houses. It was part art project, part act of preservation, part quixotic attempt to recapture a vanished past. Davis called it Red Oak II.

Though Davis passed away in 2020 (and was laid to rest here in Red Oak II), he's been survived by his salvaged hometown, which is once again a functioning village, after a fashion. A handful of folks now live there, and the church holds Sunday services and Saturday evening bluegrass jam sessions. Red Oak II's buildings are privately owned, but visitors are welcome to wander the gravel roads and admire the old edifices, imagining a past that, up close, really does seem ideal.

Phillips 66
Phillips 66
Phillips Petroleum Co.

# KANSAS

Kansas is home to the shortest stretch of Route 66, a blink-and-you'll-miss-it 13-mile (21-km) right angle through the state's southeastern corner. Don't actually blink, though, or you'll deprive yourself of the area's many attractions. Packed into this brief portion of the highway are the site of an infamous Civil War battle, remnants of a 19th-century mining boom (and its subsequent bust), and several charming sights that inspired Pixar's 2006 hit animated movie *Cars.* They're backdropped by a charming tableau of the rural Midwest: low, gently rising hills that pass country churches, open fields dotted with hay bales, and the occasional flea market or tractor dealership. With so much charm, it's no wonder that, for many, this corner of the state truly embodies Dorothy's famous declaration: "There's no place like home."

# KANSAS

**DISTANCE**
13 miles (21 km)

**DRIVE TIME (NONSTOP)**
Approx. 30 minutes

**ENVIRONMENT**
The road passes along flat terrain and through a handful of small towns as it runs across the rocky Ozark Plateau.

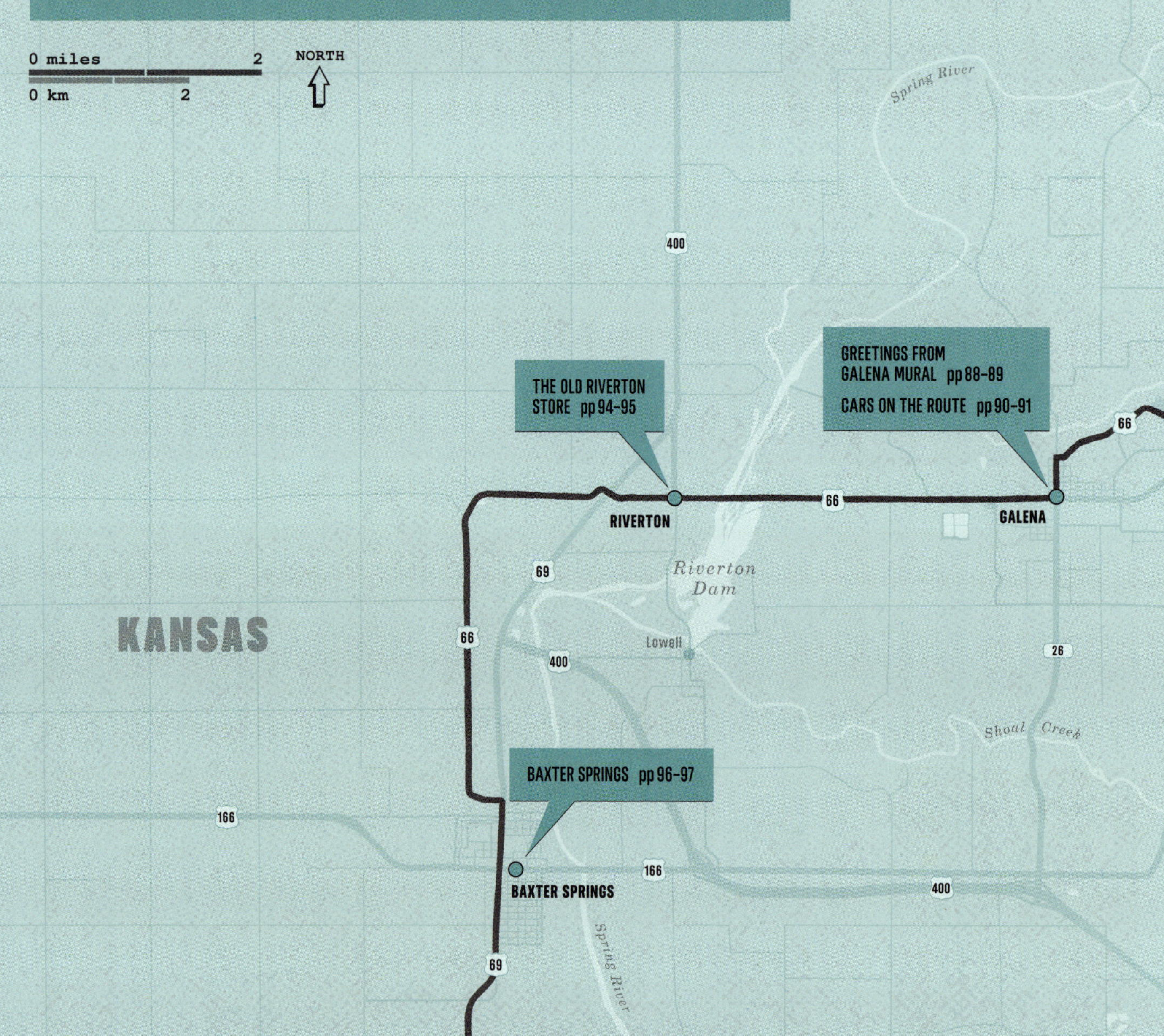

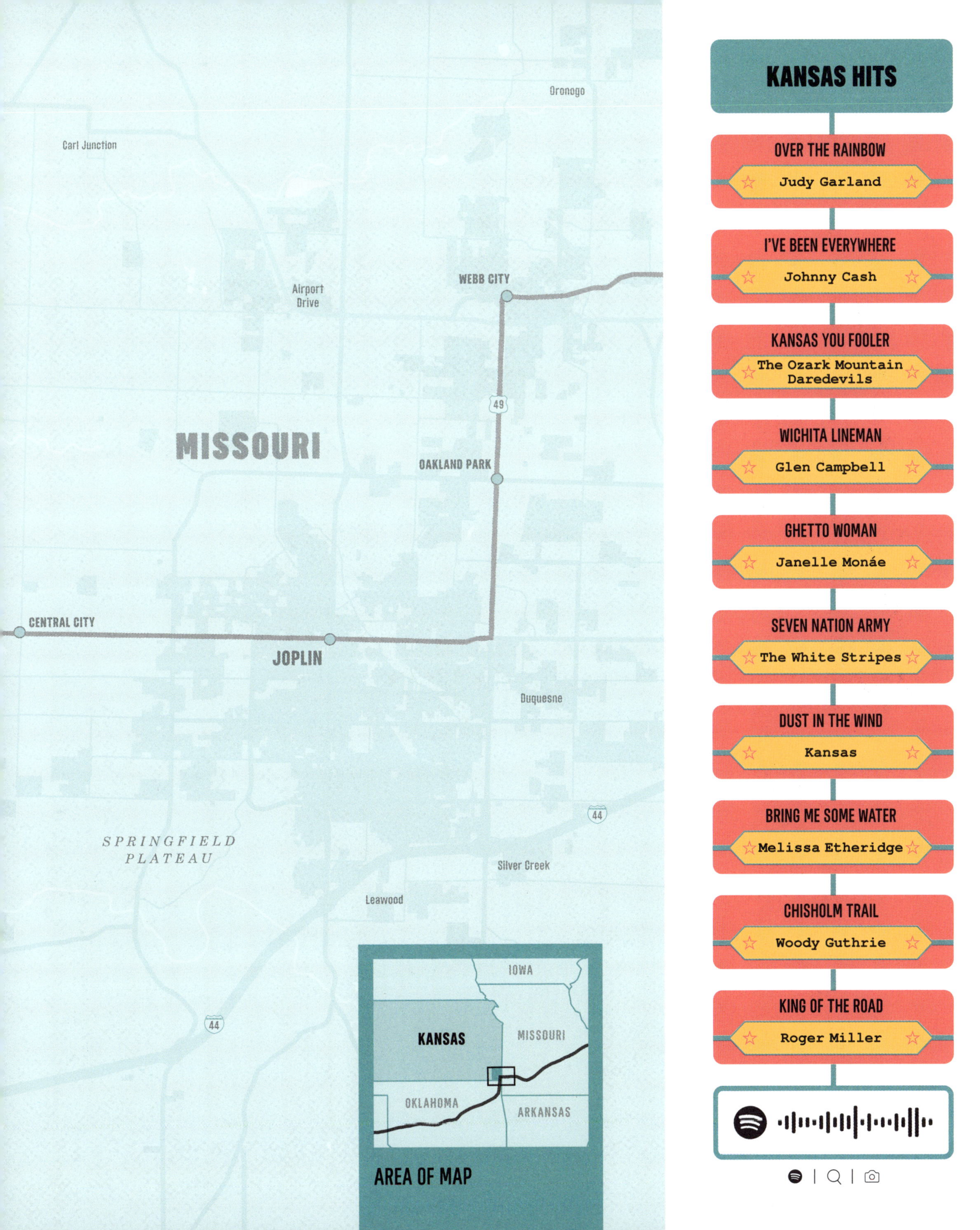

Oronogo
Carl Junction
Airport Drive
WEBB CITY
49
MISSOURI
OAKLAND PARK
CENTRAL CITY
JOPLIN
Duquesne
44
SPRINGFIELD PLATEAU
Silver Creek
Leawood
44
IOWA
KANSAS
MISSOURI
OKLAHOMA
ARKANSAS
AREA OF MAP
KANSAS HITS
OVER THE RAINBOW
Judy Garland
I'VE BEEN EVERYWHERE
Johnny Cash
KANSAS YOU FOOLER
The Ozark Mountain Daredevils
WICHITA LINEMAN
Glen Campbell
GHETTO WOMAN
Janelle Monáe
SEVEN NATION ARMY
The White Stripes
DUST IN THE WIND
Kansas
BRING ME SOME WATER
Melissa Etheridge
CHISHOLM TRAIL
Woody Guthrie
KING OF THE ROAD
Roger Miller

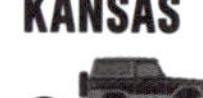

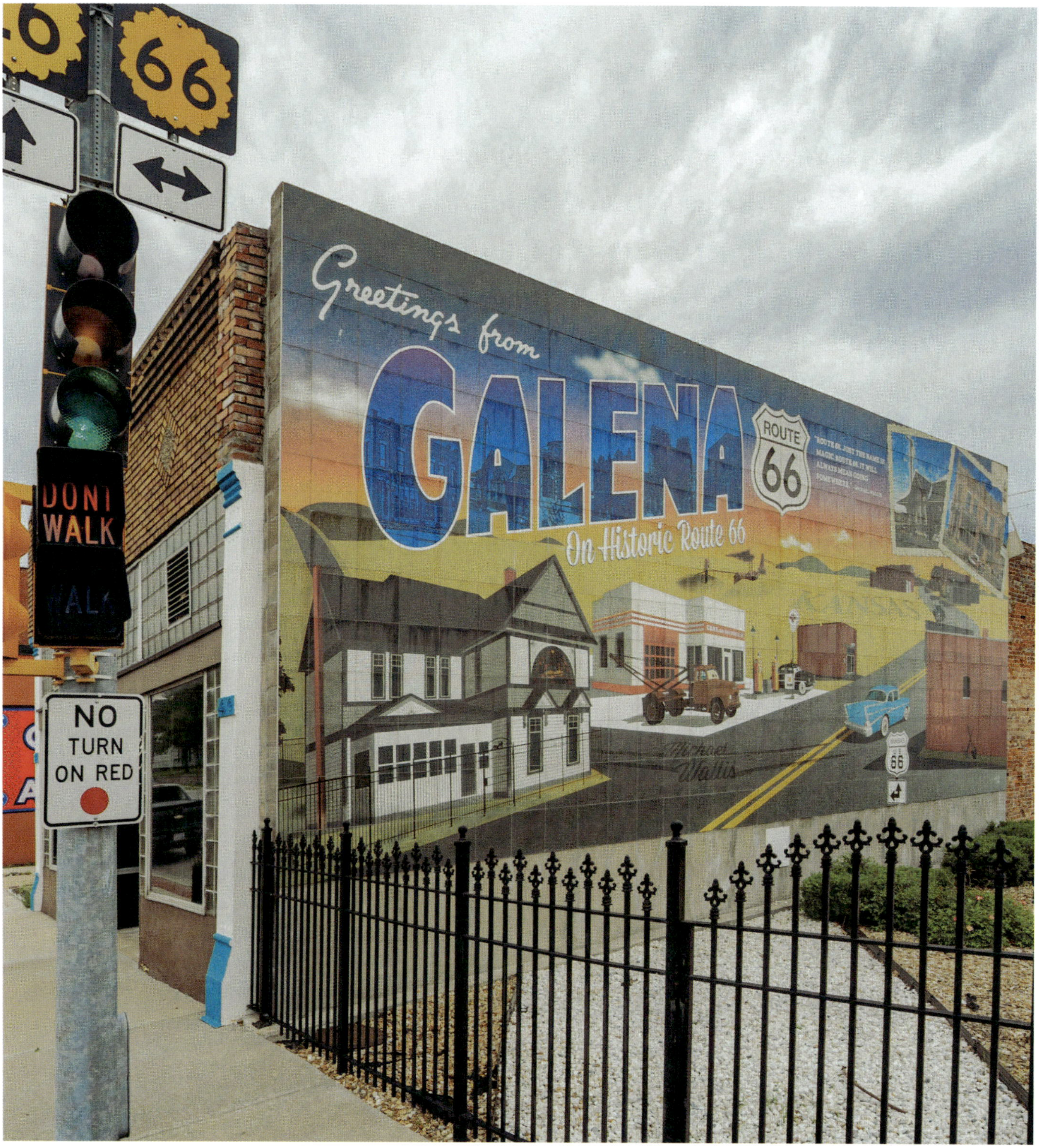
66
Greetings from
GALENA
ROUTE 66
On Historic Route 66
DONT WALK
NO TURN ON RED

# GREETINGS FROM GALENA MURAL

ODDITIES AND AMERICANA

GALENA

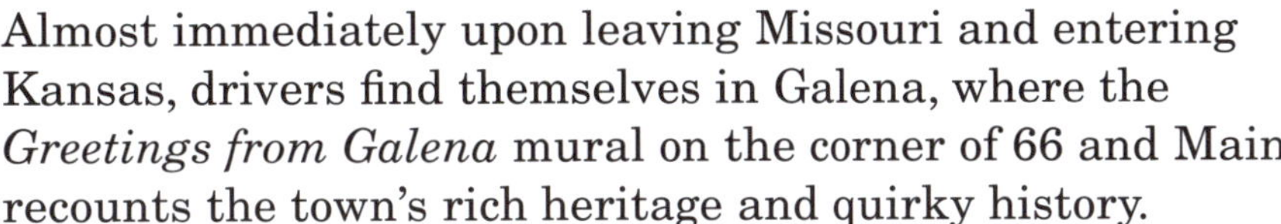

Almost immediately upon leaving Missouri and entering Kansas, drivers find themselves in Galena, where the *Greetings from Galena* mural on the corner of 66 and Main recounts the town's rich heritage and quirky history.

Murals are a common sight along Route 66. In Pontiac, Illinois, a 66-ft (20-m) mural is dedicated to Route 66 legend Bob Waldmire *(p38)*. Cuba, Missouri, has so many—of World War II veterans, a former mayor, and a local cooperage, among others—that it's been dubbed "Route 66 Mural City." In Weatherford, Oklahoma, there's even a mural on a giant wind turbine blade. No other art form is quite so suited to the highway, being visible from the car and making the ideal place to stop for a photo. They also let towns show off points of pride and commemorate their pasts. The Galena mural is the perfect example and has established itself as a firm favorite on Route 66.

The creation of artists Chris Auckerman and Jon White, the 40-ft (12-m) mural, in downtown Galena, depicts local landmarks and the rolling Kansas hills that drivers on 66 are soon to experience. At the top of the mural are the town's historic Liberty Hall and the old Missouri–Kansas–Texas train depot, now home to the Galena Mining & Historical Museum. Below is the intersection of Front and Main streets, where a baby blue '57 Chevy turns into town on Route 66's original course. On the corner are the local attraction Cars on the Route *(p90)* and the former Palace Drug Store. They're joined by a handsome home with Galena's most scandalous bit of history. Allegedly, the madam Ma Staffleback murdered as many as 50 clients in a bordello here in the 1890s. The house may never have actually been a bordello, and Ma was only ever convicted of killing one man (and dumping his body in a mine shaft for good measure), but even if the story has taken on a life of its own over the years, it's a tale you won't hear anywhere else, and that alone earns it a place on Galena's famous mural.

LEFT
Galena's cheery mural, depicting the town's key landmarks , as painted by artists Chris Aukerman and Jon White

# CARS ON THE ROUTE

MUST-VISIT MUSEUMS

GALENA

The team behind Pixar's animated film *Cars* took much of their inspiration from Route 66, and they found their model for one of the movie's most beloved characters here in Galena, Kansas. Today, drivers can visit him at this roadside attraction.

**ABOVE**
Tow Tater, or Tow Mater, the star of Pixar's 2006 animated movie *Cars*

**RIGHT**
The retro service station setting of Cars on the Route

A few years before the animation studio Pixar released *Cars*, in 2006, members of its film crew set out on a Route 66 road trip of their own. Led by Michael Wallis, the bestselling author of *Route 66: The Mother Road*, the group spent weeks cruising the highway, scouting locations, and looking for inspiration. According to the movie's co-director John Lasseter, Pixar did more research for *Cars* than for any other movie up to that point.

In Kansas, the team came across an abandoned 1951 International L-170 Series boom truck. Rusted out and unusable, it didn't look like much. Joe Ranft, the film's other director, saw something in it, though, and he went on to base *Cars*' comic sidekick, the lovable if a bit dim in the headlights Mater, on the vehicle. Today, this characterful old tow truck lives at Cars on the Route, a few blocks down from the *Greetings from Galena* mural. Occupying a restored Kan-O-Tex service station from the 1930s, it's part welcome center, part restaurant, part gift shop. Alongside its main attraction, a second tow truck and a fire engine are on display, both also having been given the *Cars* treatment with big cartoon eyes on their windshields. The L-170 no longer goes by Tow Mater, by the way. When Disney acquired the copyright to the name, Cars on the Route had to find another. Its owners held a renaming contest, which was won by a local girl. Her suggestion? Tow Tater.

*Cars* fans will find more sights around the corner at Luigi's Pit Stop on Front Street. Along with replicas of the race car Lightning McQueen and the 1959 Fiat 500 Luigi, there's a facsimile of the Sheriff, a 1949 Mercury Eight police cruiser. Its door is signed by Wallis, who voiced the character.

ROUTE 66
CARS on the ROUTE
ROUTE 66
KAN O TEX
KAN O TEX
ETHYL
REGULAR

HISTORY

# THE EAGLE-PICHER STRIKE

Galena might appear a sleepy spot, but the town saw lead smelters strike in 1935. The result? Galena's stretch of Route 66 became the only section of the highway to be placed under martial law.

1

In 1876, settlers in the hills of southeastern Kansas stumbled upon a vein of galena, transforming the formerly sleepy corner of the state. This mineral is the most important ore of lead, and an occasional source of silver. Seeing the opportunity, a mining and smelting company quickly bought 120 acres near the vein and began establishing a town; within a few weeks, some 2,000 people were living there. The settlement went through several name changes—Cornwall, Short Creek, Bonanza—before landing on one that reflected its reason for being, Galena.

Life in the town of Galena revolved entirely around mining. As many as 250 mines were established in the area, along with 65 ore crushers, two smelters, and three sludge mills, plus three railroads were constructed to handle production. May 1876 saw the launch of the town's first newspaper, the *Galena Miner*. By 1899, as many as 30,000 people lived in the town, and more than $100 million worth of lead and zinc had been mined—the equivalent of around $3.8 billion today. By some estimations, Galena was the wealthiest town per capita in the world.

Galena's prosperity continued into the first decades of the 20th century, aided by the routing of Route 66 straight down Main Street.

Just outside town, however, drivers on the highway witnessed the price of that prosperity: mountains of mine tailings, and broad swaths of cinder-covered wasteland. There was also trouble brewing within the industry. In the spring of 1935, workers at the Eagle-Picher smelter went on strike to protest poor working conditions and demand recognition of their union. Management refused, and the unrest came to a head in late June, when striking workers threw rocks and threatened to shoot those workers who refused to join the union and/or strike as they attempted to enter the plant to work. Twelve men were injured, and cars on the adjacent Route 66 were overturned, bringing traffic on the highway to a halt. In response, the Kansas governor, Alf Landon, called in the National Guard and placed Galena under military control while attempting to quash the violence. The Galena Mining & Historical Museum covers this period of the city's history in great detail.

Although the Eagle-Picher strike was suppressed, strikes at other facilities and violent confrontations between strikers and strikebreakers continued for several years. The industry fell into decline in the ensuing decades, and the last Galena mine shut down in the 1970s.

**1** Onlookers watch as striking miners are marched through the street, Galena

**2** Galena's Train Depot, today housing the Galena Mining & Historical Museum

**3** A Kansas zinc miner on strike, and holding a protest poster, 1936

**4** Mining tools, hats, and lunchboxes displayed inside the Galena Mining & Historical Museum

**5** Bustling Galena in 1898, during the height of the city's mining industry

# THE OLD RIVERTON STORE

SHOPS AND STORES

RIVERTON

**ABOVE**
The well-stocked deli counter of the Old Riverton Store

**TOP RIGHT**
Plants and retro Route 66 signs found outside the store

**BOTTOM RIGHT**
Tempting snacks and souvenirs lining the shelves around the checkout counter

Open since 1925, the Old Riverton Store has been witness to the Mother Road's entire history. It's a road-trip icon, and just a short drive from Galena, making a sandwich from this little-changed outpost an unmissable road trip pick-me-up.

A lot has changed on Route 66 in the course of 100 years, but some things remain the same, like the Old Riverton Store. While many sights and businesses have capitalized on the highway's historic legacy, by installing vintage signs and restored antiques, the Old Riverton Store is the real deal. Leo and Lora Williams built the store in 1925, selling groceries, fresh meat, and clothes, among other goods. Lora served locals her homemade chili, while her husband, Leo, made sandwiches and barbecued beef and venison in a pit out back. Through the years, the store swapped names and owners, but one thing remained constant: the store took care of locals and, increasingly, travelers, as traffic boomed on Route 66 in the middle of the 20th century. In the 80s and 90s, it was a favorite of the artist and Route 66 fixture Bob Waldmire *(p38)*, and later in the early 2000s, the store provided inspiration to the film crew behind the Pixar hit *Cars*.

Today, the Old Riverton Store is owned by Scott Nelson, president of the Route 66 Association of Kansas. The gas pumps and one of the outhouses built by Leo and Lora are gone, but the squat, redbrick building retains its polished wooden floor and pressed metal ceiling, and old ads for Bunny Bread and Lemmy brand lemonade still hang on the walls. And while potato salad has replaced Lora's famous chili on the menu, road-trippers can still pick up provisions like sugar and baking powder, or just grab a bologna and cheddar cheese sandwich to eat on the front porch, like those who came before them.

Will the Old Riverton Store still be around in another hundred years? Who's to say? If it is, though, you can bet it won't look much different.

**"The store took care of locals and, increasingly, travelers, as traffic boomed."**

# BAXTER SPRINGS

HERITAGE SITES

**BAXTER SPRINGS**

**TOP RIGHT**
A mural depicting the fateful night of October 6, 1863, at the Baxter Springs Heritage Center & Museum

**BOTTOM RIGHT**
A sign for the Fort Blair Historic Site, where Quantrill's Raiders attacked Union soldiers

**BELOW**
Outside the informative Baxter Springs Heritage Center & Museum

Last but by no means least on this short Kansas stretch is the town of Baxter Springs. Not far from Riverton, this place weaves together tales of Indigenous heritage, 19th-century miners, and a bloody Civil War.

Baxter Springs is Kansas's largest town on Route 66, and is named after John Baxter, the first settler in the area, and the mineral springs that the Indigenous Osage people were using as early as 1800. Anyone looking for a good soak will be disappointed, however. The springs dried up in the early 1900s, likely a result of local mining operations. Instead, visitors will find a rich and varied story of Kansas's history, most prominently on display at the Baxter Springs Heritage Center & Museum. Exhibits delve into 20th-century life in the area, the state's notable mining industry, and Indigenous heritage, in particular the Osage chief Black Dog, who forged an important trail linking the springs with the Great Salt Plains of north-central Oklahoma.

The museum's Civil War exhibit is devoted primarily to the region's most dramatic tale, which can also be explored at the Fort Blair Historic Site, just up the road. During the war, the fort garrisoned a contingent of about 100 Union soldiers, half of whom were white and under the command of Lt. John Crites, and half of whom were Black, under the command of Lt. Ralph Cook. As the soldiers were sitting down to lunch on October 6, 1863, the fort was attacked by Quantrill's Raiders, a loose band of 400 Confederate guerrillas, led by the notorious William Quantrill. Though the Union soldiers were outnumbered roughly four to one, they were far more disciplined (they also had a 12-lb (5.4-kg) mountain howitzer) and repelled the Raiders with few casualties. Rebuffed, Quantrill's men retreated north of the fort, where they happened upon a Union wagon train led by General James Blunt. The Raiders routed the surprised Union troops, killing dozens. Blunt survived, but it's likely this was only because he was dressed in civilian clothes.

Just weeks after the battle, the Union soldiers at Fort Blair were posted elsewhere, and the fort was decommissioned and demolished. Following the war, Baxter Springs was established where the fort had once stood.

BAXTER FLEA
COLD DRINKS
LOCALS
KANSAS
US
66
WELCOME
ANTIQUES
FROM ALL
ERAS
COLLECTIBLES
OF ALL
KINDS

Baxter Flea Market, an emporium of antiques and tchotchkes

# OKLAHOMA

Stretching for nearly 400 miles (644 km), from the Missouri border to the edge of Texas, Route 66 cuts a bold path through the heart of Oklahoma. It's here that the Mother Road starts to hit its stride—a place where grassy plains roll out to the horizon, red hills rise suddenly from the earth, and pockets of pure Americana still hum with life. In big cities like Tulsa and Oklahoma City, vintage neon flickers, signaling new energy in old haunts. And between these urban hubs, the roadside serves up an array of quirky stops: a gas station stocking hundreds of fizzy sodas, a hand-built park crowned by a towering totem pole, and friendly giants in the form of muffler men standing guard. In Oklahoma, Route 66 is less a relic and more a living, breathing tribute—proof that even the most familiar roads can still surprise you.

TULSA

# OKLAHOMA

**DISTANCE**
400 miles (644 km)

**DRIVE TIME (NONSTOP)**
Approx. 5 hours

**LANDSCAPE**
Calm, grassy prairies meet soaring red mountains across Oklahoma, with the occasional big city breaking up the rural bliss.

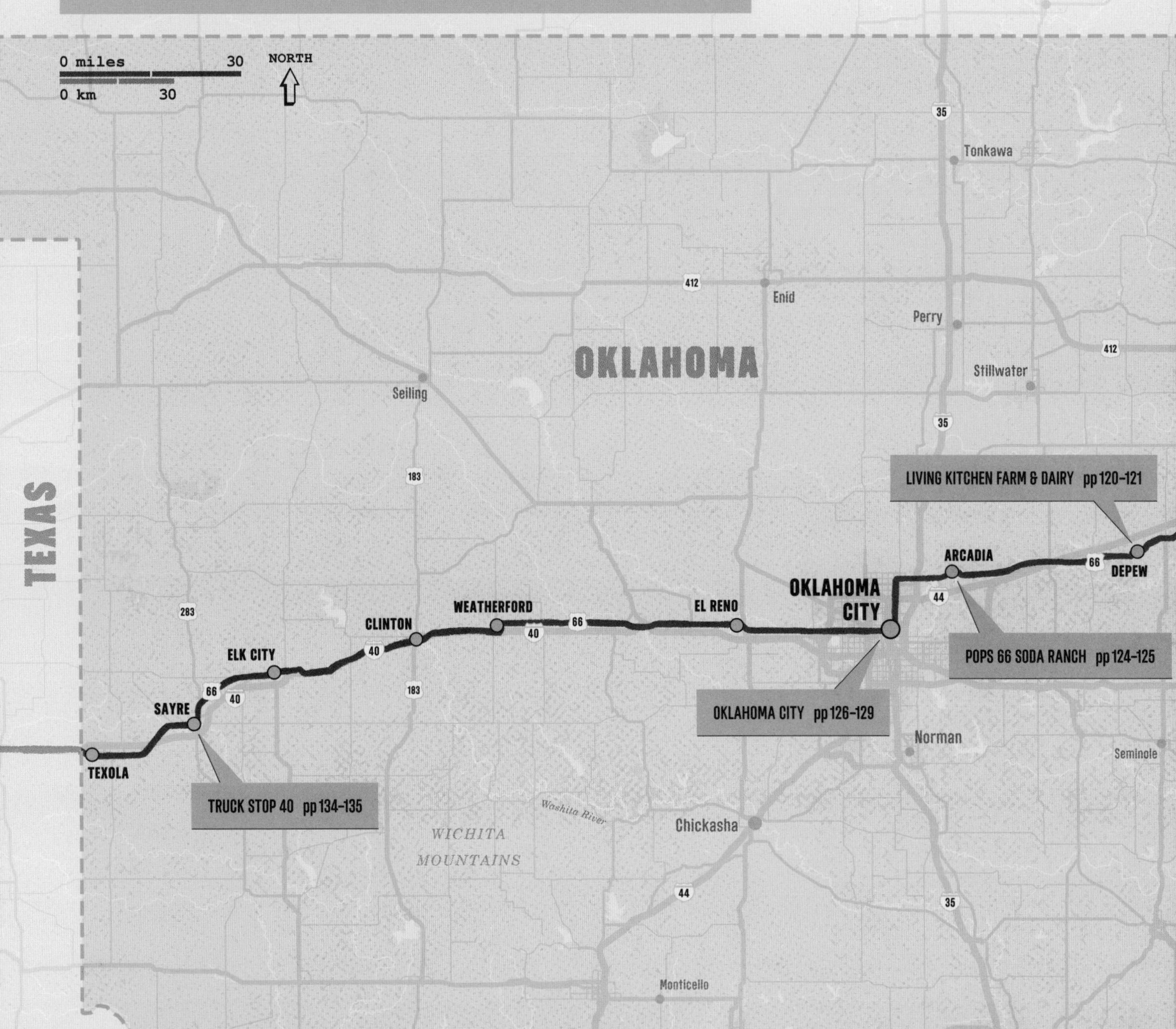

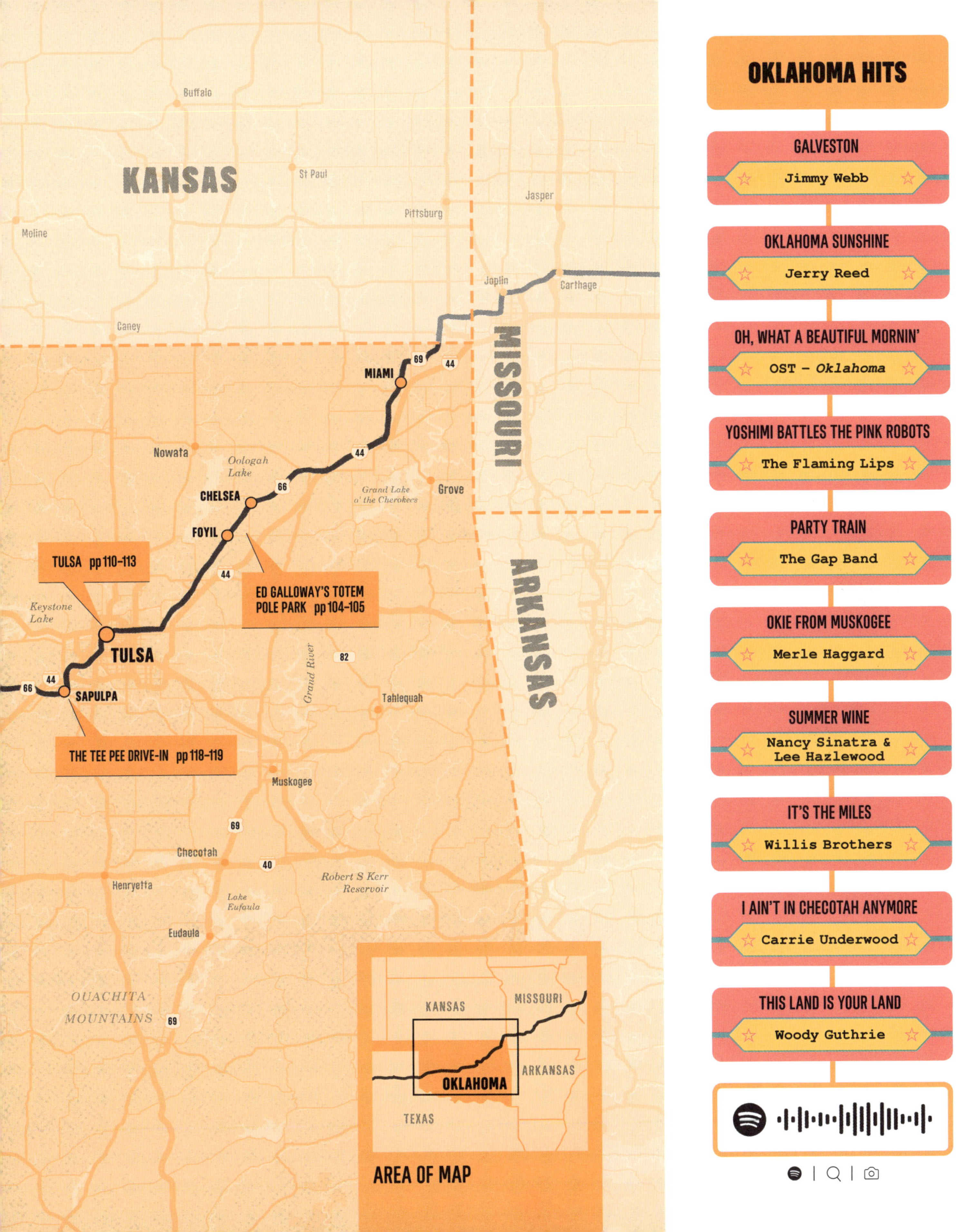

KANSAS
MISSOURI
ARKANSAS
Buffalo
St Paul
Jasper
Pittsburg
Moline
Joplin
Carthage
Caney
MIAMI
Nowata
Oologah Lake
CHELSEA
FOYIL
Grand Lake o' the Cherokees
Grove
TULSA pp 110–113
ED GALLOWAY'S TOTEM POLE PARK pp 104–105
Keystone Lake
TULSA
SAPULPA
Grand River
Tahlequah
THE TEE PEE DRIVE-IN pp 118–119
Muskogee
Checotah
Henryetta
Robert S Kerr Reservoir
Lake Eufaula
Eudaula
OUACHITA MOUNTAINS
AREA OF MAP
OKLAHOMA
TEXAS
OKLAHOMA HITS
GALVESTON
Jimmy Webb
OKLAHOMA SUNSHINE
Jerry Reed
OH, WHAT A BEAUTIFUL MORNIN'
OST – *Oklahoma*
YOSHIMI BATTLES THE PINK ROBOTS
The Flaming Lips
PARTY TRAIN
The Gap Band
OKIE FROM MUSKOGEE
Merle Haggard
SUMMER WINE
Nancy Sinatra & Lee Hazlewood
IT'S THE MILES
Willis Brothers
I AIN'T IN CHECOTAH ANYMORE
Carrie Underwood
THIS LAND IS YOUR LAND
Woody Guthrie

# ED GALLOWAY'S TOTEM POLE PARK

ODDITIES AND AMERICANA

FOYIL

Welcome to one of Route 66's most offbeat and unexpected landmarks. An early highlight on this state stretch, this totem pole park is the work of retired craftsman Ed Galloway, who spent 11 years sculpting a collection of soaring totem poles, including what might just be the world's largest.

Tucked a couple of miles off historic Route 66 in northeastern Oklahoma, Ed Galloway's Totem Pole Park has been stopping drivers in their tracks since the 1940s—and for good reason. Its centerpiece is a 90-ft (27-m) sculpture, believed to be the world's largest totem pole. Painted in bold splashes of red, blue, and yellow, this lofty landmark is covered in over 200 carved designs and balanced on the back of a sculptured turtle.

Its maker? Former teacher Ed Galloway, who crafted the icon between 1937 and 1948 using cement, steel, and sand (he collected most of the natural materials by hand from a nearby stream). Drawing inspiration from visual sources like *National Geographic* magazine and an array of old postcards, Galloway incorporated Indigenous motifs as a tribute to Turtle Island, an Indigenous name for North America. Today, the pole stands as one of Route 66's most accomplished examples of naive art, but it also raises questions about cultural appropriation, particularly since totem pole carving is a tradition among Indigenous groups in the Pacific Northwest, rather than those in Oklahoma.

Galloway's park also features some of his smaller totem poles, as well as the Fiddle House, an 11-sided building that once exhibited the artist's hand-carved fiddles; it now operates as a gift shop and micro-museum. After Galloway's death in 1961, the site fell into neglect until restoration efforts and a fresh lick of paint in the 1990s and again in 2014 brought it back to life. It's now listed on the National Register of Historic Places, and makes for one of Oklahoma's most distinctive detours.

**ABOVE**
Indigenous figures on a sculpture in the park

**RIGHT**
The park's centerpiece, believed to be the largest totem pole in the world



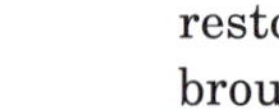

Route 66 runs through lands long inhabited by Indigenous peoples. Today, it offers travelers the chance to engage with their cultures, histories, and traditions.

HISTORY

# INDIGENOUS HERITAGE

1

The first Indigenous peoples to settle in what is now Oklahoma were the Caddo people, members of the Mississippian culture who arrived in what are now the eastern reaches of Oklahoma around 1000 CE. Over the centuries, they were joined by other groups, including the Wichita, Osage, and Plains Apache, who largely settled along the region's rivers. While these communities came of their own accord, later arrivals wouldn't be so fortunate.

The 19th century was a period of shattering upheaval for the continent's Indigenous peoples. As the U.S. government pursued westward expansion, it forced communities to leave their ancestral homes and relocate to land it had designated as Indian Territory: the Cherokee, Creek, and Seminole came from the Southeast; the Delaware, Seneca, and Wyandot from the Northeast; the Ottawa, Sauk, and Potawatomi from the Great Lakes—67 groups in all. To add insult to injury, this so-called Indian Territory didn't even remain in the hands of Indigenous peoples. The Land Run of 1889 opened the region to a flood of settlers, and in 1907, it was incorporated into the new state of Oklahoma.

Though Indigenous lands were lost, a 2020 Supreme Court ruling returned a measure of sovereignty to Oklahoma's 39 Indigenous groups,

**1** Members of the Sauk and Fox Nation dancing during a gathering known as a powwow

**2** A pond in Fort Gibson, a town in Cherokee and Muskogee counties

**3** Indigenous peoples and settlers in newly formed Guthrie, Oklahoma, just four weeks after the 1889 "Land Run"

**4** The Caddo people, who settled along the Washita River after displacement in the mid-1800s

**5** An Osage warrior by Charles Balthazar Julien Févret de Saint-Mémin, 1804

and today they have their own nations, with their own governments. Route 66 passes through many of them, including those of the Quapaw, Sauk, Cherokee, Cheyenne, and Arapaho.

Of course, Oklahoma isn't the only state where Route 66 crosses Indigenous territory, nor is it the only place where Indigenous culture is present. From 66's very beginning, Indigenous imagery has been ubiquitous along the highway, though its ability to attract tourists has almost always outweighed its accuracy. Ed Galloway's Totem Pole Park *(p104)* in Chelsea, Oklahoma, transplants the art form quite far from its home in the Pacific Northwest, while the rooms at Arizona's famed Wigwam Motel *(p196)* are shaped not like the wigwams of the Great Lakes Indigenous peoples but like the teepees of the Plains Native Americans, to take just two examples. The list is long.

Fortunately, this cultural appropriation is increasingly a thing of the past. Improved emphasis on authentic representation and the prominent place of Indigenous folk in Oklahoman society mean that the state now offers opportunities to discover the stories of these communities on their own terms. Seek out Indigenous history museums, local festivals, and annual powwows for a more accurate insight into America's oldest cultures.

# WILL ROGERS

Indigenous actor and comedian

Journey down Route 66 for long enough and you'll see the name Will Rogers cropping up everywhere—on signs, statues, and above the doorways of museums. That's because (officially) you're not just driving along Route 66; you're driving along the Will Rogers Memorial Highway. To understand why, you need to know a little about the man behind the name.

Born in 1879 on a Cherokee Nation ranch in Indian Territory (now Oklahoma), Will Rogers was one of America's most treasured actors and comedians. He roped his way from rodeos to vaudeville, before landing a slew of roles on the silver screen. By the 1930s, he was one of the most recognizable entertainment figures in the country, earning the nickname "Oklahoma's Favorite Son" for his homespun wisdom, sharp political wit, and easy charm. He also made history as the first Indigenous actor to host the Academy Awards, in 1934. So when Rogers tragically died in a plane crash in 1935, it hit the nation hard. Within days, Tulsa locals launched a campaign to rename Route 66 in his honor—by the end of that year, it was official.

Today, the road may be better known as Route 66, but Rogers's legacy remains. In Claremore, Oklahoma, the Will Rogers Memorial Museum preserves his legacy with permanent exhibits featuring his Stetson cowboy hat, regular movie screenings, and an annual street parade. Meanwhile in Santa Monica, a plaque dedicated to the actor can be found near the road's end point. Just like the famous highway that bears his name, Rogers remains a symbol of folksy wit and unwavering resilience.

PEOPLE OF THE ROAD

PEOPLE OF THE ROAD

# TULSA

CITIES OF 66

Neon signs, muffler men, old-school diners, offbeat attractions, rich multicultural history—no city combines 66's classic elements quite like Tulsa. This charismatic city is the perfect place to cut the motor and take a break from the road.

Michael Wallis, the country's foremost Route 66 historian, has called Tulsa the "heart and soul of Route 66." It's hard to find a counterargument. The iconic road may have been born in Springfield, Missouri, but it was first conceived here, by the Tulsa oilman Cyrus Avery (who helped create the Federal Highway System; *p114*). As the center of America's 20th-century oil industry, Tulsa made the highway's traffic go, and today, its complex fabric blends Indigenous, Black, and Euro-American settler history, while offbeat attractions imbue the city with 66's unique spirit. On top of all of that, there's Tulsa's location. Near the middle of the route, it's rarely a journey's beginning or end, meaning travelers have both stories to tell and miles of adventure to look forward to.

## 66 ON 11

Drivers on their way west will roll into Tulsa on 11th Street, where the four blocks between St. Louis Avenue and Peoria Avenue might just have the densest concentration of classic Route 66 culture on the highway. First up is Ike's Chili. Opened by Ike and Ivan Johnson in 1908, it's Tulsa's oldest restaurant and was a favorite of Will Rogers *(p109)*, America's favorite cowboy. It may have moved around some (it opened in its current location in 2014), and it might not sell its chili for $0.15 a bowl anymore, but it still uses the same recipe that's been passed down through four generations.

Practically next door is DECOPOLIS, a quirky museum and love letter to Tulsa's Art Deco architecture. The city's oil-fueled early 20th-century economic boom coincided with the peak of the style's popularity, leaving Tulsa with one of the country's best assemblages of Art Deco buildings.

This iconic street is also home to not one, not two, but three majestic muffler men. Beneath the neighborhood's primary landmark—30-ft (9-m)

**LEFT**
Tulsa is widely known as the unofficial "Capital of Route 66"

**LEFT**
Neon signs glowing next to Buck Atom, one of the city's three giant muffler men

**BELOW**
Tulsa's most iconic landmark, advertising Meadow Gold milk and ice cream

by 30-ft neon signs from 1934 that advertise Meadow Gold milk and ice cream—stands Meadow Gold Mack, an axe-wielding lumberjack brought south from an Illinois lumberyard. If Mack represents the classic 60s statue, his neighbors are avatars of the modern muffler man (or, rather, muffler people), with the basic fiberglass template acting as a canvas for imaginative reinterpretations. Buck and Stella Atom serve as mascots for Buck Atom's Cosmic Curios on 66, a souvenir shop housed in (what else?) a former gas station. Buck's a cosmic cowboy with a silver rocket and a ten-gallon hat perched atop his space helmet, while Stella accents her horseshoe-bedecked dress and cowboy boots with a jet pack and ray gun.

## THREE NATIONS

More history awaits just a short detour off 66, on Cheyenne Avenue. Here, drivers can find the exact spot where Tulsa was founded. Forced from their home in Alabama, the Lochapoka band of Muscogee arrived here in the early 1830s and laid the ashes from their ancestral lands' last council fires beneath a post oak on the banks of the Arkansas River. Every year, tribal leaders rekindle their sacred fire beneath the tree in what's now Creek Nation Council Oak Park.

Today's Tulsa sits at the juncture of the Muscogee, Cherokee, and Osage nations and possesses some of the richest Indigenous heritage of any U.S. city. Few did more to preserve it than Thomas Gilcrease, a wealthy oilman and member of the Muscogee Creek Nation who established the Gilcrease Museum on Tulsa's northwestern edge in 1949. Among the collection's 350,000 items are Indigenous textiles, cradleboards, pottery, and art, not just from Indigenous groups but from cultures throughout the Americas. It also holds the world's largest public collection of art of the American West.

## RISING FROM THE ASHES

When Oklahoma was opened to settlers in the Land Rush of 1889, many Black Americans sensed opportunity, and Tulsa has had a robust Black community ever since. In the early 1900s, its Greenwood neighborhood grew so prosperous that its main avenue came to be known as Black Wall Street. Success didn't exempt the community from racism, however, and on May 31, 1921, Greenwood was the site of the worst outbreak of racial violence in the country's history, the Tulsa Race Massacre. Fueled by a false rumor that a Black man had tried to rape a white woman, a mob rampaged through the district, killing as many as 300 Black residents and leaving Greenwood in ruins.

Despite the destruction, Greenwood rebuilt. Today, it's a thriving commercial center, home to Tulsa's pro soccer and minor league baseball teams and numerous Black-owned restaurants, shops, and cafés. The neighborhood also hosts the Greenwood Rising History Center and Greenwood Cultural Center, where photos, videos, and oral histories preserve the memory of the 1921 massacre and celebrate the vibrant neighborhood that Tulsa's Black community built, and then built again.

Anyone moved by the struggle for civil rights will find more inspiration just a couple of blocks west, at the Woody Guthrie Center. Born in 1912 in Okemah, Oklahoma, Guthrie was not only America's greatest folk singer but an unbending supporter of the disadvantaged and downtrodden, famously displaying the message "This machine kills fascists" on his guitar. Visitors to the center will find some of Guthrie's instruments and the original handwritten lyrics for his most enduring song, "This Land Is Your Land." There are also stations for listening to his music, the perfect addition to your Route 66 playlist.

**ABOVE**
Greenwood Rising museum, which tells the story of "Black Wall Street" both before and after the race massacre of 1921

**LEFT**
Contemplating the Black Wall Street Mural, by artist Donald "scribe" Ross, in the Greenwood District

# CYRUS AVERY

Father of Route 66

It's fair to say that without the tenacity of Cyrus Avery, a forward-thinking Oklahoma entrepreneur, Route 66 might never have been born. A slick Tulsa oilman, and visionary highway commissioner, Avery was the driving force behind the idea of connecting America's patchwork of roadways—former bike paths, wagon trails, and auto club routes—into one continuous cross-country highway. What emerged became the iconic Route 66 that we now know and love.

In typical Route 66 fashion, the idea of the road first came about in a motel. Shortly after World War I, Avery opened a motel just outside Tulsa. Gazing through the lobby window, he noticed the untapped potential of a national road system—not just for the convenience of travelers but for towns like Tulsa, poised to thrive with better connectivity. He began advocating for improved roads across Oklahoma and played a key role in developing the Ozark Trails, an early network linking St. Louis to Amarillo.

By 1925, Avery had earned a national platform as Consulting Highway Specialist to the U.S. Bureau of Public Roads. Tasked with designing a Federal Highway System and assigning route numbers, he championed a Chicago to Los Angeles corridor. It was initially designated U.S. 60, but political wrangling—particularly with Kentucky's governor—led to a renumbering of the routes *(p76)*. And so, Route 66 was born.

In 2004, the city of Tulsa renamed the Eleventh Street Bridge the Cyrus Avery Route 66 Memorial Bridge, honoring the man still fondly remembered as the Father of Route 66.

66

The space-
cowboy muffler
man Buck Atom,
wielding a
silver rocket

TEE PEE
66
DRIVE-IN

# THE TEE PEE DRIVE-IN

ODDITIES AND AMERICANA

SAPULPA

Put it in park and pass the popcorn. There's something cinematic about Route 66, so there's no better ending to a long day on the road than the retro pleasures of a movie at Sapulpa's storied Tee Pee Drive-In.

Come the weekend, folks from Tulsa and Sapulpa, Berryhill, and Sand Springs cruise down 66, passing the world's tallest gas pump before arriving at a neon sign that points the way to the Tee Pee. They'll then park in one of the rows that extend out from the screen in an arc and wait for dusk to come and the opening credits to roll.

Drive-in movie theaters are a hallmark of Route 66, and the Tee Pee, 16 miles (28 km) southwest of Tulsa, is one of the highway's most notable. It opened on May 5, 1950, with a screening of *Tycoon*, starring John Wayne. Ten years later to the day, a tornado with 200-mph (322-km/h) winds tore through the area, wrecking the theater. Incredibly, the Tee Pee reopened within a month and continued to operate for several decades. In the end, however, it wasn't an act of God, but American progress that brought about the theater's demise: the Interstate took traffic away from 66, and the proliferation of indoor theaters led to the shuttering of drive-ins across the country. The Tee Pee closed in 1999 and sat abandoned until a passionate pair of preservationists, Joni and Ben Kante, purchased it in 2021. In 2023, nearly a quarter-century after its last show, the Tee Pee's projector flickered back to life.

Like many Route 66 businesses, the restored Tee Pee is a mix of throwback delights—think foot-long hot dogs and mid-century trailers that can be rented for overnight stays—and modern touches—like a rock climbing area and margarita slushes. And while the movies and the actors have changed over the years, the Tee Pee's main draw remains exactly the same as it was in 1950: the chance to lay back on your car's hood and watch the silver screen light up as the stars come out.

**CLOCKWISE FROM TOP LEFT**
Aerial view of the Tee Pee Drive-In; the large neon sign at sunset; friends enjoying tasty snacks and drinks before a movie screening

# LIVING KITCHEN FARM & DAIRY

DINERS AND DINING SPOTS

**DEPEW**

Route 66 can sometimes feel stuck in the past, stubbornly clinging to its 1950s heyday, but drivers will also find people breathing new life into the old road, often in the unlikeliest of places.

One slight downside to a Route 66 road trip is the overabundance of diners recycling mid-century nostalgia and offering interchangeable menus of burgers, corn dogs, and milkshakes. They're great, but after a few hundred miles, motorists may find themselves pining for something served on a plate and not in a basket.

Nearly halfway between Tulsa and Oklahoma City, on a stretch of 66 that winds past farms and copses of post oak, an easily missed gravel road runs off the highway to the south. It's an odd place to find a restaurant that's twice been nominated for a James Beard Award (the country's most prestigious restaurant honor), but there it is: the Living Kitchen Farm & Dairy.

**RIGHT**
Fresh, local ingredients being served up for hungry guests

**TOP RIGHT**
Neatly landscaped vegetable patches on the farm

**BOTTOM RIGHT**
Lisa Becklund, co-owner of the Living Kitchen

Calling this acclaimed place a restaurant might be doing it something of a disservice, though. Co-owners Lisa Becklund and Linda Ford describe what they do as "un-restauranting." Becklund, a self-professed "local food sovereignty weirdo," left a restaurant career in Seattle to learn how to farm in Oklahoma in the early 2000s; she started the Living Kitchen in 2005. Ford, a Missouri transplant, joined a few years later. Since then, the partners have been raising organic heirloom vegetables and livestock on the 400-acre (162-ha) farm and periodically hosting multicourse dinners.

There's no shortage of farm-to-table restaurants around the country, but Becklund and Ford obviate the need for the preposition. Their events are just "farm table dinners." While guests mingle with the farm's goats and stroll the garden in the golden evening light, Becklund prepares the night's tasting menu using fresh ingredients from the Living Kitchen and other local farms, cooking many of her dishes over an open fire. Meals are then served on the back porch of a rustic hand-built cabin, where bushels of dried chiles hang from the wall and paper lanterns illuminate the communal table. Here, you'll find locals and travelers sharing stories over plates of delicious wild sage cavatelli and sugar snap pea sorbet. This is fine dining meets farmhouse, and while it may be a far cry from the diners, it's the sort of meal that's easy to get nostalgic about.

PEOPLE OF THE ROAD

PEOPLE OF THE ROAD

# ☆ ALLEN THREATT 

Owner of Threatt Service Station

Just east of Luther, on a rural crossroads that marks the boundary between Oklahoma County and Lincoln County, sits a plain sandstone building. It doesn't look like much, but in Route 66's early years, it was an important stop, and safe haven, for Black motorists.

When the U.S. government opened Oklahoma to settlement in 1889, many Black Americans saw the region as a land of promise; somewhere they could build a new life. Among them was Allen Threatt, a tenant farmer who used his savings to purchase 160 acres (65 ha) in 1915. He grew crops, raised livestock, sold sandstone, and built a small structure on what was then State Highway 7 (on his property's northern edge), eventually turning it into a filling station. When Highway 7 was incorporated into Route 66 a few years later, it proved a boon to business.

In turn, the Threatt Filling Station was a boon to Black travelers. The region was home to numerous sundown towns *(p40)*, and businesses that refused them service. Yet at Threatt's, they could always get their tank filled, their oil changed, or their flats fixed. Business was so good that Threatt and his family added a small café and grocery to the station, and even opened a club and barbecue (called the Brown Bomber) next door. Over time, Threatt's became not just a stop for Black travelers but a destination: on weekends, Black baseball teams would play here during the day, and at night, the Threatts would string up lights in the trees and set up a floor and jukebox for dancing.

After Threatt passed away, his descendants continued to operate the station and café until 1974. It was then added to the National Register of Historic Places in 1995 and is still standing (though not operating) today.

# POPS 66 SODA RANCH

DINERS AND DINING SPOTS

ARCADIA

Americana, but make it modern: that's POPS 66 Soda Ranch, a futuristic gas station, store, diner, and soda spot just outside Oklahoma City. Drive toward the beams of its bottle-shaped beacon to choose from a mind-boggling array of fizzy pop from all around the world.

**ABOVE**
Guests sampling the variety of sodas sold in an array of fun colors

**RIGHT**
The towering bottle statue, illuminated with LED lights

While most of Route 66's iconic stops date back to the mid-20th century, a few standout additions from more contemporary times have earned a well-deserved pin on the map. One of the most notable is POPS 66 Soda Ranch, which opened in 2007 and has quickly become a beloved, and refreshingly sweet, pit stop on the road.

Incongruously located in the tiny town of Arcadia (population 174), POPS is big, bold, and, to many a contemporary architect, beautiful. There's no denying this place knows how to make an impression: its striking sci-fi design—which includes a cantilevered truss extending 100 ft (30 m) over the gas pumps and forecourt—has earned several architectural awards. It's also easy to spot from afar, just look out for the 66-ft- (20-m-) tall neon soda bottle, illuminated every night with a dazzling LED light display—the height is no coincidence.

It's all very modern, but there's a lot of nostalgia here, too. The sleek, sloping walls are lined with an eye-popping collection of more than 700 varieties of glass-bottled sodas, displayed in a rainbow of colors. These range from nostalgic favorites like Dad's Old Fashioned Root Beer to rare imports like Japanese ramune, complete with marble stoppers. There are some left-field flavors here, too (bacon-flavored soda, anyone?).

But it's not just fizzy pop on the menu. POPS is also home to an on-site diner. Here, you'll find all the classics like juicy burgers, pulled pork sandwiches, hand-dipped milkshakes, and warm apple pie. Be sure to try the root beer bread pudding, too—it's the restaurant's signature dessert, made with root beer, raisins, and white chocolate sauce.

And one more thing. After fueling up on mix-and-match sodas and comforting diner food, give your car a bit of attention, too. POPS is a functioning gas station, after all.

# OKLAHOMA CITY

CITIES OF 66

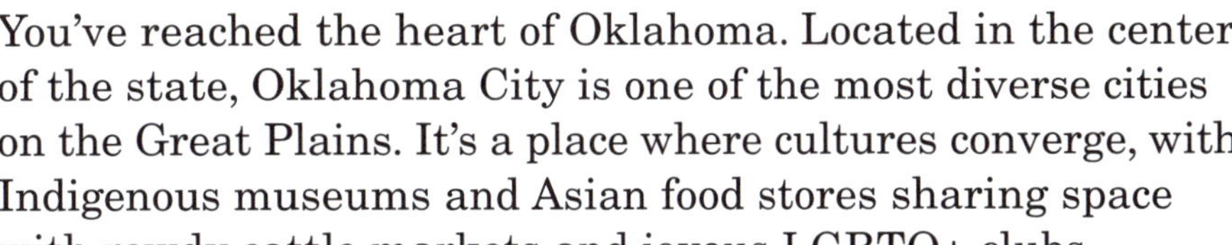

You've reached the heart of Oklahoma. Located in the center of the state, Oklahoma City is one of the most diverse cities on the Great Plains. It's a place where cultures converge, with Indigenous museums and Asian food stores sharing space with rowdy cattle markets and joyous LGBTQ+ clubs.

Oklahoma's capital (also known as OKC) has one of the country's more unusual origin stories. For a long time, it wasn't there, and then, suddenly, it was. On April 21, 1889, only three buildings and a train station stood on this patch of dirt along the Oklahoma River. The next day, the government opened the territory in the Oklahoma Land Rush, and by nightfall, thousands of settlers had staked a claim there. Abracadabra, Oklahoma City.

OKC's evolution has been equally dramatic. From its origins as a rough-and-tumble frontier town, it had grown into a bustling center of some 150,000 by the time of Route 66's inauguration. Today, it's one of the region's biggest and most cosmopolitan cities, with a population of more than 700,000 and vibrant Hispanic, Black, Asian, and Indigenous communities.

## COWBOYS AND INDIGENOUS HISTORY

Despite all the development, Oklahoma City remembers its roots: this is still a cowpoke town through and through. Across the river from downtown are the Oklahoma National Stockyards, the world's largest stocker and feeder cattle market, where cowboys in spurs and Stetsons herd cattle into a sprawling grid of corrals 24 hours a day, 365 days a year—well over 500,000 head of cattle pass through every year. The stockyards were founded in 1910, and many of the surrounding steakhouses, boot shops, and the like have been open just as long.

Road-trippers who want to dust up on more cowboy culture before the long journey West can do so at the National Cowboy & Western Heritage Museum, just off I-44/Route 66. Exhibitions here explore cowboy history and display age-old saddles, chaps, and firearms, including the Winchester Model 1873, widely known as the "gun that won the West." Other galleries

**LEFT**
The downtown skyline of Oklahoma City

cover how rodeos evolved from round-up competitions to professional events, and display works from the museum's extensive Western American art collection. Its signature piece is *End of the Trail* by James Earle Fraser, which depicts a weary Indigenous man seated atop his horse—it's one of the country's most famous sculptures.

Two of the building's major galleries are dedicated to the people who predate the cowboys: the West's Indigenous cultures. One displays objects ranging from moccasins (soft leather shoes) and olla earthenware vessels to ceremonial horse dance sticks; the other shows a rotating selection of fine art by Indigenous artists, including works by contemporary names such as Kevin Red Star and Frank Big Bear.

An even deeper immersion into Oklahoma's rich Indigenous heritage is available at the First Americans Museum, southeast of downtown. Set in a common Indigenous alignment with the cardinal directions, the museum's entrance faces the rising sun, while its main hall is designed to resemble the grass houses of the Wichita people. Exhibitions were developed by an all-Indigenous curatorial team in consultation with representatives from Oklahoma's 39 groups *(p106)* and include interactive elements that let visitors listen to oral histories or try their hands at traditional games.

**ABOVE LEFT**
*End of the Trail* sculpture by James Earle Fraser, displayed in the National Cowboy & Western Heritage Museum

**ABOVE RIGHT**
The First Americans Museum, which tells the story of Oklahoma's 39 Indigenous groups

## NEW ROUTES, NEW CULTURES

As in other cities, Route 66 changed alignments through Oklahoma City several times over the years, and two of those run through neighborhoods whose more recently emerging cultures have added to OKC's vitality.

The original Route 66 ran along Classen Boulevard, which today forms the backbone of the city's Asian District. In 1975, thousands of refugees fleeing the Vietnam War settled here, and many started food businesses. Today, the neighborhood buzzes with pho restaurants, pan-Asian supermarkets, Taiwanese bubble tea joints, and Hong Kong dim sum eateries, while Asian festivals are a common occurrence in Military Park. The district is also the site of the city's best-known oddball Route 66 attraction, the Milk Bottle Building. Across the street from the park, the triangular brick building holds up a giant milk bottle that was erected in 1948 and advertised Braum's "Oklahoma's milk."

About a mile (1.5 km) north of the Asian District, Classen runs into 39th Street, another part of early 66 alignments. Drivers who follow it west a few blocks will find themselves in the 39th Street District, the heart of OKC's LGBTQ+ scene. Among the pride flags and bike racks painted in rainbow hues, travelers can find drinks and dancing at Angles gay club, drag trivia and bingo at The Boom, and a good night's rest at the LGBTQ+ hotel and resort, The District. The strip is also dotted with several colorful murals, including a fun Route 66–themed one on the corner of 39th and Barnes Avenue that features Oklahoma roadside classics like Buck Atom and the Blue Whale of Catoosa. It's a neat tribute to this section of your journey and a fitting place to bid farewell to this state's capital.

**BELOW LEFT**
The colorful "Summer of 66" street mural by artist Nick Bayer in the 39th Street District

**BELOW RIGHT**
The famous Milk Bottle Building, built to advertise Braum's "Oklahoma's milk"

Few places in Oklahoma are better acquainted with the power of tornadoes than El Reno. This little city has been whipped up by whirlwinds multiple times; fittingly, it played a big role in the 2024 movie *Twisters*.

HISTORY

# TWISTERS & TORNADOES

1

As drivers pull into El Reno, about 40 minutes outside Oklahoma City, they may be relieved to see the city's water tower rooted firmly in place. In the climactic scene of the 2024 blockbuster *Twisters*, a monster tornado churns into town, hurling the tower into the side of a building (never mind that it was digitally moved a mile from its actual location), tossing El Reno's historic trolley down Bickford Avenue, and sending frantic citizens fleeing into the 1940s-era Centre Theatre in search of shelter. Presumably, a few fictional road-trippers were among them, as Route 66 zigzags right past the downtown blocks that were ground zero for this once-in-a-century storm.

While *Twisters* took some cinematic liberties, the basic threat is real. The Great Plains are the setting for some of North America's most violent storms—both fear-inducing and awe-inspiring in equal measure—and Oklahoma sits in the heart of a region known as Tornado Alley: in spring and summer, the state is regularly visited by supercell thunderstorms. These enormous storms roll ominously across the plains, churning up rain, hail, and sometimes tornadoes, whose winds can reach speeds of more than 200 mph (322 km/h). When filming in El Reno,

**1** The 2013 tornado, which measured 2.6 miles (4.2 km) across and was the widest in U.S. history

**2** Historic El Reno, a charming stop (when the tornadoes don't roll in)

**3** A film poster of the 2024 movie

**4** Federal officials assessing the chaos caused by the tornado of 2013

**5** El Reno's water tower, still standing despite the many storms

the *Twisters* production team ironically ended up at the mercy of these unsettled skies: a real storm swept through the city, destroying a farmers' market set. The crew quickly rebuilt it, just so they could destroy it again—only this time with the cameras rolling.

Yet for El Reno locals, the storm that interrupted *Twisters'* production would hardly rattle the EF-scale (the Enhanced Fujita scale that measures tornado intensity). This Oklahoma city is no stranger to extreme weather events. The inspiration behind the movie's El Reno tornado was in fact a real tornado that struck the city in 2013, one that, terrifyingly, outdid its fictional counterpart, reaching wind speeds of 313 mph (504 km/h) and measuring 2.6 miles (4.2 km) across. This multivortex storm wasn't El Reno's first, either. The city was hit two years earlier, in May 2011, by a rip-roaring tornado that struck the northwestern reaches, and then again, in 2019.

As global temperatures continue to rise and extreme weather events become all the more frequent, El Reno appears more vulnerable to catastrophic tornadoes than ever. Yet this little city has risen from the ruins left by the winds of 2019 and will continue to rebuild come rain or shine, or storm.

LUCILLE'S
66 HISTORIC HIGHWAY
Historic
OLD ROUTE 66
BUSINESS

# LUCILLE HAMONS 

Service Station Owner

Naturally, most folks' relationship with Route 66 is temporary, lasting only as long as their journey down the Mother Road. Yet for Lucille Hamons, this road was her life.

In 1941, Hamons and her husband, Carl, purchased a gas station and motor court fronting Route 66 just outside the town of Hydro, in the flat, lonesome plains of western Oklahoma. They lived above the station with their children, but Carl was often away (working as a truck driver), so Hamons largely ran the business herself. She pumped gas, fixed flats, changed oil, cleaned rooms, and cooked meals on a hot plate day and night. Her generosity quickly became well known among locals and journey-folk. She frequently opened spare rooms to penniless travelers in need of a bed for the night and even bought motorists' broken-down cars so they'd have money for a bus ticket.

The couple divorced in 1962, but Hamons continued to operate the gas station (originally called the Provine Station and later, Hamons' Court) even as the arrival of I-40 put a dent in the business. She pumped gas until 1986 and then continued to run the place as a souvenir shop for road-trippers, keeping it open until the day she died, August 18, 2000.

The station was added to the National Register of Historic Places in 1997, and Hamons was inducted into the Oklahoma Route 66 Hall of Fame in 1999, but her ultimate accolade was the nickname she earned for her six decades taking care of travelers along Route 66: Mother of the Mother Road.

PEOPLE OF THE ROAD

PEOPLE OF THE ROAD

# TRUCK STOP 40

DINERS AND DINING SPOTS

SAYRE

A truck stop in middle-of-nowhere Oklahoma might seem an unlikely destination for homemade Indian food, but this oasis outside the tiny town of Sayre is just that. Serving the immigrants who fuel America's economy, Truck Stop 40 is a fitting reflection of the modern trucking industry.

**ABOVE**
An empty road near Truck Stop 40, located in what appears to be the middle of nowhere

**RIGHT, CLOCKWISE FROM TOP**
Delicious Punjabi cuisine, cooked up in the *dhaba*; a large vegetarian spread; Raj and Harpreet Chhoker, who opened Truck Stop 40 in 2005

It's a long, lonely road after El Reno, with little but the empty Oklahoma horizon for company. Route 66 runs alongside I-40 here, and the chance to chew up the miles a bit faster lures many drivers away from the Mother Road and onto the freeway.

As the Interstate approaches the Texas border, a sign announces Exit 26, with access to Cemetery Road. It doesn't seem like a great place to pull off, and at first glance, nothing suggests otherwise. A black-and-white sign announces Truck Stop 40. Big rigs idle outside a garage. An American flag flaps in the dry wind. Look closer, though, and you'll notice a sign near the garage's side door that reads "INDIAN FOOD." Inside, trucker caps are replaced by turbans and greasy steaks by lentil curries. Orders are placed in Punjabi, Bollywood movies play on TVs, and the scent of cumin and turmeric fills the room.

Raj and Harpreet Chhoker opened Truck Stop 40 in 2005, with the 24-hour restaurant following a few years later. It might seem like an anomaly—an Indian American–owned truck stop and vegetarian restaurant in rural Oklahoma—but it's, in fact completely in tune with the country's contemporary trucking industry. A signficant share of truckers in America today are Punjabi, mostly first- or second-generation immigrants, and mostly Sikhs. In recent years, dozens of *dhabas*, as these roadside stops are known, have been established to serve these drivers—they sell Punjabi truck decor, provide small temples for worship, and offer a sense of community along the open road. Like Truck Stop 40, many lie along the I-40/Route 66 corridor in tiny towns like Vega, Texas; San Jon, New Mexico; and Milan, New Mexico. Their locations may be a little obscure, but these *dhabas* (so distinctly different from Route 66's kitschy diners) are destinations in themselves.

**"A significant share of truckers in America today are Punjabi."**

# TEXAS

As it snakes its way through the Deep South, Route 66 passes across the northern tip of the Lone Star State, known as the Panhandle, for 178 miles (286 km). While much of the original road has since been overtaken by the speedier I-40, towns like Shamrock, McLean, Vega, and the city of Amarillo still faithfully keep its legacy alive. Some drivers along 66 might grumble that the landscape hits the same note, with pancake-flat plains as far as the eye can see. But look closer, and the route delivers plenty of surprises: ultra-niche museums, a Texas-sized eating challenge, and even the chance to take a seat in a café booth once graced by the King of Rock 'n' Roll. With plenty of classic mom-and-pop diners to refuel at along the way, it's clear that there's more charm here than first meets the eye.

OPEN
T 6 6 X

# TEXAS

## DISTANCE
178 miles (286 km)

## DRIVE TIME (NONSTOP)
Approx. 3.5 hours

## LANDSCAPE
This northern section of the Lone Star State is a peaceful stretch, passing wide-open plains under endless skies.

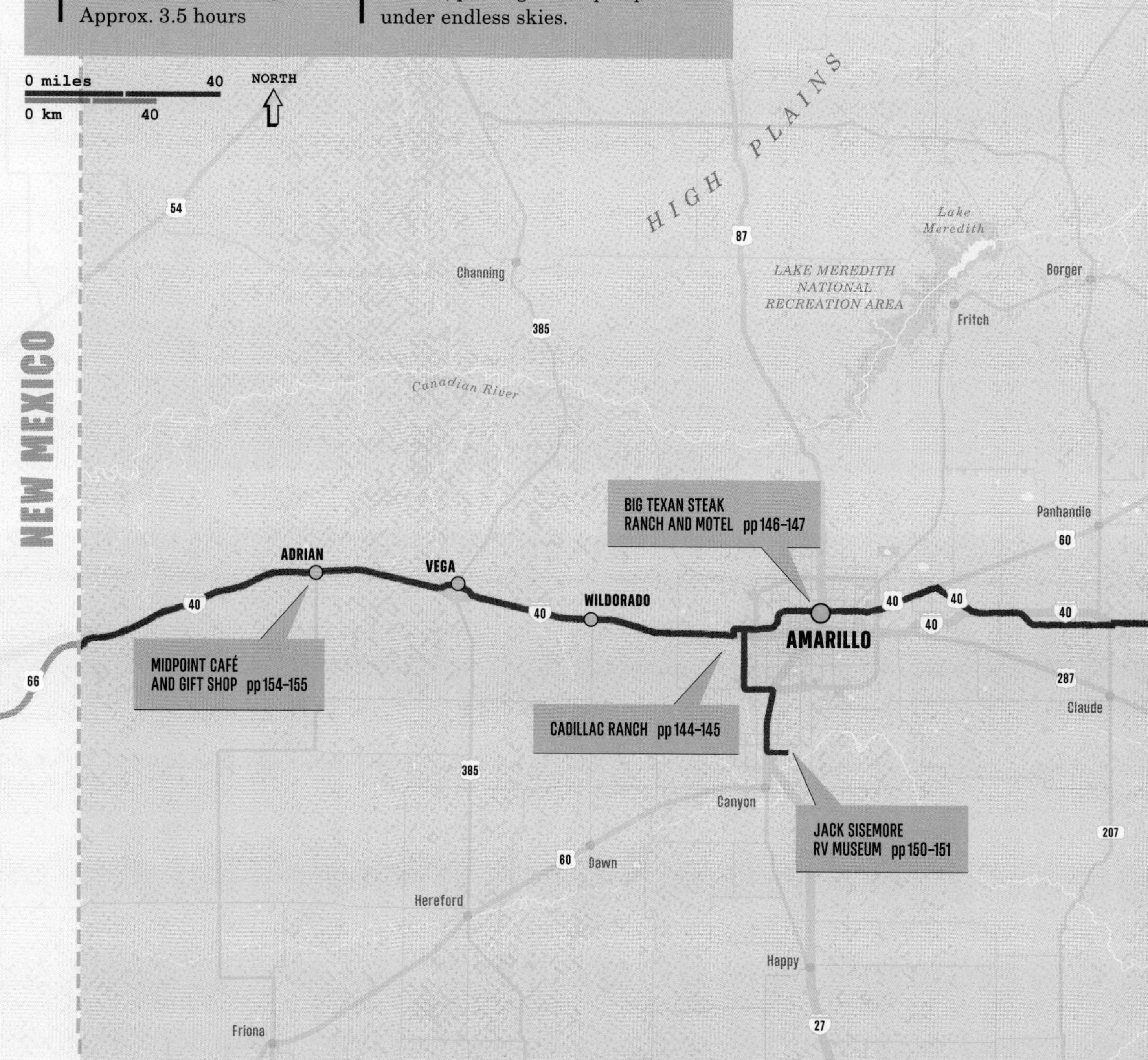

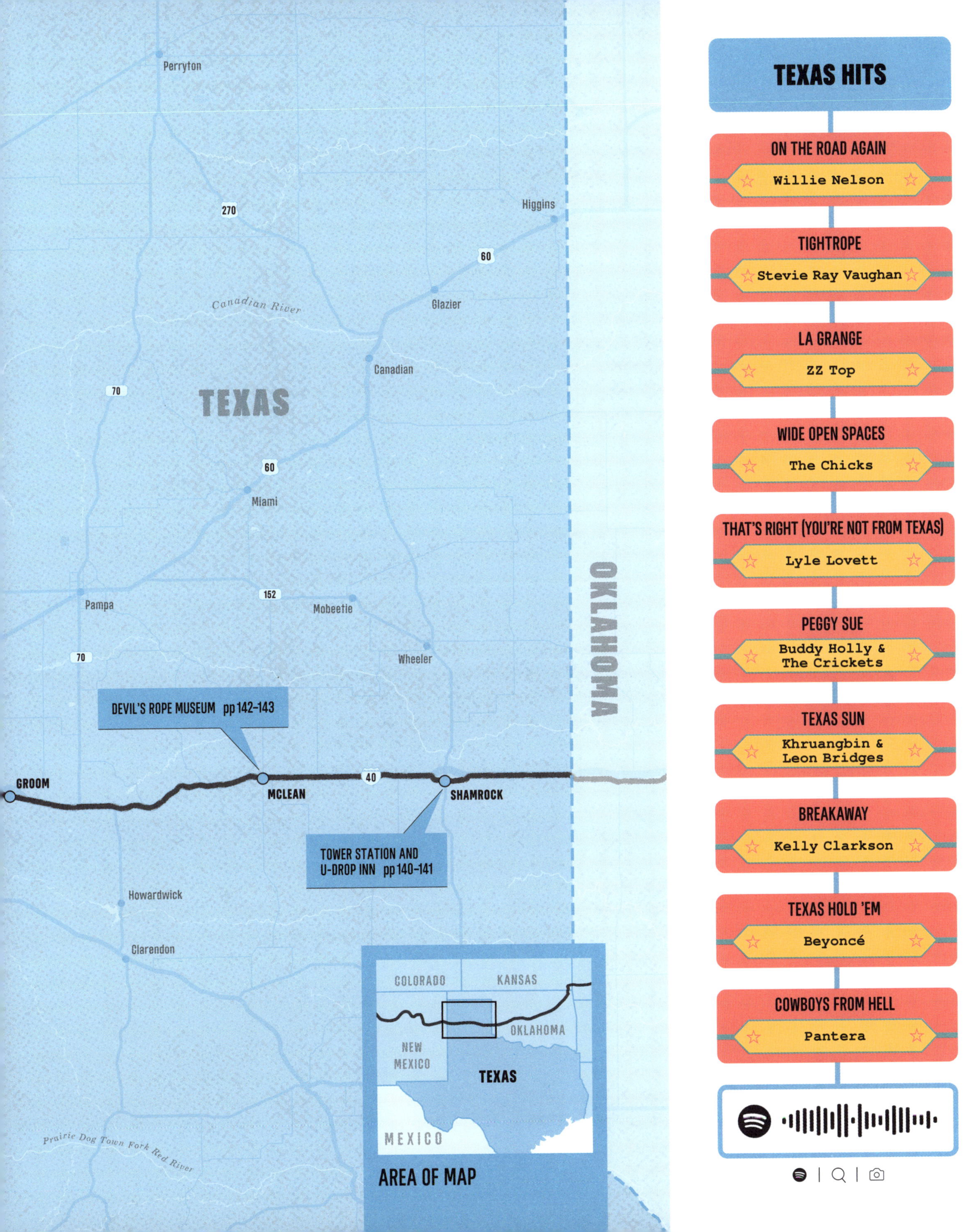

Perryton
270
Higgins
60
Canadian River
Glazier
Canadian
70
TEXAS
60
Miami
152
Pampa
Mobeetie
70
Wheeler
OKLAHOMA
DEVIL'S ROPE MUSEUM pp 142–143
GROOM
MCLEAN
40
SHAMROCK
TOWER STATION AND U-DROP INN pp 140–141
Howardwick
Clarendon
Prairie Dog Town Fork Red River
COLORADO
KANSAS
OKLAHOMA
NEW MEXICO
TEXAS
MEXICO
AREA OF MAP
TEXAS HITS
ON THE ROAD AGAIN
Willie Nelson
TIGHTROPE
Stevie Ray Vaughan
LA GRANGE
ZZ Top
WIDE OPEN SPACES
The Chicks
THAT'S RIGHT (YOU'RE NOT FROM TEXAS)
Lyle Lovett
PEGGY SUE
Buddy Holly & The Crickets
TEXAS SUN
Khruangbin & Leon Bridges
BREAKAWAY
Kelly Clarkson
TEXAS HOLD 'EM
Beyoncé
COWBOYS FROM HELL
Pantera

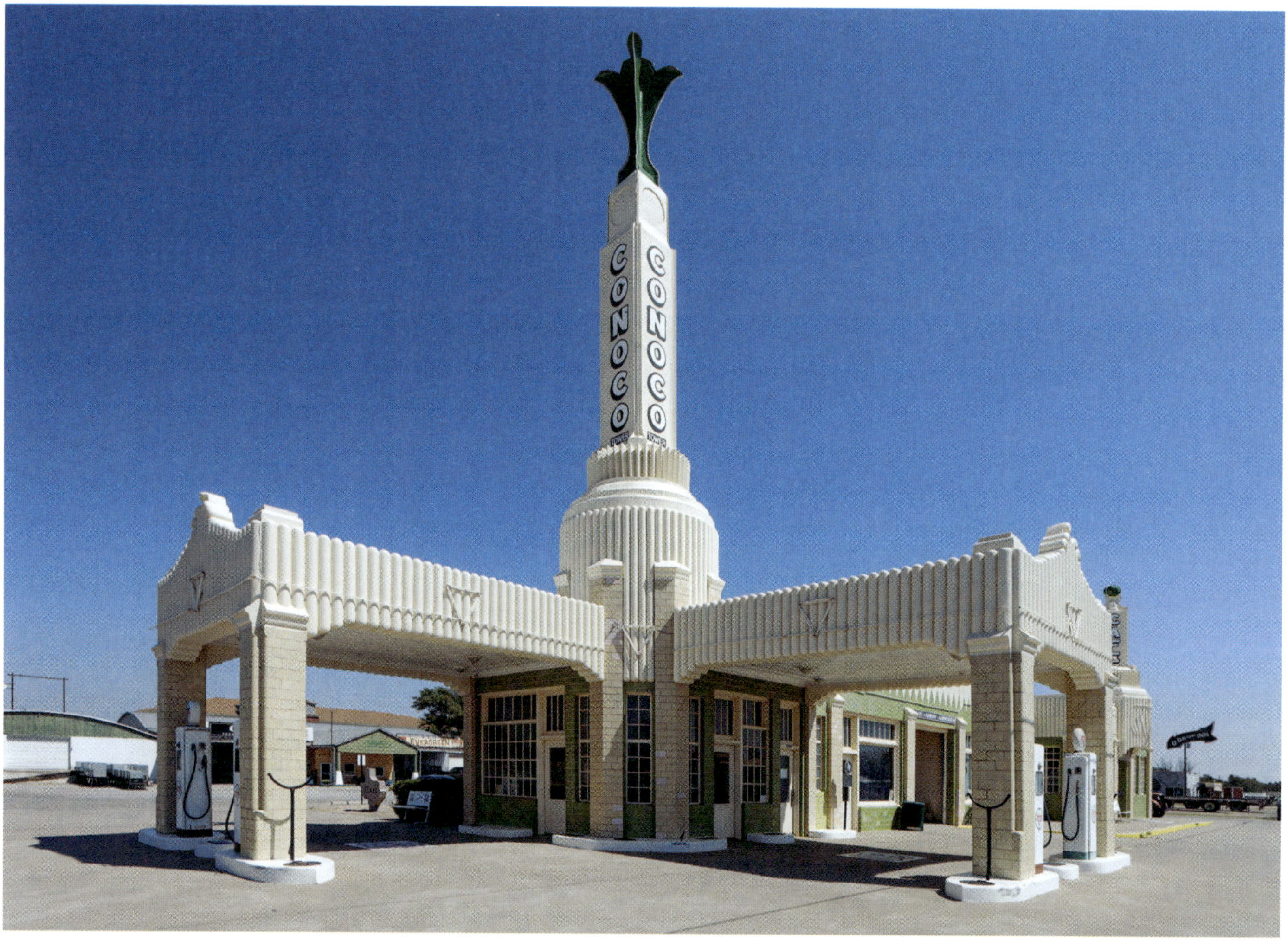
CONOCO
CONOCO

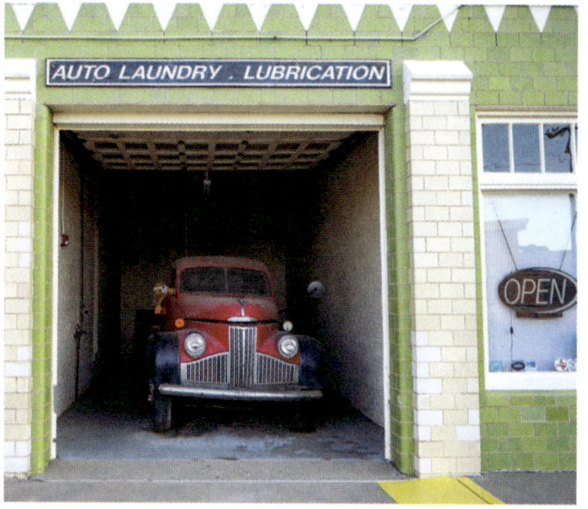

AUTO LAUNDRY . LUBRICATION
OPEN

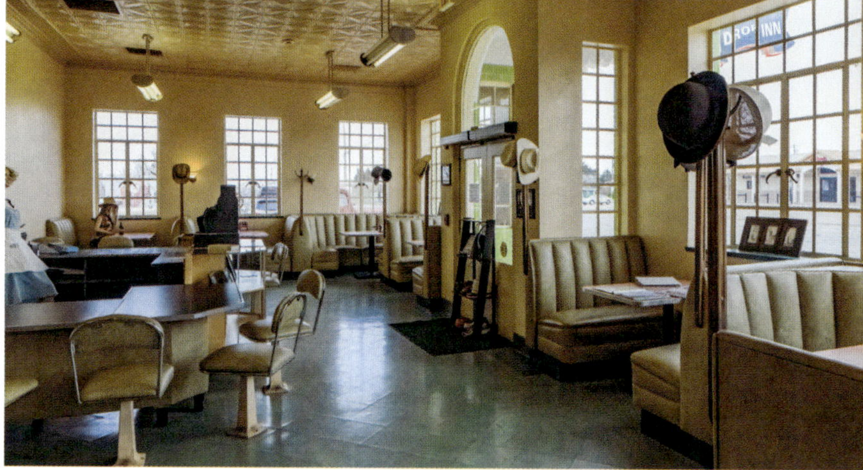

# TOWER STATION AND U-DROP INN

MUST-VISIT MUSEUMS

**SHAMROCK**

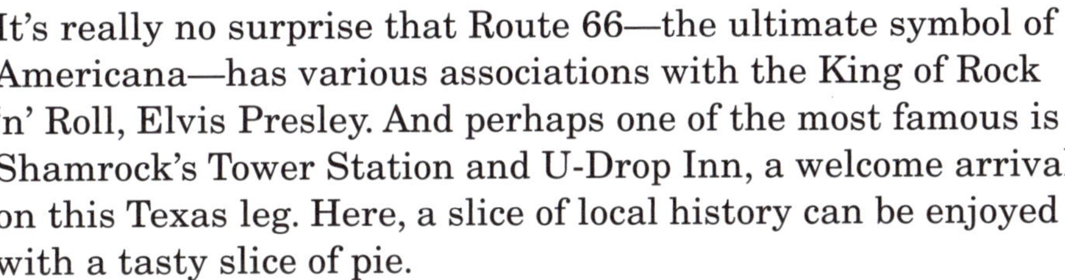

It's really no surprise that Route 66—the ultimate symbol of Americana—has various associations with the King of Rock 'n' Roll, Elvis Presley. And perhaps one of the most famous is Shamrock's Tower Station and U-Drop Inn, a welcome arrival on this Texas leg. Here, a slice of local history can be enjoyed with a tasty slice of pie.

When it first opened as a café and gas station in 1936, this gleaming Art Deco masterpiece tempted weary road-trippers with its hearty helpings of pie, coffee, and small-town charm. But it was a visit from the King during his 1963 tour that really put it on the map, with fans eager to follow in the footsteps of rock 'n' roll royalty and slide into the very same vinyl booth where the star once sat. The Tower Station and U-Drop Inn continued to thrive for decades after this visit, but, when Route 66 was decommissioned in 1985, the building slipped into disrepair, narrowly avoiding demolition.

Thanks to local conservation efforts, the landmark was restored to its former glory in the 2000s. Today, its iconic curved corners, glazed green tiles, and soaring tower make for an eye-catching highlight along the route, ready for a new generation of road-trippers to enjoy. Movie fans might recognize its unusual exterior from Pixar's *Cars*, in which Ramone's Body Shop is styled on the strikingly geometric building. Inside, there's a visitor center, a dinky museum, and a new café, where classic comfort foods like meatloaf—a favorite with Elvis—are served up while friendly volunteers dish out regional heritage stories. As the historic neon signs flicker on at sundown, casting a soft haze over the prairie horizon, the atmosphere is nostalgic; it's the kind of place where the past hasn't left the building.

**CLOCKWISE FROM TOP LEFT**
The Tower Station and U-Drop Inn with its sign for Conoco fuel; booths and tables inside the Tower Station and U-Drop Inn's restored café; a historic pickup tow truck parked inside the gas station

# DEVIL'S ROPE MUSEUM

MUST-VISIT MUSEUMS

MCLEAN

One of the unexpected delights of exploring Route 66 is stumbling upon its wonderfully niche museums. Few, however, are more specific than the Devil's Rope Museum in McLean. Housed in a former brassiere factory, this offbeat museum has been dedicated to the history of barbed wire since 1991.

Rolled up, strung out, or rusting, barbed wire might seem too mundane an item to warrant an entire museum dedicated to the stuff. But, once inside the Devil's Rope Museum, it all starts to make sense. Barbed wire, nicknamed "the Devil's Rope," was once a game changer in the American West, and this specialist museum sheds some light on its lasting impact on the region. The spiky wire allowed settlers to fence off vast, open lands swiftly and cheaply, transforming the endless stretches of frontier into a patchwork of private property, and reshaping the livelihoods of the people who called it home in the process. Its use also had a lasting impact on warfare, ranching, and law in the American West.

A staggering 2,000-plus varieties of barbed wire carefully collected from enthusiasts across the country are housed in the museum, alongside fencing tools and examples of historic wires once used in warfare. For those looking to dig a little deeper into the history of this type of fencing, there's also a useful reference library on-site, jam-packed with documents and information on patents. It's not just about barbed wire here, though: the museum sets the historical scene through displays on the Dust Bowl era and artifacts from Texas's involvement in the Main Street America program.

McLean, where the museum is located, has a compelling origin story itself. The town was founded in 1901, thanks to an English rancher, Alfred Rowe, who donated land near a cattle rail stop. Tragically, Rowe perished aboard the *Titanic*, but the town he helped create—likely with the help of barbed wire—lives on.

**RIGHT, CLOCKWISE FROM TOP LEFT**
A display of early electric fencing; tools once used to install barbed wire fencing; outside the entrance to the Devil's Rope Museum in McLean

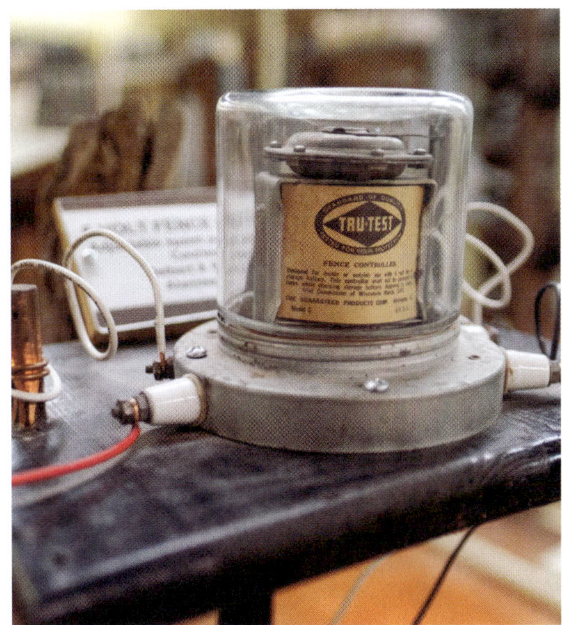

TRU-TEST
FENCE CONTROLLER

SADDLE FENCING TOOLS

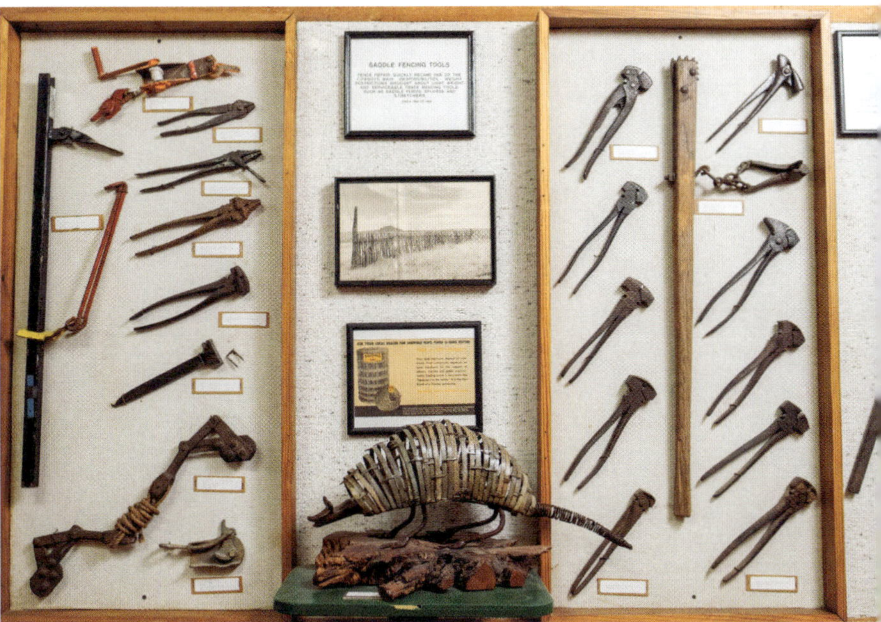

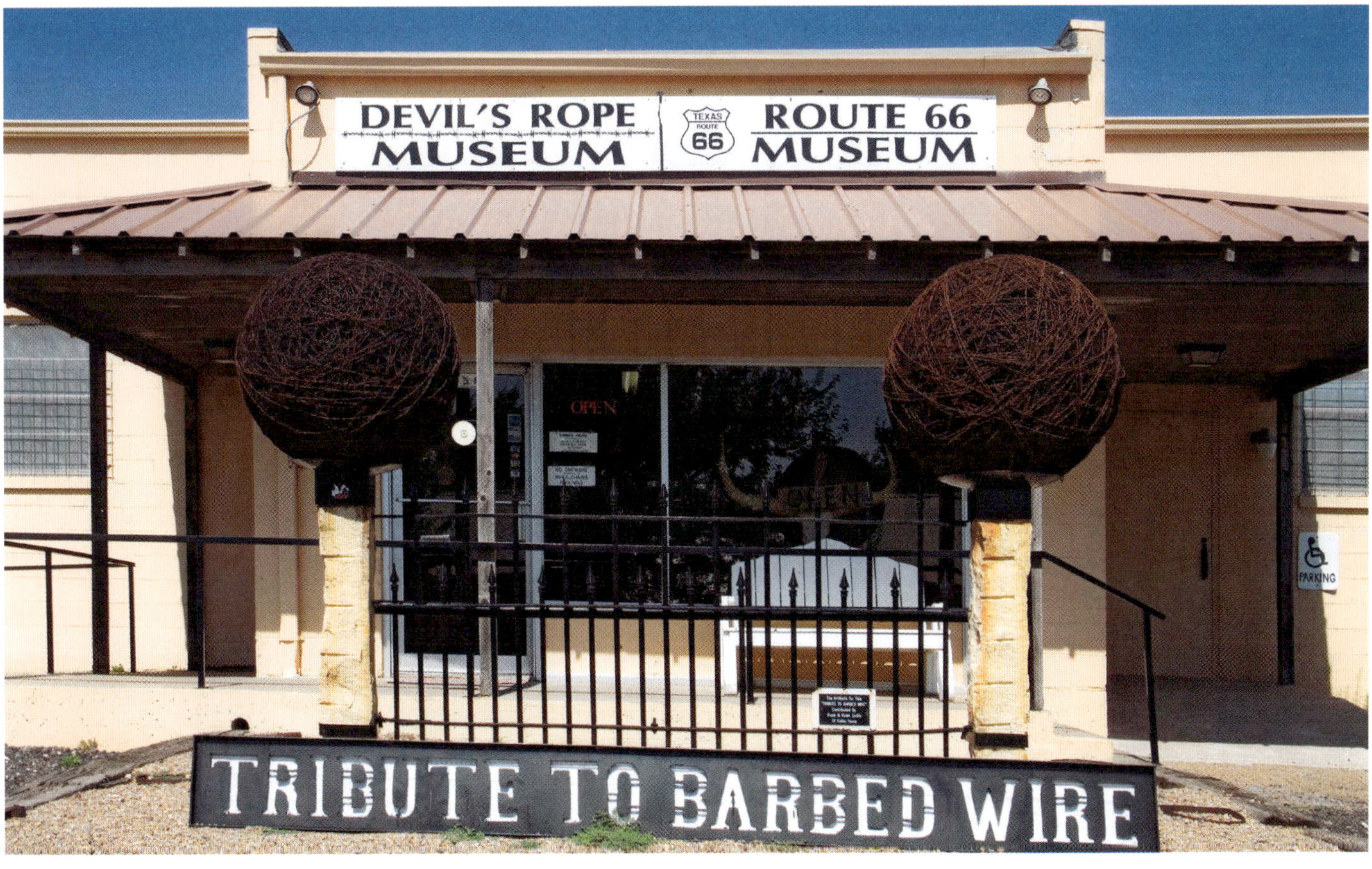
DEVIL'S ROPE
MUSEUM
TEXAS
ROUTE
66
ROUTE 66
MUSEUM
OPEN
PARKING
TRIBUTE TO BARBED WIRE

# CADILLAC RANCH

ODDITIES AND AMERICANA

AMARILLO

Bright, bold, and imbued with the freewheeling spirit of the 1970s, Cadillac Ranch demands your attention. Like an automotive Stonehenge rising from the plains, this art installation today is a Route 66 icon and a magnet for road-trippers, artists, and the curious.

Route 66 and America's postwar countercultural underbelly have crossed paths many times. Jack Kerouac's definitive Beat novel *On the Road* (1957) mythologized the idea of the cross-country road trip, while the 1969 film *Easy Rider* later solidified the route's rebellious image. Filmed largely in Santa Monica and Flagstaff, its story of two biker-hippies riding in search of freedom helped to establish Route 66 as a symbol of nonconformity and alternative ideals.

One of the most enduring physical monuments to some of these countercultural legacies of the highway is Cadillac Ranch, a striking art installation located just outside of Amarillo. Created in 1974 by the San Francisco–based art collective Ant Farm—made up of the artists and architects Chip Lord, Hudson Marquez, and Doug Michels—it was funded by eccentric local millionaire Stanley Marsh 3, who was drawn to the uniqueness of the concept. The piece features 10 brightly painted Cadillacs, positioned nose-first in the ground. There's good reason behind the cars' distinctive, bottoms-up placement: the artists wanted to highlight the evolution of the tail fin design on the rear of the Cadillacs. It quickly became an Amarillo staple, gaining even greater popularity when Bruce Springsteen named a song after it in the 1980s.

Today, the much-photographed installation remains a constantly evolving work of art. In homage to the project's irreverent spirit, layer upon layer of neon shades of paint are splattered on by visitors eager to leave their mark like those before them. Don't worry if you haven't brought spray paint—there's usually plenty available nearby. While the original hippies and beatniks may have moved on from Route 66, the spirit of counterculture and creativity is still alive and kicking in this Texan field.

**ABOVE**
Spray painting a car at the installation

**RIGHT**
The graffiti-covered cars of Cadillac Ranch

# BIG TEXAN STEAK RANCH AND MOTEL

DINERS AND DINING SPOTS

**AMARILLO**

**ABOVE**
A sign at the motel, foreshadowing what's to come inside

**RIGHT, CLOCKWISE FROM TOP LEFT**
Giant cowboy boot statue outside the motel; the infamous 72 oz steak challenge; diners in the kitschy steakhouse, complete with taxidermied deer

A true test of Texan appetite, the Big Texan Steak Ranch and Motel offers a free meal if you can conquer its massive steak challenge within the allotted time. Grab a cowboy hat, pull up a chair, and prove you've got what it takes.

Like a Wild West spin on Alice's Wonderland, the Big Texan Steak Ranch and Motel plays tricks on your mind from the moment you roll in. A giant green dinosaur statue (complete with cowboy boots, of course) welcomes drivers to this surreal slice of Amarillo while a towering cowboy boot sculpture stands proud in the sunny courtyard. The fully functioning motel, meanwhile, looks like the set of a spaghetti western—all Technicolor facades, swinging saloon doors, and lamps shaped like cowboy boots—and across the lot, ranchers check their ponies into the on-site "horse hotel." Even the outdoor pool doesn't play it straight, being shaped like the state of Texas.

But it's inside the motel's legendary steakhouse where the fun really ramps up. Since 1960, diners have flocked here to attempt the iconic 72 oz (2-kg) steak challenge: a feast featuring an intimidatingly hefty hunk of beef, plus three fried shrimp, a baked potato, a bread roll, and a bowl of salad. It's all to be consumed within 60 minutes, if you want the server to tear up the check. The current record? A jaw-dropping 4 minutes and 18 seconds, set by competitive eater Molly Schuyler in 2015. It's no challenge for the fainthearted (only about 10 percent triumphantly clean their plates within the hour), but it's fun all the same: around the Old West–style dining room, taxidermied stags watch on as hundreds of hopefuls dig into their platters; friends and family cheering them on at every mouthful.

As the saying goes, everything's bigger in Texas, and nowhere is that more true than at the Big Texan, whether it's the steak dinners, cowboy-themed statues, or all the star-spangled spectacle that comes with it.

BIG
TEXAN
BIG TEXAN
TRADING POST
WELCOME

Howdy Y'all!

DODGE
CATTLEMENS HOTEL
LILLY'S HOTEL

The themed facades of Amarillo's Big Texan Motel

1954 HARLEY DAVIDSON KH
SPORTSTER BOAT TAIL
This motorcycle was only produced in 1971.
This one was found in a barn in White Deer, Texas.
It has 787 original miles.
Gornicke

# JACK SISEMORE RV MUSEUM

MUST-VISIT MUSEUMS

AMARILLO

You don't need to be cruising Route 66 in an RV to enjoy this one-of-a-kind museum. Both a celebration of vintage motor homes and a tribute to classic family road trips, the Jack Sisemore RV Museum is one of 66's most nostalgic pit stops.

For decades, American families have bundled into RVs packed with snacks and suitcases and set off on the open road, and Route 66 has long been a favorite for family vacations. Flat and with a steady stream of campgrounds, the Mother Road is made for motor homes. Many of these are on display in the (fittingly family-run) Jack Sisemore RV Museum.

This free museum is packed with more than 20 beautifully restored vintage motor homes, campers, and trailers from the 1930s to the 1970s. Step inside the iconic bus from the 2006 Robin Williams movie *RV*, get up close with the oldest Airstream trailer in existence—a stunning 1935 Torpedo—and check out the very first Itasca motor home ever built by Winnebago. Each set is also filled with authentic period details, such as antique spice tins and retro decor, offering an immersive glimpse into the golden age of American road travel. And it's not just RVs. Thanks to a partnership with the Amarillo Area Motorsports Hall of Fame, the museum also hosts nearly 40 gleaming chrome motorcycles, classic cars, and rare race cars, making it a true celebration of all things on wheels.

For many, however, the museum isn't just about the vehicles; it's a journey back in time to those carefree childhood vacations—when the biggest drama was tumbling out of the top bunk or sharing out the snacks—and a vivid reminder of why Route 66 remains the ultimate American road trip.

LEFT
Choose your road-trip vehicle: family-ready campers and speedy motorcycles in the museum

Traveling from the Great Plains to California, hundreds of thousands made the long journey along Route 66 during the Dust Bowl. This exodus shaped the highway for decades to come.

HISTORY

# ROUTE 66 AND THE DUST BOWL

Five years after Route 66 was inaugurated, America went dry. Between 1931 and 1940, the country experienced four major droughts; with them came dust storms and widespread crop failure. The period came to be known as the Dust Bowl, and though few parts of the country's middle were spared, it was the region just north of Amarillo and Route 66 (where the Texas and Oklahoma panhandles meet), that bore the brunt of this catastrophe.

The Dust Bowl was as much a human-made disaster as it was a natural one. Settlers had been lured to the Great Plains with misleading accounts of its agricultural potential, and many brought with them farming practices unsuited to the arid environment. As the topsoil was depleted and overgrazing decimated prairie grasses, farmers and ranchers moved onto ever poorer land, a trend exacerbated by low crop prices that required farmers to cultivate more and more acres to continue seeing a profit. This left the earth dry, depleted of nutrients, and vulnerable to erosion. So, when drought came, it was merciless. Crops died and winds blew the thin soil into billowing dust storms that darkened the sky and swallowed up homes.

With farms and local economies decimated, people left their homes in

L. A. Police Slug College Girls

Daily News

DUST STORM SWEEPING TOWARD CALIFORNIA

As Patrolman Knocked Co-Ed Unconscious

Dense Clouds of Midwestern Silt Blanket Arizona

Clubs Wielded At Anti-War Gathering

Berlin Makes Concession For Peace

New Tuberculosis, Anemia Cures Announced

U.S. Campuses In Pacifist Turmoil

**1** Two Dust Bowl refugees walking along the highway toward the fabled Los Angeles

**2** A postcard (dating from the 1930s) showing the enormous size of an approaching dust storm in the American Midwest

**3** Refugees from Abilene, Texas, making their way to California for agricultural work

**4** A 1935 article from the *Daily News* (a Los Angeles paper) highlighting the sheer scale of the dust storms

**5** A photograph from 1935 showing a young boy in overalls and a cap standing in the dry agricultural land that came to characterize the Great Plains in the 1930s

droves to search for work, especially in California (the so-called "promised land" where agricultural jobs and a better climate awaited). Cutting a direct line from the Dust Bowl's epicenter to the west coast, Route 66 became an indispensable escape route, one that at least 200,000 people took during the drought years. It was largely this exodus that cemented the highway's reputation as a road of opportunity in the American imagination. It was also when Route 66 acquired its famous moniker—though when John Steinbeck dubbed it "the Mother Road" in *The Grapes of Wrath,* he wasn't celebrating 66 as the original highway but canonizing it as the last chance of the destitute. For "refugees from dust … from the thunder of tractors and shrinking ownership, from the desert's slow northward invasion, from the twisting winds that howl up out of Texas … 66 is the mother road, the road of flight."

Not everyone fled, however, and one of the Dust Bowl's most unexpected legacies was how it turned 66 into a thriving commercial artery. Some of those who stayed opened businesses to service the many migrants heading to California or returning home, and while towns off the highway suffered amid the era's destitution, those with the good fortune to be on 66 often flourished.

# MIDPOINT CAFÉ AND GIFT SHOP

DINERS AND DINING SPOTS

ADRIAN

"When you're here, you're halfway there," reads the slogan at the Midpoint Café in Adrian. Weary travelers will be pleased to hear it's true: it may look like you're in the middle of nowhere, but you're actually at the very heart of Route 66.

Just outside the speck of a town that is Adrian sits the Midpoint Café, a pint-sized retro diner and gift shop perched precisely halfway between Chicago and Santa Monica—there's 1,139 miles (1,833 km) still to go in either direction. Reaching the café is a rite of passage for road-trippers tracing the Mother Road, and it's much more than just a photo opportunity.

**RIGHT**
The colorful interior of Midpoint Café, the half-way point along Route 66

The Midpoint Café is both an icon of the road and a lovely place to linger. Inside, a cowbell jingles as the door swings open, and diners slide into one of six booths or perch on red leather counter stools. The welcome is warm and genuine, thanks to owner Brenda Hammit, who started out flipping burgers in the kitchen before buying the café in 2018. Now, she's the keeper of the flame—and the secret recipe for the café's prized flaky-crust pies.

Originally opened in 1928 as Zella's, the café has had several names over the decades but never lost its role as a haven for travelers halfway there. It's the oldest continuously operating café on Route 66 between Amarillo, Texas, and Tucumcari, New Mexico, and it's long welcomed road-trippers from all over the world. It continues to do so today, with folks drawn in by double-stacked Angus burgers, creamy milkshakes, and slices of Elvis pie, layered high with peanut butter and banana.

The café also offers a side of movie history. Former owner Fran Houser inspired the big-hearted character Flo in Pixar's *Cars*, and Disney's California Adventure Park even modeled its version of Flo's V-8 Café after the spot, complete with "ugly crust pie" on the menu.

Before you hit the open road again, stop by the adjacent gift shop to browse Route 66 patches and bumper stickers declaring "We made it halfway!"—a tiny souvenir for a big moment on America's fabled highway.

**ABOVE LEFT**
Retro Route 66-themed goodies in the café's gift shop

**ABOVE RIGHT**
A quirky tribute to Pixar's *Cars* parked outside the café

# NEW MEXICO

Dusty desert landscapes and red rock mesas define the route as it stretches for nearly 400 miles (644 km) through New Mexico, also known as the Land of Enchantment. From the low-key town of Tucumcari, it's on to the azure waters of the Blue Hole sinkhole, in Santa Rosa. It's not long after the Blue Hole that Route 66's alignment shifted, significantly diverting motorists away from Santa Fe, in the 1930s. We prefer to take the long and winding road, and journey via Pecos National Historical Park before continuing onto Santa Fe—it's this, the original and more scenic route, that the following pages honor. After Santa Fe, you'll then make your way to Albuquerque, where diners and neon signs keep the 66 spirit alive, before the town of Gallup offers a flavor of Hollywood's Golden Age at El Rancho Hotel.

NM

# NEW MEXICO

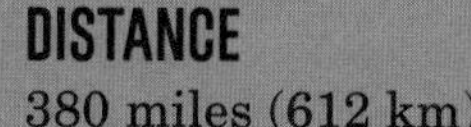

**DISTANCE**
380 miles (612 km)

**DRIVE TIME (NONSTOP)**
Approx. 5 hours

**LANDSCAPE**
Dusty high desert plains and rugged mountains are punctuated by Pueblo architecture and thriving cities.

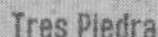


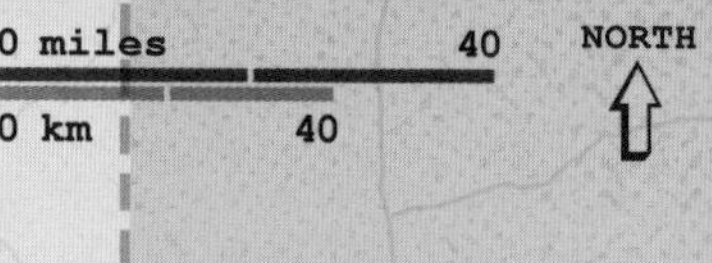

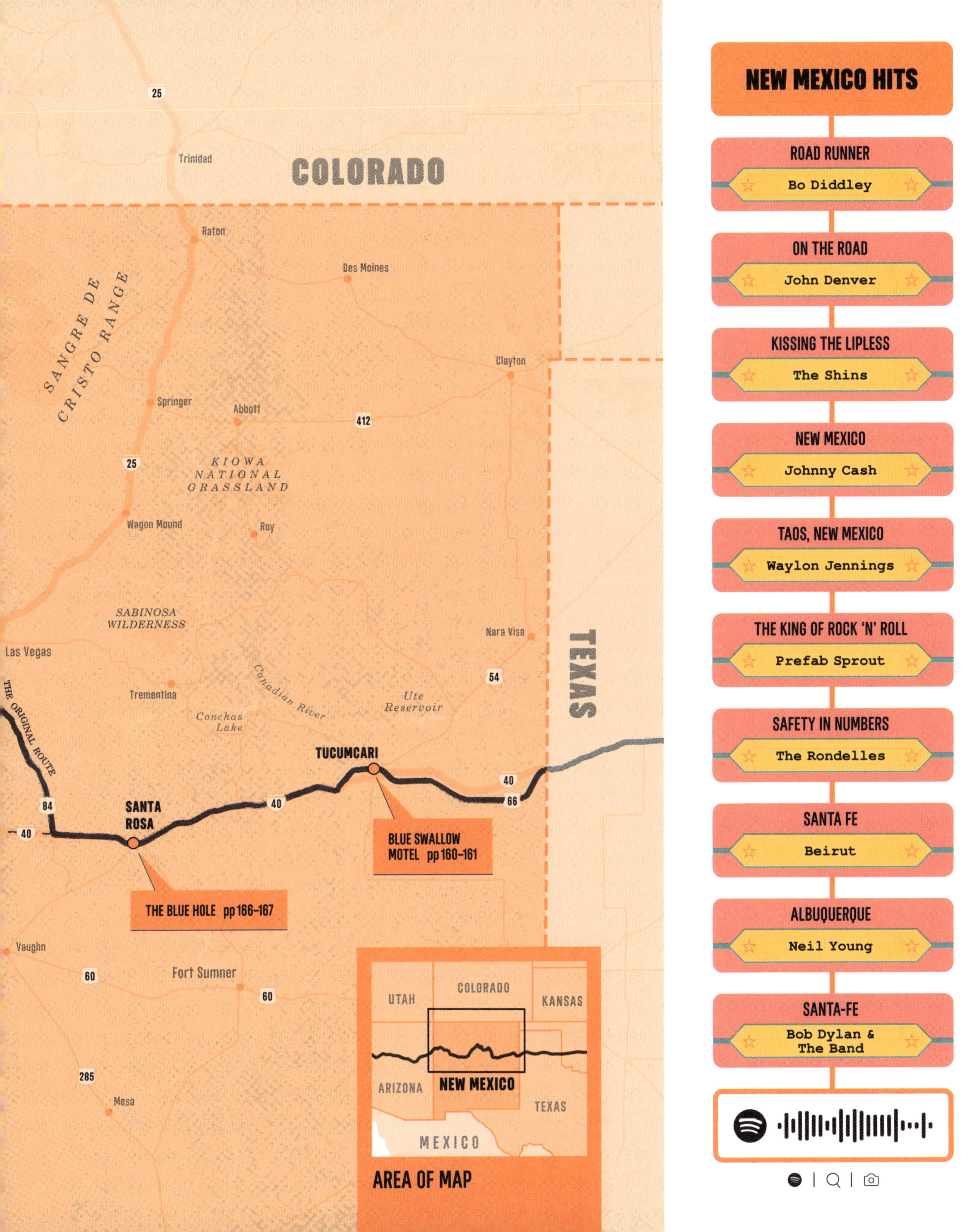

25
Trinidad
COLORADO
Raton
Des Moines
SANGRE DE CRISTO RANGE
Clayton
Springer
Abbott
412
25
KIOWA NATIONAL GRASSLAND
Wagon Mound
Roy
SABINOSA WILDERNESS
Nara Visa
TEXAS
Las Vegas
THE ORIGINAL ROUTE
Trementina
Canadian River
Ute Reservoir
54
Conchas Lake
TUCUMCARI
84
SANTA ROSA
40
40
40
66
BLUE SWALLOW MOTEL pp 160–161
THE BLUE HOLE pp 166–167
Vaughn
60
Fort Sumner
60
285
Mesa
UTAH
COLORADO
KANSAS
ARIZONA
NEW MEXICO
TEXAS
MEXICO
AREA OF MAP
NEW MEXICO HITS
ROAD RUNNER
Bo Diddley
ON THE ROAD
John Denver
KISSING THE LIPLESS
The Shins
NEW MEXICO
Johnny Cash
TAOS, NEW MEXICO
Waylon Jennings
THE KING OF ROCK 'N' ROLL
Prefab Sprout
SAFETY IN NUMBERS
The Rondelles
SANTA FE
Beirut
ALBUQUERQUE
Neil Young
SANTA-FE
Bob Dylan & The Band

# BLUE SWALLOW MOTEL

HOTELS AND MOTELS

**TUCUMCARI**

One of Route 66's most photogenic landmarks, the Blue Swallow Motel has defied the odds to keep its lights aglow. Nowadays, it stands as a shining testament to the Mother Road's plucky staying power and makes for a welcoming first stop as you cross the border into New Mexico.

Twilight is prime time for spotting Route 66's vintage signs, which flicker on to lure in nighttime drivers. Few, however, are as instantly recognizable as the Blue Swallow's. This blazing insignia shows a bright blue bird in midflight above radiant cursive promising "100% Refrigerated Air"—it's hard to miss and hard to resist slowing down in admiration.

Originally opened in 1940 by carpenter W.A. Huggins, the Blue Swallow is a standout example of Southwest Vernacular design: blush-pink stucco walls dotted with seashells and garage bays nestled between rooms to park your car (many still featuring their original wooden overhead doors). It began as a classic motel and café in the tiny city of Tucumcari, and for a number of years, it flourished on Route 66. Yet as with much of the Mother Road, the highway's course was rerouted in the late 1960s and the new I-40 meant Tucumcari was bypassed. It spelled the end of the road for many local businesses in the area, but (despite changing hands several times over the years) the Blue Swallow endured.

Today, the guest rooms have been restored with care and a collector's eye: atomic chalkware lamps, 1940s rotary phones, and vintage chenille bedspreads nod to the motel's original era, while plush mattresses keep pace with 21st-century expectations. There's hardly a more atmospheric place to bed down for the night, but you don't need to stay over to enjoy the Blue Swallow's charms. In a hurry? Make it a quick pit stop to snap photos and grab souvenirs like pins, mugs, and room key tags from the on-site shop.

Rumor has it James Dean stayed here before fame came calling, but nowadays, it's not celebrities who keep the Blue Swallow busy—it's classic car convoys, overseas visitors on the trip of a lifetime, and cross-country families. The Interstate may be quicker, but, as is clear to see from the shimmering no-vacancy sign, there's no road quite like Route 66.

**ABOVE**
Guest rooms featuring baby-blue doors and shell-decorated walls

**RIGHT**
A classic car under the Blue Swallow sign

BLUE SWALLOW MOTEL
TUCUMCARI - HWY. 66 EAST - NEW MEXICO
BOOT SALE
COME TO
TUCUMCARI
Marlboro
Marlboro
GENERAL Junior

PEOPLE OF THE ROAD

PEOPLE OF THE ROAD

# LILLIAN REDMAN

Blue Swallow Motel Owner

As far as engagement presents go, Floyd Redman set the bar high when, in 1958, he gifted his bride-to-be Lillian the Blue Swallow Court. It turned out to be a good omen—the couple enjoyed a long, happy marriage and ran what became the Blue Swallow Motel for decades, welcoming generations of road-trippers with splashy neon signage and warm hospitality.

Lillian became the motel's most devoted caretaker, with a natural instinct for service. Long before Floyd popped the question, she had worked as a Harvey Girl—one of the young women employed by entrepreneur Fred Harvey who made it his mission to elevate the passenger rail experience, opening up fine-dining restaurants, curio shops, and grand hotels across the American West. Thanks to her training, Lillian brought professionalism and poise to railroad hotels and dining rooms across the American West.

After their wedding, the Redmans changed the name from Blue Swallow Court to Blue Swallow Motel and installed the motel's now-iconic neon sign. They were generous hosts: if a guest couldn't pay, they might accept a keepsake, or simply hand over the room key anyway. "I end up traveling the highway in my heart with whoever stops here for the night," Lillian once said.

When Floyd died in 1973, Lillian guided the motel through tough years as Tucumcari faded from the map. Although she died in 1999, Lillian's legacy lives on. Today, the motel's swankiest suite bears her name—complete with a vintage vanity and bubblegum-pink claw-foot tub. A fitting tribute for this motel queen.

The LEGENDARY RO
GET YOUR
KICKS
ROUTE
66
TUCUMCARI
TONIGHT

Driving past a Route 66-themed mural by Doug and Sharon Quarles in Tucumcari

# THE BLUE HOLE

NATURAL WONDERS

SANTA ROSA

The Blue Hole is a sapphire gem seemingly lost amid the rusty terrain of New Mexico's arid High Plains. For centuries, the pool has tempted travelers, from Indigenous peoples and cowboys to scuba divers and thrill seekers, so jump on in, the water's fine!

After an hour spent driving through the dry, desolate expanse of eastern New Mexico, Santa Rosa's welcoming Blue Hole suddenly appears. Nestled amid a sea of stone and sand, this brilliant blue pool might leave travelers doubting their senses, but don't worry; it's real. This inviting oasis has become an irresistible stop for the road-weary, plenty of whom leap off the rock shelf and plunge into the perpetually 62°F (17°C) water.

The Blue Hole is roughly 80 ft (24 m) wide and equally deep, narrowing slightly at the middle to form an hourglass shape. It's a sinkhole (akin to Mexico's cenotes), formed as groundwater eroded the limestone bedrock until the surface caved in—a process that took many thousands of years. A spring at the hole's bottom pumps out 3,000 gallons (11,356 liters) per minute, enough to completely recycle its water every six hours (so the water really is fine), and underground channels connect it to six other lakes in Santa Rosa.

New Mexico's inhabitants have long utilized the pool. Centuries ago, the Blue Hole was an important water source for nomadic Indigenous peoples; later, it provided the same respite to cowboys driving herds of cattle across the lonely land. Of course, Route 66 also ran right past the pool, turning it into a tourist attraction—though, somewhat ironically, anyone visiting during the highway's golden era would have been disappointed. From 1952 to 1967, it was used as a fish hatchery.

Nowadays, the Blue Hole is a rather unexpected scuba diving destination, and it's not uncommon for people to drive half a day just to dive here. Thanks to the frequent recycling of the pool's water, visibility can reach an impressive 100 ft (30.5 m), allowing divers at the bottom of the pool to peer right up at any travelers jumping in to wash off the dust of the road.

**RIGHT**
A blue dot in a sandy state: Santa Rosa's dazzling Blue Hole

# PECOS NATIONAL HISTORICAL PARK

NATURAL WONDERS

PECOS

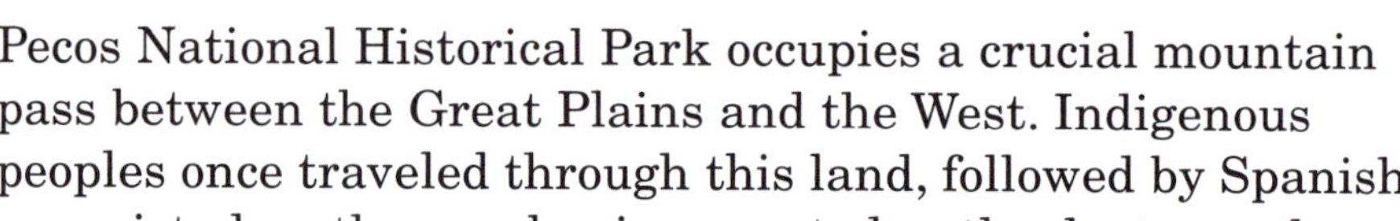

Pecos National Historical Park occupies a crucial mountain pass between the Great Plains and the West. Indigenous peoples once traveled through this land, followed by Spanish conquistadors then early pioneers; today, the dusty earth reads like a miniature history of North America.

Amid a featureless expanse of scrubland 18 miles (29 km) from Santa Rosa, drivers heading west on Route 66 have a decision to make. They can continue straight toward Albuquerque on I-40, or they can take the U.S. Route 84 exit and follow 66's original alignment to Santa Fe. Unless they're in a hurry—and if they're road-tripping on Route 66, why would they be?—the choice is clear.

But before Santa Fe, another must-visit: Pecos National Historical Park. The park is perched nearly 7,000 ft (2,134 m) above sea level, at the Glorieta Pass, a historically important route through the southern reaches of the Sangre de Cristo Mountains that links the Great Plains in the east with the Rio Grande Valley in the west. Route 66 did not blaze any new trails here. The pass has seen hunters, traders, conquistadors, missionaries, settlers, soldiers—in short, all manner of humanity—travel through here for centuries. Beginning in the mid-1400s, it was the site of the Pecos Pueblo, one of the region's largest and most important Indigenous settlements, which grew prosperous facilitating the trade of buffalo hides, crops, and turquoise through the pass. Eventually, Spaniards and their new religion arrived. The Puebloans revolted against the Spanish in 1680, sending them back to Mexico, but both eventually lived in peaceful cohabitation *(p182)*, and today, relics of the Spanish mission and Puebloan ancestral sites can still be seen in the park.

Park visitors can also stop by the Trading Post; now an information center and museum, it was originally built to serve as a stop on the

Santa Fe Trail, which ran from Independence, Missouri, to Santa Fe in the mid-1800s. Glance at a chart of the famed trail, and you'll see that in this part of New Mexico, it maps almost exactly onto turn-of-the-century rail lines, the original Route 66 alignment, and I-25. It's a fascinating testament to the Glorieta Pass, and the centuries' worth of travelers who have passed this way.

**"Relics of the Spanish mission and Puebloan ancestral sites can still be seen in the park."**

**LEFT**
Leafy Glorieta Pass, in the Pecos National Historical Park

**ABOVE**
The Spanish colonial Mission Nuestra Señora de los Ángeles Porciúncula

ONE WAY
STOP
STOP

# SANTA FE

CITIES OF 66

Route 66 ran through Santa Fe only for a decade, but it's worth taking the long way around to explore a city that somehow manages to combine 400 years of history with one of America's best contemporary art scenes.

Nestled between the Rio Grande and the southern tip of the Rocky Mountains, the city of Santa Fe is a true high-desert oasis. Surrounded by forests and hills covered in juniper, aspen, piñon, and cottonwood, it's one of the country's oldest cities, having been founded by the Spanish in 1610, but it wears its years with ease. It's also long been a magnet for artists and travelers, and it remains a major tourist destination, renowned for its museums, galleries, and restaurants.

## ROUTE 66 REMNANTS

Route 66 runs in an inverted U through the center of town, skirting the state capitol and Santa Fe Plaza, where locals people-watch from shaded benches and a stone marker denotes the terminus of the old Santa Fe Trail. Facing the plaza's western edge is the Plaza Cafe, which has been serving Route 66 travelers since the highway's inception. Opened in 1905, it's the state's oldest restaurant. The café specializes in New Mexico classics like Hatch green chile cheeseburgers, while its Greek salad is a nod to Dionysus Razatos, the immigrant who bought the place in 1947 and whose family has run it ever since.

Another highway classic is El Rey Court, whose sense of location was better than its timing. Fronting Route 66 (now Cerrillos Road) on the city's southwest side, it debuted in 1936, just a year before the highway was rerouted to bypass Santa Fe. Like the Plaza Cafe, though, the motel has weathered the decades well, reinventing itself with expansions and upgrades, first through additional rooms and enclosed carports and, later, facilities like a pool and a tequila bar that hosts live music and a weekly LGBTQ+ night. El Rey's combination of traditional

**LEFT**
Santa Fe's rose-colored buildings and pretty cathedral, illuminated by street lights

architectural features, such as viga rafters and *kiva*-style fireplaces, with contemporary decor in earthy Southwestern tones arguably makes it the most stylish motor court anywhere on 66.

## TIME CAPSULE TOWN

Route 66 was redirected to run from Santa Rosa to Albuquerque in 1937, so with a mere decade on the highway, Santa Fe doesn't possess that many 66-related sites. But it compensates with one of the richest histories of any city in the country.

Bordering Santa Fe Plaza to the north is the Palace of the Governors, the oldest continually used public building in the U.S. Upon founding the city in 1610, Spanish colonists erected the squat adobe structure to serve the territory's governor. Following the Mexican–American War, it served the same purpose for American territorial governors. It's now part of the New Mexico History Museum.

Just off 66 on the way out of town, El Rancho de las Golondrinas is a living link to that past. Centuries before Route 66 was even a glint in Cyrus Avery's eye *(p114)*, travelers plied the Camino Real de Tierra Adentro, and the ranch was established in the early 1700s as a *paraje*, an official stop where caravanners could rest and trade. It's now a living history museum, where original restored buildings share space with historic structures—houses, mills, a one-room schoolhouse—relocated from elsewhere in the state, while staff members demonstrate traditional trades like tanning and tinsmithing.

With a name like Santa Fe (meaning "Holy Faith"), it's hardly a surprise that several of the city's most important historical sites are

**ABOVE**
Unwinding by the pool in the design-focused El Rey Court motel

religious. Just a few blocks south of the plaza is another "oldest," this one the oldest church in the U.S. San Miguel Chapel's origins are hazy, but it's thought to date to the first years of the 17th century. Its current form can be traced back to 1710, when the bell tower was added. Mass is still held on the first Sunday of the month, but the chapel is open daily for visitors to find a moment of calm or admire its altar screen, a colorful aberration in the humble adobe edifice. Gifted by Lieutenant José Antonio Ortiz in 1798, it features four oil paintings of saints and a small niche holding a statue of the Archangel Michael.

Just up the road is the strikingly different Loretto Chapel. Constructed in the 1870s, the Gothic Revival structure was modeled on the royal Sainte-Chapelle in Paris. It's most famous for the spiral staircase leading from the nave to the choir loft. Legend says that after the chapel's sisters prayed for nine days straight, a carpenter arrived in town and built the stairs, which have no center pole or other structural support. Then he vanished, just as mysteriously as he had appeared.

**BELOW**
Leading a donkey through El Rancho de las Golondrinas

## CENTURIES OF CREATION

Contemporary pilgrims largely come to Santa Fe not for the churches, but for the art. In fact, the city is home to the country's third-largest art market. Not bad for a town of just 90,000. Walking around, it can often feel as if Santa Fe is just one big art fair. Local Indigenous artisans sell jewelry

**BELOW LEFT**
A photograph of the artist at the Georgia O'Keeffe Museum

**BELOW RIGHT**
The neon-lit interior of Meow Wolf, where art installations take a psychedelic turn

## "Pilgrims largely come to Santa Fe not for the churches, but for the art."

and pottery in the Palace of the Governor's portico, and galleries line downtown's cozy streets. The city is also home to multiple arts districts. The most famous is Canyon Road, where nearly 100 galleries and studios squeeze into a half-mile (800-m) stretch, selling and displaying everything from traditional pieces by local artists to abstract contemporary works.

Travelers without space for a new canvas in their trunk can content themselves with a spin through the city's top-tier art museums. The collection at the New Mexico Museum of Art spans Indigenous photography, regional Southwestern works, and art produced under the Works Progress Administration. Then there's the Museum of Indian Arts & Culture, home to one of the world's finest collections of Southwestern pottery and Navajo and Pueblo weavings, which it uses to illuminate the distinct cultural traditions of the region's various Indigenous peoples. Meanwhile, the Museum of Contemporary Native Arts focuses on the creations of modern Indigenous artists and how they draw on, defy, and redefine traditional forms and aesthetics.

Undoubtedly, Santa Fe's headline art venue is the Georgia O'Keeffe Museum, devoted to one of America's most important 20th-century artists. The Wisconsin-born creator spent the latter half of her life living near Santa Fe, and this acclaimed museum is filled with her lyrical New Mexico landscapes, which vividly capture the texture

of the land and the gradations of the desert light. The large collection (featuring nearly 150 paintings) encompasses her local landscapes, as well as her famous floral paintings, abstract sculptures, and still lifes. These are complemented by displays of O'Keeffe's personal items, from prized paintbrushes and clothing to bones she collected and photographs of the artist at home.

O'Keeffe has long been Santa Fe's most celebrated artist. Arts and entertainment company Meow Wolf, on the other hand, began as a struggling band of sculptors, painters, filmmakers, technologists, media artists, and graphic designers operating outside the traditional art market. The coterie has since become the country's coolest art collective, applauded for its immersive, hyper-maximalist interactive installations. It created the first of these, the House of Eternal Return, in a former Santa Fe bowling alley bought and donated by *Game of Thrones* author George R. R. Martin. Entering the house—to solve the fictional mystery of a family's disappearance or simply to explore and experiment—might inadequately be described as traversing a multidimensional and technologically augmented Salvador Dalí painting while under the influence of ayahuasca (a psychoactive brew). In case the trip down 66 hasn't been long and strange enough already.

**ABOVE**
A large statue of an Apache warrior, standing guard over the Museum of Indian Arts & Culture

The highway snaking through endless deserts in New Mexico

# ALBUQUERQUE

CITIES OF 66

Albuquerque is where Route 66 comes together. The highway's old north–south road from Santa Fe and its later east–west alignment from Santa Rosa converge here, in a fascinating desert city that blends Native and Hispanic heritage with signature Route 66 sights.

Route 66's original north–south path has a pedigree. It roughly follows a late-19th-century Atchison, Topeka, and Santa Fe Railway track, which in turn roughly followed the Camino Real de Tierra Adentro, a Spanish colonial trade route that linked Mexico City with Santa Fe between 1598 and the late 1800s. That, in turn, followed even older trails blazed by the region's Indigenous peoples. This north–south alignment only predominated for a decade, in the early 20th century, so most of Albuquerque's typical Route 66 attractions are found along Central Avenue. It does, however, run past a pair of cultural centers dedicated to groups that have played major roles in shaping the city, both past and present.

The Indian Pueblo Cultural Center is a few blocks west of 4th Street, near I-40. New Mexico is home to 19 Pueblo tribes, each a sovereign nation. (What's now Albuquerque was originally the territory of the Sandia Pueblo.) The center's permanent exhibition introduces the tribes' legacies through their pottery, textiles, foodways, and instruments. Displays delve into Pueblo architecture and the Tewa and Keresan languages, while the center's gallery hosts rotating exhibitions of work by Pueblo artists. Traditional dance performances are also held on weekends.

Three miles (4.8 km) to the south, and right on 4th Street, the National Hispanic Cultural Center does much the same for New Mexico's Hispanic and Latino communities, which make up nearly half of the state's population. A permanent collection of 3,000-plus artworks is augmented with rotating shows that explore everything from the all-important history of tequila to street art.

**ABOVE**
An artist performing a traditional dance at the city's Indian Pueblo Cultural Center

**LEFT**
Stopping to admire the view of the city of Albuquerque from a hiking trail

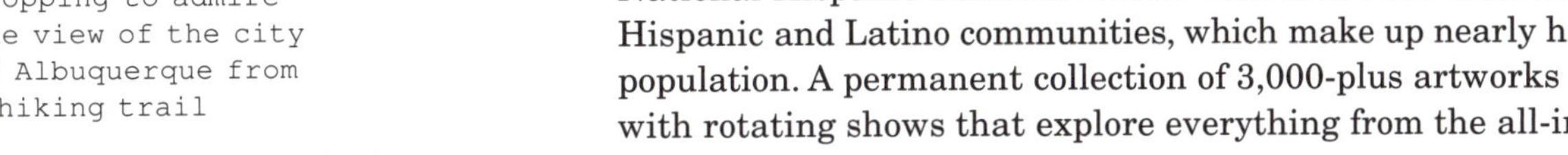

## "RETRIBUTION ROAD"

Why Route 66 was rerouted to avoid Santa Fe is one of the Mother Road's great stories. The bureaucratic account is that it was done as part of a federal highway safety project, as the new path lopped more than 100 miles (161 km) and four hours off the journey. Much better is the version that might be called "Hannett's Revenge." Arthur T. Hannett became New Mexico's governor in 1925, and when his reelection bid failed, he blamed his loss on a conspiracy by politicians in Santa Fe. As payback, his last act in office was to draft the plan that would send Route 66 straight to Albuquerque, along I-40. To this day, the alignment is sometimes referred to as "Retribution Road."

The Central Avenue alignment is Route 66's longest urban drive, running for 18 miles (29 km) across the city. Anyone driving it on a Sunday night shouldn't expect a quick jaunt across town, though. That's when the avenue becomes the scene for the city's weekly lowrider cruise, with dozens of cars rolling low and slow to show off their gleaming paint jobs, custom rims, and souped-up hydraulics.

**ABOVE**
Driving along Central Avenue, otherwise known as Retribution Road

# "The avenue becomes the scene for the city's weekly lowrider cruise, with dozens of cars rolling low and slow."

**BELOW**
A retro road sign advertising vacancies at El Vado Motel

Central cuts right past Albuquerque's Old Town, where the city was first established as a Spanish colonial settlement in 1706. It still has something of the 18th century about it, thanks to low adobe buildings and the San Felipe de Neri church, which watches over the central plaza, just as it has done since 1796.

## NEON AND NOSTALGIA

To the east and west of the Old Town, Central plays the Route 66 hits. There are restaurants in refurbished 1930s- and 40s-era service stations, like M'tucci's Bar Roma, which still maintains the station's original lettering above its dining room, and 66 Diner, which, despite opening after Route 66 had already been decommissioned, leans into the mid-20th-century nostalgia with a Wurlitzer jukebox and staff in vintage uniforms.

Classic motels are well represented, too. The city's first motor lodge, El Vado, built in 1937 in the Spanish Pueblo Revival style, is still around, as is Monterey Motel, practically next door, though it's had a stylish makeover and even serves its very own gin in its lounge. A mile and a half (2.4 km) to the east, ARRIVE Albuquerque is the new spin on the Downtowner Motor Inn, built in 1965. On one of its walls, Nanibah Chacon's giant mural of a lowrider and Navajo blanket patterns pays tribute to Indigenous and Hispanic cultures.

Central also serves up a glowing parade of neon signs that befits a city of 66. Take El Vado and Monterey Motel, both of which have strong offerings, the first with an Indigenous person framed by a sunburst, the latter, classic red arrows. El Don Motel has a multicolored, lasso-twirling cowboy, while Westward Ho! Motel has a life-size saguaro cactus. Naturally, the Dog House Drive In, open since 1948, advertises its hot dogs with a neon wiener dog that wags its tail. Then, Downtown's storied KiMo Theatre lights up its name in blazing red and gold. And drivers leaving town pass beneath a neon red, blue, pink, and turquoise Route 66 arch that spans the highway near the intersection with State Road 45, a blazing goodbye to the city before the road heads into New Mexico's remote western reaches.

HISTORY

# NEW MEXICO'S PUEBLOS

New Mexico—and, significantly, this particular region of Route 66—is suffused with the culture of the Pueblo peoples, who have lived in the state for hundreds of years, long before roads were built.

1

Nineteen Pueblo tribes call New Mexico home, each a sovereign nation with its own culture, traditions, and, in some instances, language. Yet all share a common heritage and history.

The Pueblo peoples are believed to have descended from the Ancestral Puebloans, who settled across the Four Corners region beginning in the early centuries of the Common Era. They established an agricultural society centered on corn and formed permanent settlements of terraced, multiroom stone and earthen dwellings, often along cliffs or atop mesas. Settlements were governed by religious councils, which met in subterranean ceremonial chambers called *kivas*. When the first Spanish colonists came upon these settlements in the mid-16th century, they called them Pueblos, the Spanish word for "village" or "people," which they've been referred to as ever since.

As the Spanish and their missionaries sought to convert the Puebloans to Catholicism, their rule grew more oppressive. Colonists burned the Puebloans' *kivas* and sacred objects and, in the worst instances, they whipped, mutilated, or executed their holy men. Such actions pushed a normally peaceful people to violent revolt. In 1680, the holy man and war captain Po'Pay led a rebellion that overthrew

Spanish rule and drove the colonists out of Pueblo lands. The Pueblo Revolt remains the only successful uprising by an Indigenous people against a colonial power in North American history. When the Spanish returned 12 years later, and reclaimed New Mexico after the revolt, it was a changed dynamic. The Spanish were again the ruling power but realized cruel policies wouldn't get them anywhere. Puebloans were still encouraged to adopt Christianity but could maintain many of their traditional ways of life.

Today, Puebloan culture remains an important part of the New Mexico fabric (the sun symbol of the Zia Pueblo appears on the state flag), and a Route 66 road trip is a great way to see it. Pueblo communities continue to conduct traditional dances and religious ceremonies, some of which are open to the public. Galleries and art markets are filled with Puebloan jewelry, weaving, and pottery. The original Santa Fe alignment *(p171)* passes through seven different Pueblos, providing travelers with the opportunity to, for example, discover the renowned turquoise jewelry of the Santo Domingo (Kewa) Pueblo or visit the Sky City Cultural Center in Acoma Pueblo, thought to be the oldest continuously inhabited settlement in the country.

**1** A photograph of the San Ildefonso Pueblo community, taken by photographer Ansel Adams in the 1930s or 40s as part of a photo series capturing U.S. national parks and monuments

**2** The Pueblo of Laguna, not far from Albuquerque, with the Mission San José de la Laguna crowning the hill

**3** A vintage postcard depicting life in the cliff dwellings of the now abandoned Puye Pueblo, near Santa Fe

**4** People of the Zuni Pueblo performing the sacred ceremonial Parrot Dance in Gallup

**5** A photograph of the Zuni Pueblo's community, taken in the late 19th century

# EL RANCHO HOTEL

HOTELS AND MOTELS

GALLUP

Ride back through time to Hollywood's Golden Age with a stay at the rootin'-tootin' El Rancho Hotel, where legends like John Wayne once kicked up dust. Lovingly restored, the hotel now features whimsical Route 66–themed rooms, transporting guests to a bygone era.

**ABOVE**
The hotel's cozy lobby, inspired by Southwestern ranch life

**RIGHT**
El Rancho Hotel, tempting Hollywood stars and weary road-trippers for almost 100 years

Two hours of scrubland and mesas from Albuquerque, the city of Gallup sits amid red sandstone and hogback cliffs, landscapes that lured many a director of Westerns here in Hollywood's Golden Age. It was this booming industry that inspired El Rancho. Built in 1936 by the brother of famed director D.W. Griffith, and with employees trained by the highly regarded Fred Harvey company, the hotel was intended for movie crews and stars filming in the region. Its guestbook soon read like a true Tinseltown cast list: Katharine Hepburn, John Wayne, Humphrey Bogart, Gene Autry, Spencer Tracy, Kirk Douglas, and Gregory Peck all checked in while working on set.

While El Rancho remained connected to Hollywood until the mid-1960s, the decline of the Western genre led to the hotel's slow decay. Then in 1988, it was purchased and meticulously restored, eventually earning a place on the National Register of Historic Places. Nowadays, guests soak up the quintessential Old West ambiance of the lobby, surrounded by rustic ranch-style furnishings, sepia-toned photographs of A-list visitors, and a life-size cardboard cutout of John Wayne for photo ops. Ranch-style aesthetics continue in the hotel rooms, though some rooms come with a dollop of Route 66 fun—listen out for vinyl record players spinning Nat King Cole's timeless hit "Get Your Kicks on Route 66."

Whether stopping for the night, or simply passing through before hitting the road once more, a drink at the hotel's 49er Lounge is a must. It was here that, legend has it, John Wayne once rode his horse inside, ordering a beer for himself—and then one for his horse.

HOTEL
el Rancho
CHARM OF YESTERDAY ... CONVENIENCE OF TOMORROW
El Rancho Hotel
NATIONAL HISTORIC SITE
"Charm Of Yesterday,
Convenience Of Tomorrow"

# GEORGE GALANIS MULTICULTURAL CENTER

INDIGENOUS HERITAGE SITE

GALLUP

Gallup is a hub of regional Indigenous culture, where members of the Navajo, Hopi, Zuni, and other nations have long gathered. At the city's heart is this cultural center, which delivers an engaging overview of their arts, history, and contributions to the country.

Sure, El Rancho Hotel welcomed many a Hollywood star *(p184)*, but the town of Gallup's origins themselves are perfectly suited for a movie picture. Originally an ordinary stagecoach stop, a nameless town sprang up when the spot was made an office on a new rail route in 1881. The office's paymaster was David L. Gallup, and when workers went to get their paycheck, they'd say they were "going to Gallup." The name stuck. Gallup is situated between Navajo, Hopi, and Zuni homelands, and it has

been an important center of Indigenous culture since at least the stagecoach days, when lively trading posts were established here. Several of those trading posts are still around, and more than half of the city's population is Indigenous. Right on Route 66, the George Galanis Multicultural Center (often simply referred to as the Gallup Cultural Center) introduces visitors to this rich heritage.

The center occupies an old railroad headquarters dating from 1918, part of which still serves as the train station. Inside, exhibits explore the art and culture of Southwestern tribes through displays of pottery, baskets, sandpaintings, rug weaving, and kachina dolls. These dolls are striking representations of spiritual messengers that the Hopi believe have the power to bring rain, provide aid, or issue punishment.

Much of the center is dedicated to the Navajo Code Talkers who served in the Marines during World War II, transmitting messages in a code they had developed based on their native Navajo language. Efficient and unbreakable, it proved a major asset in the Pacific theater, including during the pivotal Battle of Iwo Jima. The Marine Corps had enlisted roughly 400 Navajo Code Talkers by the end of World War II, but the program had begun with just 29 men. That small first cohort departed for the front lines from this very spot, boarding a train to a San Diego Marine base from the Gallup train station in 1942.

**ABOVE**
The first 29 Navajo Code Talkers being sworn into the U.S. Marine Corps at Fort Wingate, on May 4, 1942

**LEFT**
Flags and a statue of a soldier standing outside the center

# ARIZONA

As Route 66 rolls into Arizona, it enters one of the most dramatic stretches of the highway. This is a state defined by its wide desert skies, Indigenous strongholds, and old Wild West towns. Things certainly start with a bang—not long after crossing the state border, road-trippers find themselves winding through the surreal colors of Petrified Forest National Park and the ancestral lands of the Navajo and Hopi peoples. Respite from the road comes in the form of the kitsch Wigwam Hotel in Holbrook, before a crater and canyon compete for attention at Meteor Crater National Landmark and Walnut Canyon. But it's the stretch beyond where the spirit of 66 really comes to life. The community of Seligman is passionate about preserving the highway's history, while Oatman serves up nostalgia with a smile.

# ARIZONA

**DISTANCE**
401 miles (645 km)

**DRIVE TIME (NONSTOP)**
Approx. 7½ hours

**LANDSCAPE**
Sun-scorched deserts, rugged canyons, meteor craters, and historic cowboy towns promise endless adventure.

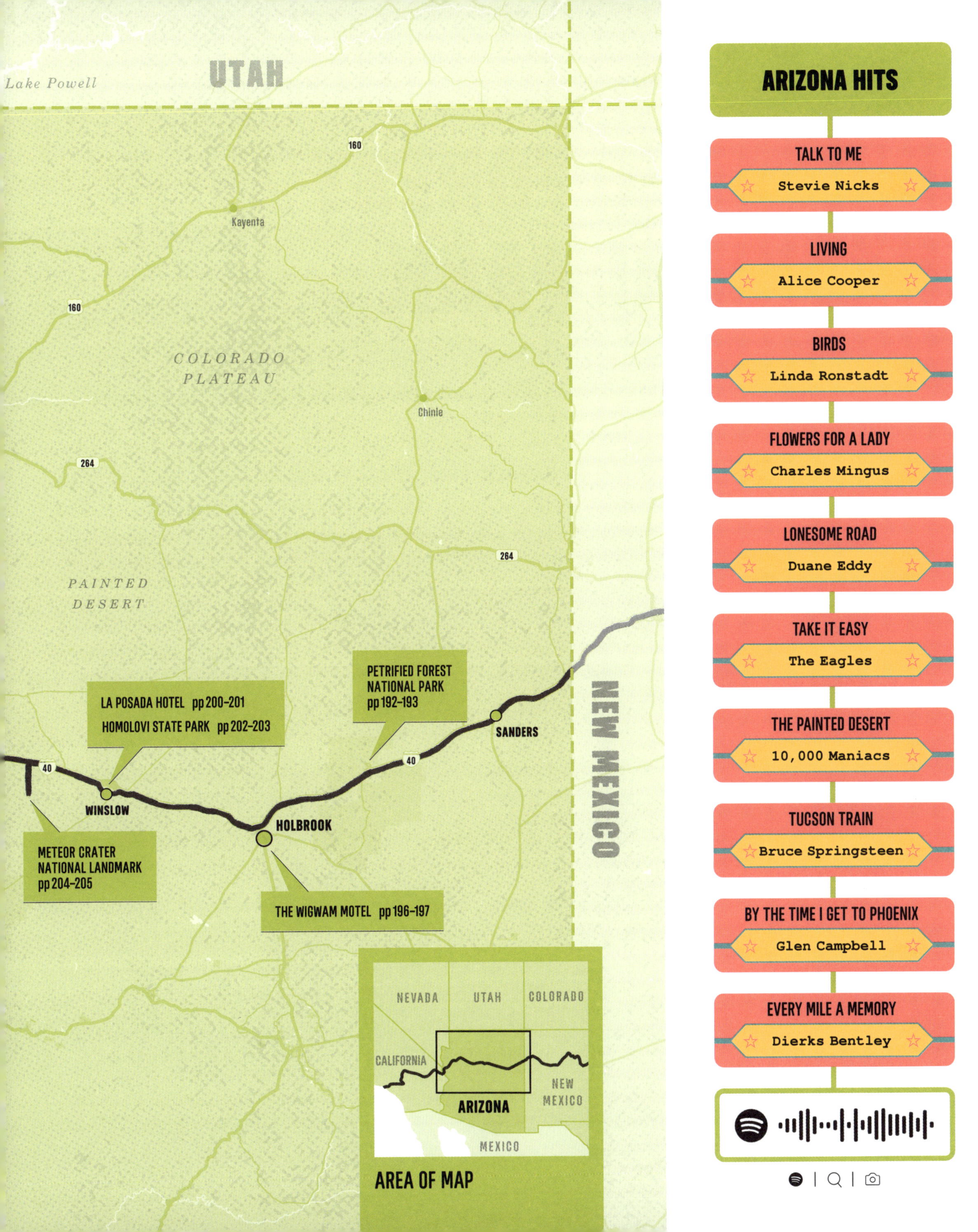

UTAH
Lake Powell
160
Kayenta
160
COLORADO PLATEAU
Chinle
264
264
PAINTED DESERT
PETRIFIED FOREST NATIONAL PARK pp 192–193
LA POSADA HOTEL pp 200–201
HOMOLOVI STATE PARK pp 202–203
SANDERS
NEW MEXICO
40
40
WINSLOW
HOLBROOK
METEOR CRATER NATIONAL LANDMARK pp 204–205
THE WIGWAM MOTEL pp 196–197
NEVADA
UTAH
COLORADO
CALIFORNIA
ARIZONA
NEW MEXICO
MEXICO
AREA OF MAP
ARIZONA HITS
TALK TO ME
Stevie Nicks
LIVING
Alice Cooper
BIRDS
Linda Ronstadt
FLOWERS FOR A LADY
Charles Mingus
LONESOME ROAD
Duane Eddy
TAKE IT EASY
The Eagles
THE PAINTED DESERT
10,000 Maniacs
TUCSON TRAIN
Bruce Springsteen
BY THE TIME I GET TO PHOENIX
Glen Campbell
EVERY MILE A MEMORY
Dierks Bentley

# PETRIFIED FOREST NATIONAL PARK

NATURAL WONDERS

Soon after arriving in Arizona, you'll find yourself at a rare crossroads of ancient geology, paleontology, and Indigenous history. Often overlooked in favor of its more famous neighbors, Petrified Forest is as epic a national park as they come.

**ABOVE**
Stunning colors inside the cross-section of a petrified tree log

**RIGHT**
A section of the highway passing through Petrified Forest National Park

A detour to the Grand Canyon might seem like a good idea; after all, it's only 80 miles (129 km) northwest of Flagstaff *(p209)*, Arizona's main city on the historic highway. But why wait until Flagstaff, and why sign up for such a detour when the road delivers you straight to a sublime alternative? Just 70 miles (113 km) west of Gallup, New Mexico, the highway brings motorists to the doorstep of Petrified Forest National Park, a seriously striking but lesser-known natural wonder without the elbow-to-elbow hustle. The highway cuts straight through the national park, treating motorists to sweeping views of the Painted Desert, in all its rusty red and rose-colored glory. For those tempted to do more than admire it through their windshield, swing into the visitor center (where you will need to pay an entrance fee; driving along the Interstate is free, however) and venture into the park itself.

Petrified Forest is home to the planet's largest concentration of fossilized conifer trees—towering titans from a time when this land was lush and stalked by dinosaurs. A natural phenomenon occurred over 200 million years ago, when volcanic ash turned these ancient forests into glimmering quartz logs, now scattered like gemstones across the parched desert floor. There's more than prehistory beneath your boots, too. Though the park is not located on a reservation—and today is solely managed by the National Park Service—reminders of the park's early residents remain evident, giving this otherworldly landscape a human touch. Etched into stone are petroglyphs dating back thousands of years, left by the Ancestral Puebloans, and visible from the Puerco Pueblo and Newspaper Rock areas.

HISTORY

# NAVAJO AND HOPI CULTURE

Northeastern Arizona is the realm of the Navajo and Hopi tribes, and a drive through the region gives travelers the chance to discover their stories.

Route 66 enters Arizona in the Navajo Nation. Covering an area of more than 27,000 sq miles (69,930 sq km) across three states (Arizona, New Mexico, and Utah), it's the country's largest reservation and contains some of the West's most iconic sights, including Monument Valley and Antelope Canyon, both on or near the Arizona–Utah border.

The Navajo, or Diné as they refer to themselves, meaning "the people," likely migrated to the Southwest from western Canada between 1100 and 1500, together with the people who would become the Apache, with whom they share linguistic similarities. In their new home, they came into contact with Pueblo tribes *(p182)*, acquiring their agricultural and artistic practices, before then encountering the Spanish, from whom they adopted sheepherding and horsemanship. Like their Apache relatives, the Navajo occasionally raided other Indigenous and settler communities. In response, U.S. Colonel Kit Carson began a scorched-earth campaign against the Navajo in 1863, burning their crops, killing their livestock, and forcing 8,000 Navajo to walk 300 miles (482 km) to Fort Sumner, New Mexico, where they were imprisoned for four years. The Navajo signed a treaty with the government establishing their reservation in 1868.

Encircled by the Navajo Nation, but some distance from Route 66, is the Hopi Reservation, home to the westernmost Pueblo people. The Hopi represent one of the oldest cultures in North America and have occupied this area for thousands of years; their settlement of Old Oraibi is thought to be the oldest continuously inhabited village in the U.S., having existed since at least 1150. Both Hopi and Navajo clans are matrilineal, and men would become part of their wives' families after marriage. Unlike the Navajo, who are widely dispersed due to limited water resources and grazing land, the Hopi have traditionally lived in self-governing villages.

Today, 12 villages occupy three mesas, called, from east to west, First, Second, and Third mesa. First Mesa is especially known for its pottery, Second for its basketry, and Third for its weaving and kachina dolls. The Hopi are most renowned for the innovative agricultural techniques they use to grow crops in the arid environment.

Remember, you are a guest on these tribal lands. If you're planning to veer off the highway and explore more, prior research is necessary, and a local guide is highly recommended, particularly as some areas have limited access and strict photography laws. Always practice Leave No Trace.

**1** A group of Hopi people building a house in Old Oraibi

**2** Manuelito, a former chief of the Navajo

**3** Imprisoned Navajo people, who were led to Fort Sumner, New Mexico, in 1864

**4** Members of the Navajo Nation Band

# THE WIGWAM MOTEL

HOTELS AND MOTELS

HOLBROOK

If you thought Pixar's *Cars* was long behind you, you'd be wrong. The Wigwam Motel in Holbrook was the inspiration for the movie's Cozy Cone Motel. Beyond its novelty and silver-screen value, it's also a place where the room rates seem frozen in time, offering plenty of bang for your buck.

"Have You Slept in a Wigwam Lately?" That's the burning question written in swirling script on the motel's overhead sign. If your answer is no, maybe it's time to pull over, check in, and spend the night at a spot that feels like something straight out of a Wes Anderson movie.

The Wigwam Motel is a crescent of 15 white concrete teepees, each one with a vintage car parked out front, as if its owner just wandered off for a slice of pineapple upside-down cake at the diner down the road. Built in 1950 by Chester Lewis—a Holbrook local who licensed the design from a chain stretching from Florida to California—this is one of just three original Wigwam Motels still standing. The only other one on the Mother Road is farther west, in San Bernardino, California.

Each wigwam stands 28 ft (8.5 m) tall and is roomier than you might expect. Most fit a double bed or two, dressed in Southwestern-print blankets; a tiny, tiled bathroom; and even a small desk, should the urge to work-from-wigwam strike. At sunset, the Arizona sky mirrors the rust-red of the nearby badlands in Petrified Forest National Park *(p192)*. Freight trains moan across the surrounding desert, and travelers gather in foldout camp chairs outside their teepees, chatting road-trip routes and sipping cold beer; the scene feels plucked from another era.

It's not, however, all just kitsch and Kodak moments. The teepee design draws inspiration from nomadic Native American tribes of the Great Plains in North America, although not from local tribes such as the Hopi and Navajo. The current owners are mindful to steer clear of presenting it as any kind of Indigenous experience, instead focusing on celebrating the motel's role in mid-century roadside culture. Today, this carefully preserved piece of Americana is listed on the National Register of Historic Places.

**ABOVE**
A vintage car outside Holbrook's Wigwam Motel

**RIGHT, CLOCKWISE FROM TOP**
Two of the teepees that make up the motel; beds inside a teepee

**"The Wigwam Motel is a crescent of 15 white concrete teepees, each one with a vintage car parked out front."**

# JOY NEVIN

Pilot and Businesswoman

Joy Nevin wasn't your average ranch hand—or your average anything, for that matter. A Rhode Island farm girl turned World War II pilot, she brought sky-high ambition to the dusty byways of Arizona's Route 66.

After a bout of polio, Joy headed west to convalesce at a friend's ranch in Heber, Navajo County, and quickly fell for the wide-open landscape in the process. Within months, she had gone from recovering patient to roping cattle, and she never looked back. But, in true Joy fashion, that was just the beginning.

She decided to convert a truck into a rolling supply shop, and stocked it with everything a working rancher might come to need, from rope to rifle cartridges, before hitting the highway. Stockmen's Supply Service was officially born: a one-woman traveling store rolling down Route 66. Clad in jeans, boots, and a cowboy hat, Joy sold her goods with the flair of a circus ringmaster, leaving ranchers amused and amazed in equal measure.

Over time, Joy became a local legend. One day, spotting a pilot in distress overhead, she coolly orchestrated an emergency landing, sending cars racing to block traffic on Route 66 so the plane could touch down safely.

Joy eventually married a cowboy and helped run the Painted Desert Trading Post in Holbrook, where they sold rugs, jewelry, and gasoline to passing motorists. But her greatest legacy wasn't in the goods she peddled—it was in the roles she refused to accept. In an era that kept women at home, Joy carved her own path along Route 66, inspiring others to take the wheel and head west.

# LA POSADA HOTEL

HOTELS AND MOTELS

WINSLOW

With a history almost as old as the Mother Road itself, this landmark hotel preserves the legacy of a pioneering female architect from Route 66's early days. It remains one of the premier places to stay along the legendary highway.

During the 1920s, the Santa Fe Railway marched from the Midwest to the Pacific, unlocking the desert-wrapped Southwest as a top American tourist destination. In 1929, entrepreneur Fred Harvey—who later became known as "the Civilizer of the West"—set his sights on Winslow, a modest railroad town 30 minutes in the car from Holbrook, that also happened to be along Route 66.

Harvey hired contemporary architect Mary Colter (one of the few women operating in her field at the time) to design the hotel. Already celebrated for her rustic, Indigenous-inspired buildings in Grand Canyon National Park, Colter dreamt up a sprawling property that fused Mission Revival and Spanish Colonial Revival styles. From its opening in 1930, the hotel drew a stellar guest list, including showbiz heavyweights like John Wayne and Gene Autry, President Franklin D. Roosevelt, and revered physicist Albert Einstein.

It soon earned the nickname "The Last Great Railroad Hotel," but this golden era was short-lived. Railroad travel was in sharp decline, and even its prime Route 66 location couldn't save La Posada. By 1957, it had shuttered. Over time, Colter's masterpiece fell into disrepair, until the 1990s, when husband-and-wife entrepreneurs Allan Affeldt and artist Tina Mion bought and meticulously restored the property.

Mary Colter (who passed in 1958) would surely have approved of the results. The tangle of rooms and corridors are once again decked out with plant-filled alcoves; patterned Zapotec rugs; and bold, Southwest-inspired artworks. The grounds are alive with sagebrush, mesquite trees, and a rose garden bright with blooms. The 2018-opened Affeldt Mion Museum in the 1930s train depot showcases regional artworks, while the Turquoise Room restaurant dishes up plates of chicken mole and stuffed squash blossoms. It's a true Mother Road icon, enjoying a dazzling new lease on life.

**ABOVE**
Inside the foyer of the restored La Posada Hotel

**RIGHT**
The red-tiled roof and apricot-colored stucco of the hotel

# HOMOLOVI STATE PARK

INDIGENOUS HERITAGE

A 10-minute drive from La Posada Hotel, Homolovi State Park is the perfect place for a welcome stretch of the legs before hitting the road once more. Home to Ancestral Puebloan dwellings in the high desert, this site remains sacred to the Hopi.

It's thought that the ancestral Hopi people (known today as the "Hisat'sinom," or "those who lived long ago") began building Pueblo villages from around 1260. These villages were once elaborate—indicative of the advanced civilizations who lived here—with sprawling residences, plazas, and *kivas* (usually round chambers used for important ceremonies).

Today, the remains of these settlements dot the desertscape and continue to be sacred to the modern Hopi people. Of the hundreds that

can be found within the grounds of Homolovi State Park, there are two which are now open to visitors: Homolovi I and Homolovi II. Both sites offer intriguing windows into this distinctive past. Wandering around, you'll be able to spot intricate stone walls and complex foundations, while trails strike out to reveal ancient petroglyphs and pottery.

But these sites are much more than archeological relics. In 2011, the word "ruins" was dropped from the park's name to reflect the fact that it remains a living and sacred part of Hopi culture. More than 19,000 people identify as Hopi today; you can take a deep dive into that culture and heritage at the Homolovi Visitor Center, located within the park. Exhibits inside the center showcase artifacts, from baskets to tools, alongside contemporary Hopi handicrafts, like carvings and pottery.

Back outside, Mother Nature puts on a fine display in the park grounds. Homolovi is named after a Hopi word meaning "Place of the Little Hills," and those little hills are replete with myriad forms of wildlife and natural wonders. Red-tailed hawks and kestrels soar overhead, while road-runners scamper through the grasslands, and prairie dogs and pronghorn antelope make fleeting appearances across the open plains. Among these natural wonders, an afternoon in this desert park feels a world away from the kitsch curiosities of Route 66.

**ABOVE**
The foundations of a 14th-century chamber, located inside the park

**LEFT**
Walking along one of Homolovi State Park's trails with a ranger as a guide

# METEOR CRATER NATIONAL LANDMARK

NATURAL WONDERS

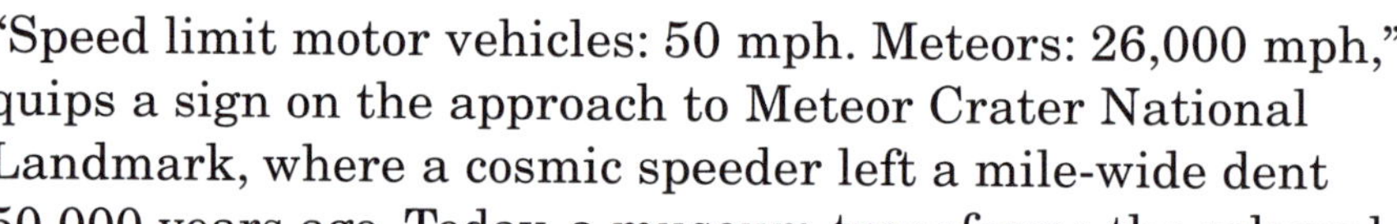

"Speed limit motor vehicles: 50 mph. Meteors: 26,000 mph," quips a sign on the approach to Meteor Crater National Landmark, where a cosmic speeder left a mile-wide dent 50,000 years ago. Today, a museum transforms the colossal impact into a daytrip.

It's not every day you get to stand on the edge of a hole made by a rock from outer space. But at Meteor Crater National Landmark near Winslow, that's exactly what you do. Just over 30 miles (48 km) from Homolovi State Park *(p202)*, this vast geological scar is one of the best-preserved meteorite impact sites on the planet, gaping nearly 1 mile (1.6 km) across and more than 550 ft (168 m) deep.

Access to the rim is via the on-site museum, from where ticketed tours with expert guides lead visitors to the crater's very edge. There, gazing into the windswept bowl of jagged rock and desert silence, it's easy to forget that you're still on Earth. Viewing platforms with mounted telescopes help bring the twisted rock formations into sharp focus. Inside the museum, you'll find fragments of the original space rock, some weighing hundreds of pounds, along with interactive exhibits and a surprisingly immersive 4D film that recreates the moment of impact (spoiler: it's loud and dramatic). Kids can test their balance on the gravity floor exhibit, simulating lunar movement, and aspiring space historians can marvel at a real Apollo 11 test capsule on loan from NASA. There's even an astronomical scavenger hunt, where younger visitors collect clues to win a souvenir.

Just down the road, the Meteor Crater RV Park and its dome-shaped convenience store offers a delightfully sci-fi detour, stocked with UFO magnets, astronaut ice cream, and plenty of alien merch. Epic and extraordinary, Meteor Crater is a reminder that sometimes, the universe really does drop in unannounced.

**RIGHT, CLOCKWISE FROM TOP LEFT**
An aerial view of the Meteor Crater; an Apollo test capsule on display at the crater; taking in the epic proportions of the Meteor Crater

BOILER PLATE 29
PLEASE KEEP OFF
APOLLO TEST CAPSULE

# WALNUT CANYON NATIONAL MONUMENT

INDIGENOUS HERITAGE

A portal to the past, this national monument protects a series of ancient cliff dwellings. It's a worthy detour off the Mother Road before arriving in the city of Flagstaff *(p209)*, and promises history and natural beauty in spades.

Walnut Canyon can trace its beginnings back around 5 to 6 million years, when the snaking Walnut Creek began sculpting layers of ancient limestone rock. Over the course of millennia, the canyon began to take its modern shape: a dramatic ravine that plunges downward for about 394 ft (120 m). Its craggy walls are speckled with greenery, the north-facing slopes carpeted with Douglas firs, and the south-facing walls heaving with juniper and ponderosa pines. Above the canyon floor, hawks and falcons soar, while coyotes and bobcats stalk the rugged canyon rim.

Indigenous peoples have moved through the area for millennia, while it's estimated that the first permanent inhabitants moved here in around 600 CE. The Sinagua—who are descendants of modern Puebloan peoples, including the Hopi—are thought to have lived here for around 800 years. From about 1100, they began forging cliff dwellings that remained until the modern day.

The fruits of their labor are the intricate, multiroom structures hewn from limestone and mortar that can still be seen today. The strenuous, 1-mile (1.6-km) Island Trail is the best way to spot around 25 cliff dwellings. Walkers can tackle the copious stairs along the trail, which drops down almost vertically for 184 ft (56 m) before heading up and out the same way, to see these vestiges of the past, where snug limestone alcoves and crumbling remnants of old walls and doorways remain. Archeologists cannot be certain why the Sinagua left Walnut Canyon—it might have been drought, crop failure, or the threat of warfare—but these material echoes of their culture continue to live on.

**ABOVE**
A tour group descending to the floor of the ravine

**RIGHT**
Hiking through the verdant Walnut Canyon

# FLAGSTAFF

CITIES OF 66

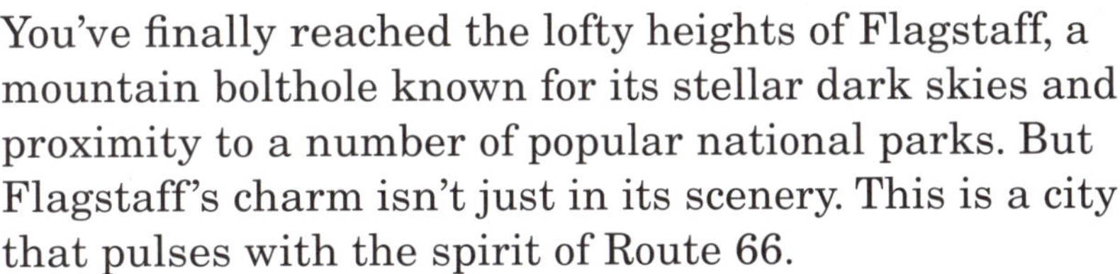

You've finally reached the lofty heights of Flagstaff, a mountain bolthole known for its stellar dark skies and proximity to a number of popular national parks. But Flagstaff's charm isn't just in its scenery. This is a city that pulses with the spirit of Route 66.

Nestled amid towering pines and framed by rugged mountain peaks, Flagstaff proudly wears the nickname "The City of Seven Wonders." As Route 66 winds its way into this lively college town, you're instantly embraced by some of the Southwest's most breathtaking natural treasures. Wrapped in the vast green arms of the Coconino National Forest, Flagstaff boasts the dramatic silhouette of the snowcapped San Francisco Peaks to the north. Just 80 miles (129 km) away, the awe-inspiring South Rim of the Grand Canyon beckons, while closer still the fiery red cliffs of Oak Creek Canyon create a picture worthy of a painting. History and nature intertwine here, with Walnut Canyon's ancient cliff dwellings, the mysterious volcanic landscapes of Sunset Crater, and the sprawling ruins of Wupatki National Monument all within easy reach.

## ON THE ROAD AGAIN

Route 66 charges through the heart of Flagstaff—striking the city from east to west—revealing a store of classic Americana along the way, from old-school motels to neon-trimmed diners. The roots of the Mother Road run deep here. Flagstaff was the location for the first-ever Muffler Man, an axe-wielding giant built to represent the folkloric North American lumberjack Paul Bunyan, installed in 1962. And while this Muffler Man is now long gone, countless other reminders of Route 66's heyday remain. Take the Coconino Rowhouse, a once-bustling boarding house that was constructed from local Moenkopi sandstone in 1926. Next door, the Sierra Vista Motel is equally evocative; although it's long been shuttered, its striking red sign remains evocative of a bygone era. Flagstaff's Our Lady of Guadalupe Chapel has been around as long as Route 66. A fine example of the American Craftsman architectural style, dating back to 1926, the church is a stone's throw from 66's original alignment.

LEFT
Biking around the smooth bends of Route 66 near Flagstaff, Arizona

As you make your way west, the road reveals further retro flourishes. With its exterior drenched in red neon and crowned by a giant clock, the Galaxy Diner could be pulled straight from the 1950s. Inside, you'll find checkered floors, a rainbow jukebox, and a sweeping chrome bar. The decor is an act of pure nostalgia: though the diner opened back in 1958, the vintage details enjoyed today were added to the diner only in the 1990s. Nearby, the 1960s Americana Motor Hotel offers up more mid-century appeal. Renovated and reopened in 2023, the space is all disco balls and retro artwork, while the swimming pool adds a splash of its own with eye-popping color.

## WINDOW TO THE STARS

Not all of Flagstaff's wonders can be enjoyed at ground level. The inky, star-spangled skies that stretch above the town earned the area an accreditation as the world's first International Dark Sky City (which it was designated back in 2001). Fittingly, Flagstaff is also the home of the Lowell Observatory's Astronomy Discovery Center. It was here that young astronomer Clyde Tombaugh discovered Pluto in 1930. His breakthrough compounded the work of master astronomer Percival Lowell, after whom the observatory is named. On a tour of the site, you'll see the famous Lawrence Lowell Astrograph, the 13-inch (33-cm) telescope through which Tombaugh first spied the dwarf planet, as well as the impressive Clark Refractor, which Lowell used to study Mars.

**ABOVE LEFT**
The Galaxy Diner, replete with an old-school jukebox and neon lighting

**ABOVE RIGHT**
Bright sun loungers lining the pool at the Americana Motor Hotel

## COLLEGE TOWN VIBES

Plenty more studious folks have followed in Lowell and Tombaugh's footsteps. At its heart, Flagstaff is a college town, home to Northern Arizona University and its more than 28,000 students. That lends the city a lively energy, and also means there are many patrons for its countless downtown coffee shops, bars, vintage stores, and arty boutiques. A favored hangout is the Mother Road Brewing Company, a funky brewery that leans into its Route 66 theme with its collection of vintage license plates and artwork depicting the open road.

Before you sink a pint, though, it's worth stopping off at the Museum of Arizona. This thoughtful museum offers a deep dive into cultures of the Colorado Plateau, touching on Indigenous heritage, natural history, and even Route 66 itself. It's an ideal way to ground yourself in a city where the past and present are fueled by its connection to the Mother Road.

**BELOW**
The interior of Flagstaff's Mother Road Brewing Company, filled with quirky decor

HISTORIC
U S
66

A section
of Route 66,
near the town
of Seligman

# SELIGMAN

TOWN OF 66

**The tiny town of Seligman, an hour's drive from Flagstaff and passing through leafy woodland, punches well above its weight when it comes to Route 66 attractions, offering a joyride through some weird and wonderful businesses.**

Seligman might just be the closest thing you'll find to a Route 66 theme park—minus the roller coasters, and with a lot more Betty Boop memorabilia. The town's charm comes from the way its 445 residents have wholeheartedly embraced the retro-fueled revival of their little stretch of the Mother Road.

The result? A place where nearly every square inch is devoted to preserving, celebrating, and selling the spirit of mid-century Americana. No wonder, then, that it was used as the inspiration for the fictional town of Radiator Springs in Pixar's *Cars*.

It's here that road-trippers will find the original Route 66 Gift Shop, opened by local barber-turned-Route-66-conservator Angel Delgadillo *(p217)* and his wife, Vilma. A slice of the road's history comes with the option to buy a snow globe, or three, in this emporium of tchotchkes. A stone's throw away is the Rusty Bolt, a treasure trove crammed with mannequin vignettes, retro signage, and enough Elvis ephemera to launch a second Graceland. Across the street, you'll find the Roadkill Café, which may not sound appetizing at first but is where you can tuck into a mean buffalo burger before knocking back a drink at a rootsy saloon bar plastered with fluttering dollar bills and Route 66 memorabilia.

Be sure to make a stop at Delgadillo's Snow Cap Drive-In, the brainchild of Angel's brother, Juan. Built from railroad scraps back in 1953, it's part café, part slapstick sketch. The sign on the door reads "Sorry, We're Open," and the condiment bottles may or may not squirt string. Order a refreshing cup of flavored crushed ice, and don't be surprised if it comes with a side of rubber chicken.

There's nowhere else quite like Seligman along Route 66, a place where the entire town joins in on the theatrics, blurring the line between commerce and stage set.

**ABOVE**
Bikers parked up outside Seligman's Route 66 Gift Shop

**RIGHT**
A classic car outside a vibrant Seligman mural

**"A slice of the road's history comes with the option to buy a snow globe, or three."**

ANGEL
US
66

PEOPLE OF THE ROAD

# ☆ ANGEL DELGADILLO ☆

The "Guardian Angel of Route 66"

Most people breeze through Seligman in northern Arizona without giving it too much thought—just another speck along the ribbon of Route 66. But for local Angel Delgadillo, this small town was worth staging a fight of David and Goliath proportions.

Born in 1927, Delgadillo grew up at the curb of the Mother Road. He watched Seligman thrive during the golden age of American road trips, then opened his own barbershop in 1950, snipping hair while chrome-finned Chevys rumbled past the window. That easygoing rhythm came to an abrupt halt in 1978, when the newly built I-40 bypassed the town entirely. It siphoned off the traffic and, as Angel later reflected, handed a death sentence to his treasured hometown.

Where others packed up, Angel dug in. In 1987, he founded the Historic Route 66 Association of Arizona from the tiny back room of his barbershop, igniting a new era for the road with his trademark optimism and tireless spirit. Part activist, part storyteller, he sparked a preservation movement: rallying communities, promoting tourism, and advocating for the road's historic designation, all with a glinting pair of scissors in hand.

Angel retired in his 90s, but a cutout of the smiling barber now stands beside his cutting chair (similar cutouts pop up in Seligman's Route 66 Gift Shop). Tourists come to snap a selfie with the man who never lost faith in the Route 66 dream, even when the road itself seemed all but lost.

# OATMAN

TOWN OF 66

**An hour's drive from Seligman *(p214)*, and about 40 minutes from the California border, is the almost abandoned mining town of Oatman. Just 100 people call this place home—them, and a large population of free-roaming donkeys.**

After gold was discovered in the Black Mountains in 1863, mines quickly sprang up in the region, and, by the early 1900s, Oatman was booming with some 10,000 residents. The town's mines produced a total of more than $10 million worth of gold in their heyday, making Oatman one of the largest producers of gold in the American West. Money talks, and, in 1939, Hollywood royalty arrived: Clark Gable and Carole Lombard honeymooned at the Oatman Hotel, which still stands today.

Not long after the newlyweds left, World War II ushered in a nationwide war effort. The government ordered the town's gold mines to shut down in order to prioritize other metals critical to the war. Though less financially prosperous, Oatman continued to flourish, with Route 66 cutting straight through the town and bringing passing trade with it. However, like so many places, it was bypassed by I-40, and, by the 1960s, almost all of the town's residents had abandoned it for bigger communities with more job prospects.

Distant relatives of those who worked the mines are still around, however, though perhaps not the ones you might think. Descendants of once-domesticated beasts left behind after the miners threw down their pickaxes, wild *burros* (the Spanish word for donkeys) now run this town. Officially protected as living symbols of the pioneer spirit, they saunter in daily from the rocky Black Mountains, clogging traffic, nosing into car windows, and demanding snacks from startled tourists (compressed hay pellets can be purchased from various stores).

Today, Oatman greets travelers with Route 66 nostalgia, Wild West quirk, and twice-daily gunfights staged by local actors dressed in cowboy garb. That, and the chance to meet the town's unofficial mayor, Walter the Wonder Donkey, hand-reared by shop owners Brad and Kelly Blake after being orphaned in 2019. It's little wonder half a million inquisitive visitors roll through Oatman each year—perhaps you'll be one of them.

**ABOVE**
A donkey peering into one of Oatman's stores

**RIGHT, CLOCKWISE FROM TOP**
Oatman, with the Black Mountains beyond; a donkey warning sign

**"Half a million inquisitive visitors roll through Oatman each year."**

# CALIFORNIA

This is the home stretch. But before travelers reach the long-awaited California coast, they have to contend with a lonely drive through the sunbaked Mojave Desert, with little but the occasional Joshua tree, roadside relic, or old ghost town for company. From the desert outpost of Barstow, the highway veers south and crosses the San Gabriel Mountains, where the seemingly endless sprawl of Los Angeles glitters ahead. L.A.'s historic Route 66 alignments give road-trippers a glitzy send-off, carrying them down Sunset Boulevard, through the palm-lined roads of Beverly Hills, and beyond, before the Pacific Ocean finally comes into view. The lights of Santa Monica Pier's Ferris wheel twinkle ahead, inviting travelers to switch off their engine, breathe in fresh sea air, and take in the final scene of an unforgettable road trip.

# CALIFORNIA

**DISTANCE**
315 miles (507 km)

**DRIVE TIME (NONSTOP)**
Approx. 6 hours

**LANDSCAPE**
The flat, arid Mojave Desert gives way to the San Gabriel Mountains before the metropolis of Los Angeles leads drivers to the coast.

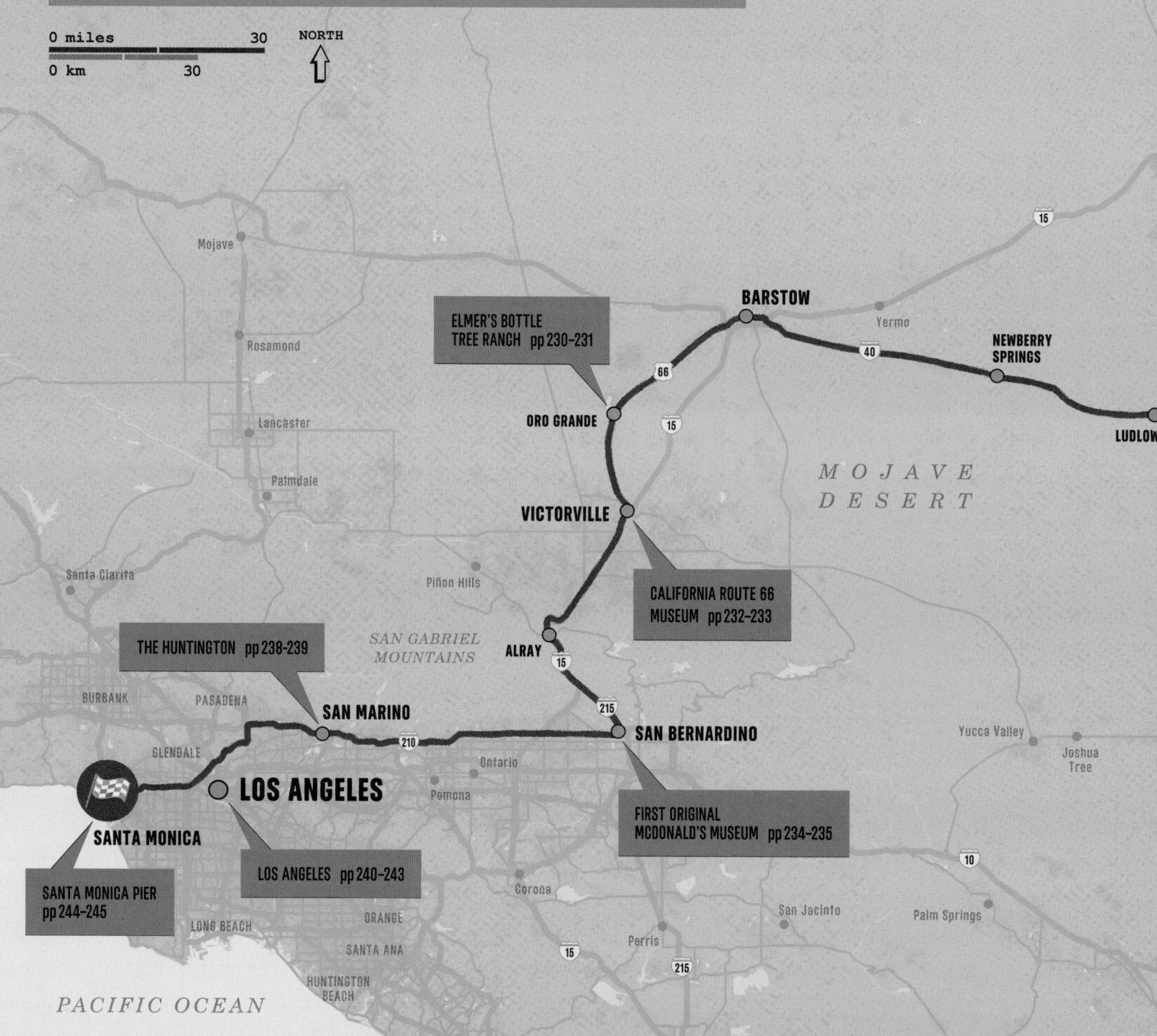

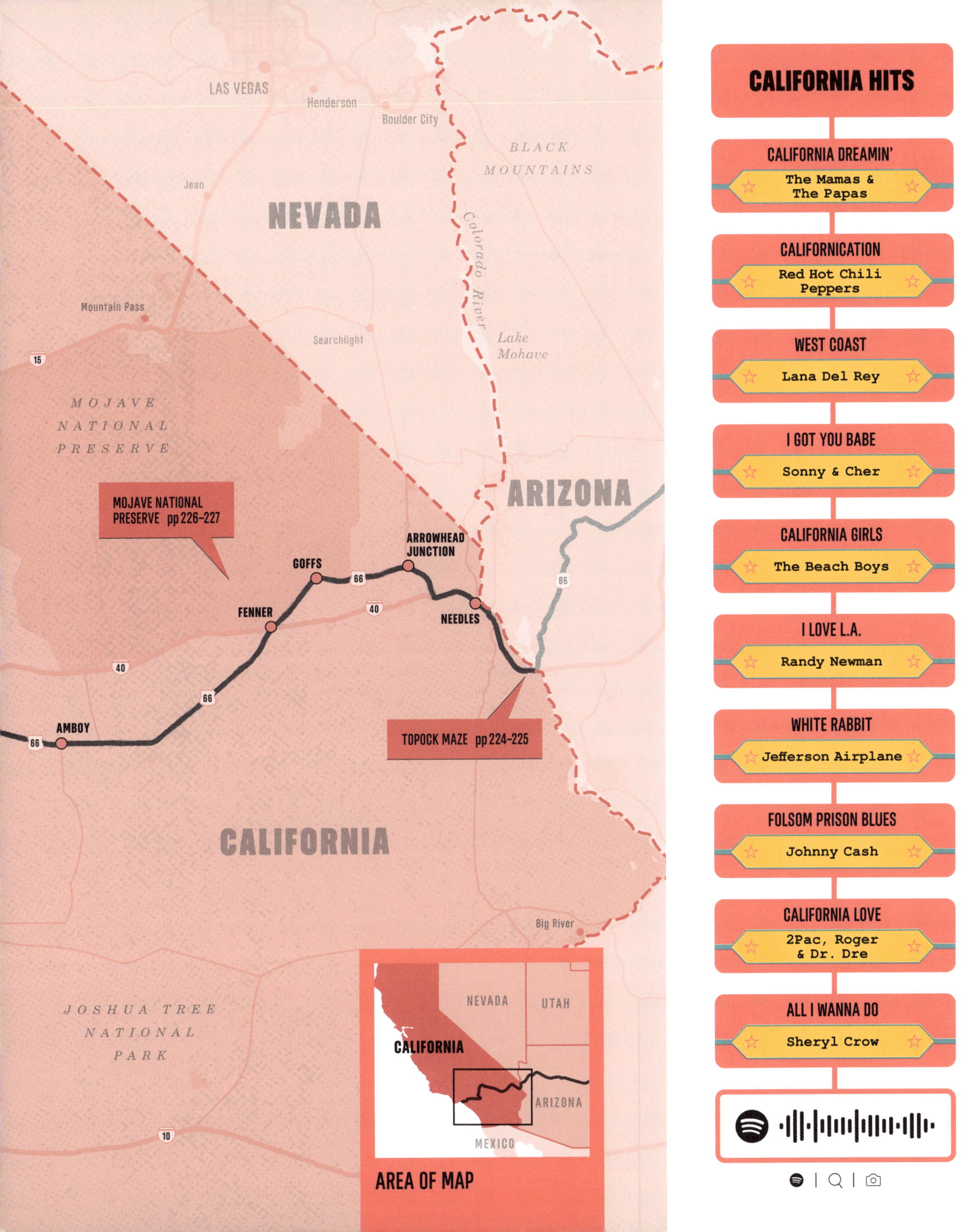
LAS VEGAS
Henderson
Boulder City
BLACK MOUNTAINS
Jean
NEVADA
Colorado River
Mountain Pass
Searchlight
Lake Mohave
15
MOJAVE NATIONAL PRESERVE
MOJAVE NATIONAL PRESERVE pp 226–227
ARIZONA
ARROWHEAD JUNCTION
GOFFS
66
66
FENNER
40
NEEDLES
40
66
AMBOY
66
TOPOCK MAZE pp 224–225
CALIFORNIA
Big River
JOSHUA TREE NATIONAL PARK
10
NEVADA
UTAH
CALIFORNIA
ARIZONA
MEXICO
AREA OF MAP
CALIFORNIA HITS
CALIFORNIA DREAMIN'
The Mamas & The Papas
CALIFORNICATION
Red Hot Chili Peppers
WEST COAST
Lana Del Rey
I GOT YOU BABE
Sonny & Cher
CALIFORNIA GIRLS
The Beach Boys
I LOVE L.A.
Randy Newman
WHITE RABBIT
Jefferson Airplane
FOLSOM PRISON BLUES
Johnny Cash
CALIFORNIA LOVE
2Pac, Roger & Dr. Dre
ALL I WANNA DO
Sheryl Crow

# TOPOCK MAZE

INDIGENOUS HERITAGE

NEEDLES

Almost as soon as drivers cross the state border into California, they'll pass a curious "maze" that unfolds right off Route 66. This phenomenon remains a sacred site and is a further reminder that—long before roads were constructed—this land belonged to the region's Indigenous peoples.

In the depths of the Mojave Desert, the Topock Maze unfolds in a series of raised gravel strips. Well, it's called a maze, but most believe these wavy dirt tracks, called windrows, were nothing of the sort. Most archeologists date the markings back around 600 years and the oral histories of the Indigenous Fort Mojave people—whose ancestral lands span California, Arizona, and Nevada—corroborate this, too. The nation's stories describe the site as a kind of sacred portal, through which departed spirits must pass. It's also said that the souls of revered Indigenous warriors would have been cleansed here before they returned home from battle.

Whatever its inspiration, the roadside "maze" is still a site of significance to Indigenous peoples, particularly as it is shrinking; though the site once stretched for 2,178 sq ft (202 sq m), it has reduced in size by 80 percent. This is in part thanks to modern development, including the construction of Route 66 in the early 20th century and, before that, the Southern Pacific Railroad, in the 1880s (with some arguing that the gravel tracks were, in fact, made during the construction of the railroad). Add in desert winds and a series of monsoons, and the Topock Maze is, sadly, slowly being erased from the landscape. Despite this, the maze's mystique persists, inviting passing motorists to ponder over its purpose.

**RIGHT**
Zigzagging across the desert, and sitting alongside the highway, the mysterious Topock Maze, near Needles

**"The roadside 'maze' is still a site of significance to Indigenous peoples."**

LUNCH
ROOM

# MOJAVE NATIONAL PRESERVE

NATURAL WONDERS

Vast and untamed, the Mojave National Preserve feels like one of California's best-kept secrets. A 50-minute drive from Topock Maze *(p224)*, this dramatic desert landscape offers a change of pace from the quirkier towns and attractions of Route 66.

A short drive from the historic highway, the Mojave National Preserve spans a whopping 2,410sq miles (6,243 sq km), with dramatic scenery at every turn. Motorists pass collections of crooked, almost cartoon-like, Joshua trees (a lynchpin in California's desert ecosystem) before finding themselves marveling at giant volcanic cinder cones or vast, shimmering dunes. And among it all, slow-moving desert tortoises—a threatened species—amble around, even crossing the highway (so be vigilant).

The preserve's southern boundary is traced by the original Route 66 alignment, with an easy access point near the Mojave Trails National Monument (and Barstow, if you're driving west to east). From there, Kelbaker Road weaves deep into the preserve, connecting it to the ghost town of Amboy. Once a busy Route 66 stopover, Amboy is now mostly deserted, known best for the retro-futuristic glow of the Roy's Motel and Café sign—a striking relic of mid-century Americana. But history in the Mojave isn't limited to fading highways. The restored Kelso Depot, a 1920s Spanish Mission–style train station, now serves as a visitor center and a gateway to the preserve's human history (though the center is under refurbishment at the time of publication).

Don't be afraid to stay a while. Mojave National Preserve is as stellar at night as it is during the day, with dark, unpolluted skies that make for unforgettable stargazing. The preserve offers three main campgrounds—Mid Hills, Black Canyon, and Hole-in-the-Wall—that welcome both tent campers and RV travelers eager to sleep under a blanket of stars. Such an experience might just be the true magic of the Mojave.

**CLOCKWISE FROM TOP**
Joshua trees, a defining feature of the Mojave Preserve; Kelso Depot's original lunch room sign hanging outside the visitor center today; a trail of footsteps crossing Kelso sand dunes

Road Runner's Retreat
RESTAURANT

A fading
road sign for
Road Runner's
Retreat in the
ghost town
of Amboy

R R

# ELMER'S BOTTLE TREE RANCH

ODDITIES AND AMERICANA

**ORO GRANDE**

One man's trash is another man's treasure, or so the saying goes. Few places embody that idea better than Elmer's Bottle Tree Ranch, just north of Victorville, a whimsical forest of "trees" crafted from salvaged iron and thousands of colorful glass bottles, collected over decades by a father and son.

It all began in the 1950s, when a young Elmer Long went camping in the Mojave Desert with his father. Driving the family Jeep across the dry expanse, they stumbled upon all kinds of abandoned odds and ends—rusted car parts, scraps of metal, and, most notably, glass bottles of many different colors. Elmer Long Sr. began collecting these desert relics, a hobby that slowly overtook his home and rubbed off on his son. When his father passed away, Elmer inherited his vast collection. The question was: what to do with it all?

In 2000, Elmer began experimenting with junk modeling (literally creating art from junk), a popular pastime in the Mojave. Drawing inspiration from his father's collection, he welded iron "trees" and decorated them with bottles in every shape and color. One tree led to another, then another, until a surreal, shimmering forest emerged along Route 66. Over time, the Bottle Tree Ranch became a roadside icon and a symbol of creativity, resilience, and reuse. Not that it's all bottles here. Tucked away throughout the ranch are vintage typewriters, handmade wind chimes, and even the original family Jeep that once hauled the father and son's desert finds. Every object tells part of a story—a tribute not only to Elmer's vision but to a shared journey between parent and child.

With his flowing wizard's beard and jaunty hat, Elmer became something of a Route 66 legend. When he passed away in 2019, his son Elliott took up the mantle, continuing to preserve and share this colorful legacy with travelers from around the world.

**LEFT**
Long-abandoned scrap, rusting road signs, and bottle trees galore at Elmer Long's self-styled "ranch"

# CALIFORNIA ROUTE 66 MUSEUM

MUST-VISIT MUSEUMS

**VICTORVILLE**

**ABOVE**
A hodgepodge of old wooden signage displayed inside the museum

While there are Americana-filled museums up and down the highway, there's something about California's tribute to Route 66 that perfectly captures the Mother Road's spirit of freedom and reinvention.

Just 15 minutes down the highway from the quirky charm of Elmer's Bottle Tree Ranch *(p231)*, the city of Victorville emerges as a long-time desert transportation hub. In the heart of Old Town, the California Route 66 Museum has been welcoming travelers for three decades, offering an immersive journey through the history of America's most legendary road. Stepping inside is like entering a time capsule. Displays trace the evolution of Route 66, from its early beginnings, through the droughts of the Dust Bowl era and the devastation of World War II, to the route's eventual decommissioning in 1985. But this isn't just a museum about the road—it's also a love letter to the Mojave Desert town of Victorville and its role in shaping the story of the West.

The exhibits are a tactile blend of highway history and Americana. Vintage gas pumps and license plates line the walls, alongside old road maps and weathered postcards that tell of long trips and roadside stops. One highlight is a beautifully restored 1917 Ford Model T—the car that put America on wheels. Affordable, reliable, and revolutionary, it was a common sight on Route 66 in its infancy. Nearby, a classic Volkswagen camper van evokes the free-spirited energy of the 1960s, when the road became a symbol of counterculture and escape. There's even a retro diner setup, complete with red vinyl booths and a working jukebox. Fittingly, the building used to be home to the Red Rooster Café, which made a cameo in the 1980 film *The Jazz Singer*, with Neil Diamond playing a young musician chasing his dreams.

**"One highlight is a beautifully restored 1917 Ford Model T—the car that put America on wheels."**

**ABOVE**
The museum, occupying a former roadside diner, in Old Town Victorville

# FIRST ORIGINAL MCDONALD'S MUSEUM

MUST-VISIT MUSEUMS

SAN BERNARDINO

Nothing says "road trip" like the famous golden arches, beaming from the roadside with the promise of a tasty refuel. McDonald's is one of the U.S.'s most iconic fast-food chains—and where better to delve into its history than the place where it all began, on the homestretch of Route 66?

San Bernardino hides a tasty slice of history, on the site that changed the way that America—and much of the world—eats. This is the place where brothers Richard and Maurice McDonald flipped their first burgers and cooked up a global phenomenon in the world's very first McDonald's.

Back in 1940, long before Ronald and his clown shoes came onto the scene, the McDonald brothers introduced the "Speedee Service System" to their drive-in. It was a revolutionary concept built around efficiency and affordability. At first, their menu included everything from barbecue ribs to pork sandwiches, served by a fleet of carhops in jazzy uniforms. But in the late 1940s, they stripped things back to the basics: burgers, fries, and sodas, all served up in minutes. Fast food, as we know it, was officially born.

Today, the site is home to the First Original McDonald's Museum, a playful, free-to-enter shrine dedicated to the humble quarter pounder, opened by Albert Okura *(p237)* in the late 1990s. Out front, giant sculptures of burgers and hot dogs greet visitors. Inside, glass cabinets are stuffed with decades' worth of Happy Meal toys and vintage menus, largely donated by customers from around the world. You'll find plenty of international curiosities, like 1960s Hawaiian saimin noodle soup boxes and a miniature plastic Snoopy figurine from the Czech Republic. Props from *The Founder*, the biopic about Ray Kroc, who helped the brothers build their empire, are also on display, along with a gold-painted Big Mac immortalized as modern art. Spend an hour or two marveling at this fast-food temple. You'll leave full of fun facts—with room left for a cheeseburger, of course.

**ABOVE**
The original 1960s take-out bag

**RIGHT, CLOCKWISE FROM TOP**
Outside the first-ever McDonald's; a costume for Grimace, one of the chain's early characters; glass tumblers on display

## “Burgers, fries, and sodas all served up in minutes. Fast food, as we know it, was born.”

HISTORIC SITE OF THE
McDonald's
ORIGINAL McDONALD'S
15¢
SELF SERVICE SYSTEM
HAMBURGER
have Sold OVER 1 MILLI
SAN BERNARDINO - CALIFORNIA
1398

# ALBERT OKURA 

Restaurant owner and philanthropist

A visit to the First Original McDonald's Museum *(p234)* is a chance to raise a McFlurry to Albert Okura, a fast-food tycoon and Route 66 preservationist. Okura, a third-generation Japanese American, grew up in Los Angeles in modest circumstances. He began working in the fast-food industry after dropping out of college, rising through the ranks at Burger King and other chains. Inspired by Richard and Maurice McDonald's story, he set out to launch his own restaurant, and, in 1984, he and his brother-in-law opened Juan Pollo, a Mexican-style rotisserie chicken restaurant that would grow to 25 locations across Southern California.

Okura's ambitions extended beyond business; he was passionate about preserving American roadside traditions, too. In 1998, he bought the site of the original McDonald's after learning it had fallen into disrepair. Okura saw potential in the dilapidated spot and transformed it into the eccentric museum seen today, a celebration of not just McDonald's but the culture of quick-service dining in general. He was also fascinated by Route 66 and the stories left behind in its fading roadside towns. When I-40 started to divert traffic away from the Mother Road, the once-busy town of Amboy in the Mojave Desert faded into a ghost town. Okura saw something worth saving, so in 2005, he bought the place and hoped to bring Roy's Motel and Café—a classic mid-century stop—back to life.

Albert Okura passed away in 2023, but, like many who champion Route 66, he has left his mark. Travelers along Route 66 can stop in Amboy, where a mural of Okura watches over the highway, or call in at the First Original McDonald's Museum. Both are fitting tributes to a man who believed that history—even in the form of fast-food wrappers—is worth saving.

PEOPLE OF THE ROAD

PEOPLE OF THE ROAD

# THE HUNTINGTON

MUST-VISIT MUSEUMS

**SAN MARINO**

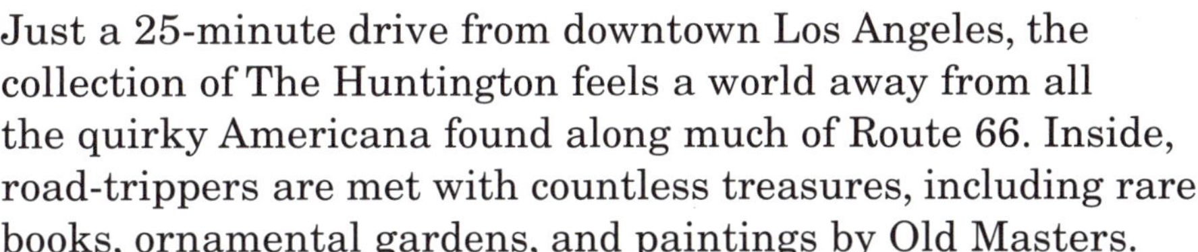

Just a 25-minute drive from downtown Los Angeles, the collection of The Huntington feels a world away from all the quirky Americana found along much of Route 66. Inside, road-trippers are met with countless treasures, including rare books, ornamental gardens, and paintings by Old Masters.

Before Route 66 was in the thick of its road-tripping heyday, America's railroad industry was booming. That's how railroad magnate Henry Edwards Huntington made his fortune, and he—along with his wife, Arabella—spent that fortune amassing a fine collection of artworks, curios, and books. After some two decades, Huntington bestowed his store of treasures along with his entire estate upon the public in 1919.

Fast-forward to today, and that same sprawling estate is now a book-worm's dream. The Huntington holds some 12 million items in the Library, from medieval masterpieces such as Geoffrey Chaucer's *The Canterbury Tales* to poetry-filled tomes from the likes of William Blake, plus precious political works, including the first manuscript of Benjamin Franklin's autobiography.

It's not just about books, either. Around 50,000 objects fill the Art Museum, spanning two millennia of art history. Visitors can pore over works by European Masters like Thomas Gainsborough or drink in decorative arts produced by the lauded William Morris company. American greats are well represented, with Edward Hopper's striking coastal landscape *The Long Leg* and one of Andy Warhol's iconic Campbell's soup cans *Small Crushed Campbell's Soup Can (Beef Noodle)* on display.

Outside, the grounds artfully unfold into a tangle of carefully curated gardens, covering more than 200 acres (80 hectares) of land with flora from all over the world. Cacti and succulents fill the Desert Garden, while classical Chinese garden Liu Fang Yuan (translating to "the garden of flowing fragrance") is a swirl of bridges, waterfalls, and striking pavilions. The Japanese Garden is similarly intricate and traditional, with bonsai trees and a teahouse. Altogether, it makes for a refined detour from the Mother Road's famous kitsch—one well worth taking.

**LEFT, CLOCKWISE FROM TOP**
The tranquil pond of the Chinese Garden; a flower-lined path of the Desert Garden; paintings by Thomas Gainsborough on display

Civic Center
Hill Street
EXIT ONLY
EXIT 24C
110 SOUTH
Downtown
Stadium Way
Dodger Stadium
1/4 MILE
EXIT 24D

# LOS ANGELES

CITIES OF 66

Los Angeles is a city that needs no introduction. After driving for thousands of miles and through hundreds of towns, its vast sprawl signals your arrival in one of America's most iconic cities. A place of constant movement and change, L.A. has always marked a turning point—a city where journeys shift gears and new chapters begin.

The glittering promise of Los Angeles—land of Hollywood royalty, vintage convertibles, and lapped by the sun-drenched Pacific—is the perfect place to draw to a close weeks spent on the road. As is common for Route 66, there have been several alignments in the Los Angeles area over the past century, but the most iconic iteration plows its way through the Arroyo Seco valley (on what's now the Arroyo Seco Parkway, State Route 110). That first glimpse of L.A.'s cluster of soaring skyscrapers from this busy, multilane section of the road is a sure sign that you've made it to the legendary metropolis and you're closing in on the finishing line of Route 66.

From the Arroyo Seco Parkway, you'll strike through Downtown L.A. before pushing southwest onto glitzy Sunset Boulevard, that palm-lined home of Hollywood glamour filled with everything from legendary music venues to high-end boutiques. Next, you'll cruise onto Santa Monica Boulevard, as you inch toward the highway's showstopping finale: the sweeping beaches that open to the Pacific Ocean and the colorful Santa Monica Pier *(p244)*. There's no need to rush, though. The City of Angels has plenty of classic pit stops and hidden gems that offer a taste of the Mother Road's storied past.

**ABOVE**
Enjoying a sunset beside one of the palm-lined roads of Los Angeles

**LEFT**
Traffic lining Arroyo Seco Parkway, one of the U.S.'s oldest freeways

**"You'll reach the original terminus of Route 66, right on the intersection between 7th Street and Broadway."**

**BELOW LEFT**
Outside the historic Clifton's Republic today, with its fading old signage

**BELOW RIGHT**
The impressive Art Deco interior of L.A.'s Union Station

## NOSTALGIA HIT

As you enter pockets of L.A. on historic Route 66, you'll feel as though you've driven straight into a time gone by. Arranged along the Arroyo Seco Parkway, Highland Park certainly has the feel of a neighborhood that's been plucked from a past decade. Here, gloriously faded motels and flashes of neon signs line the road. The beloved Highland Theatre may have shuttered in 2024, but its hulking sign remains a symbol of the Roaring Twenties, while Galco's Soda Pop Stop promises a hit of nostalgia with its rows of fizzy drinks in a dizzying array of colored bottles.

Continuing southwest, the route brings you close to one of Downtown L.A.'s most recognizable buildings. It's easy to see why the 1939-built Union Station—a dazzling blend of Art Deco, Mission Revival, and Spanish Colonial architectural styles—is hailed as "The Last of the Great Train Stations." It still functions as a working rail station, in case you want to zip off somewhere after your Route 66 trip wraps up.

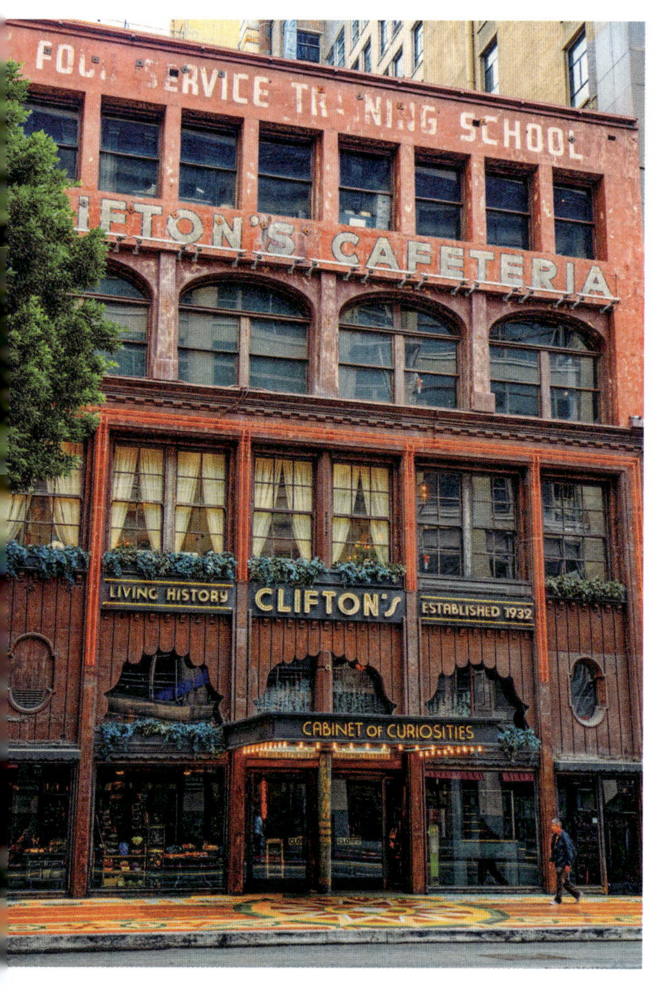

## MOTHER ROAD EATS

After a continued push southwest, you'll reach the original terminus of Route 66, right on the intersection of 7th Street and Broadway. Although the route no longer ends here, this spot endures as a foodie landmark. Beginning life in the 1930s, when the Mother Road was booming, Clifton's Brookdale (now Clifton's Republic) was a cafeteria and Route 66 venue renowned for its whimsical decor—think dense thickets of faux trees and cascading waterfalls. It was also well known for offering free meals to locals who couldn't pay, as well as being a key venue for Black travelers, as listed in the Green Book *(p40)*. Eventually, it transitioned from cafeteria to nightclub, filled with a tangle of elaborately decorated lounges before closing for a short while. It reopened again in 2024, retaining its playful, woodsy 1930s interiors, now replete with fanciful decor.

It's worth making a few short detours from the original alignment to get your teeth into other historical bites nearby—several vintage diners pepper the surrounding area. Rae's Restaurant is a 1950s confection; the epitome of the mid-century American diner, it's complete with classic red diner booths, turquoise bar stools, and bold neon sign outside. Just off Santa Monica Boulevard, you'll also find the Apple Pan, a no-frills 1947 diner with a traditional U-shaped counter and a menu full of belt-busting sandwiches and pies. Then it's onto the city of Santa Monica *(p244)*, just west of downtown Los Angeles, the final stop on America's most historic highway...

**ABOVE LEFT**
The neon diner sign for the Apple Pan

**ABOVE RIGHT**
A bustling crosswalk on Santa Monica Boulevard

# SANTA MONICA PIER

HERITAGE SITES

SANTA MONICA

There's no better place to end a legendary road trip—or to simply feel like you're at the end of one—than the Santa Monica Pier. This is the symbolic finale to Route 66, where the historic highway meets the blue shimmer of the Pacific.

**ABOVE**
The End of the Trail sign, marking the symbolic finishing point of Route 66

**RIGHT**
The sun setting over Santa Monica Pier

Few places scream California louder than this cheerful, chaotic boardwalk. But the pier hasn't always been about carnival rides and cotton candy. When it first opened in 1909, its purpose was far less glamorous: it was built to dispose of sewage into the ocean. Thankfully, that practice ended in the 1920s. Despite its first intention, people were drawn to the pier, from the very beginning. On opening day, navy warships paraded offshore, surfers rode the waves nearby, and locals came to fish, stroll, and soak in the surroundings. It was clear the pier was destined for greater things.

In 1916, entrepreneur and carousel builder Charles Looff started to construct an adjoining amusement pier, replete with an ornate merry-go-round, roller coasters, and a fun house. The new pleasure pier captured imaginations immediately. Over the decades, it evolved, passing through various owners and boasting additions like the lavish La Monica Ballroom.

By the 1970s, however, the good times had faded. The pier had become weatherworn and forgotten, and plans were drawn up to demolish it entirely. But the community wouldn't let it go without a fight. Locals rallied to save their beloved landmark, and their efforts paid off: the pier was rescued and restored, becoming stronger than ever. It enjoyed a further renaissance in 1996, with the opening of Pacific Park, a retro amusement park full of kitschy charm. The Pacific Wheel, a solar-powered Ferris wheel glowing with color, soon became an icon in its own right. Add in snack shacks, a roller coaster, and arcade games, and you've got the ultimate nostalgic playground.

In 2009, the now-famous "End of the Trail" sign was installed, cementing the pier as Route 66's unofficial, photogenic finale. Technically, the highway's endpoint is a few blocks inland at Olympic and Lincoln Boulevards, but let's be honest: this is where the journey really ends. With the sun setting over the Pacific, waves crashing below, and the lights of the Ferris wheel spinning above, the Santa Monica Pier offers a cinematic closing scene to America's greatest road trip.

Stunning ocean views running parallel to the road in Santa Monica

# PREPARING FOR YOUR ROAD TRIP

While there's plenty to be said for just jumping in your car and hitting the road, planning ahead will ensure you make the most of your Route 66 road trip. To help you prepare, we've put together some handy pointers.

## PLANNING A ROAD TRIP

Stretching across eight states, Route 66 is 2,400 miles (3,862 km) long in total. It's possible to drive the entire route in about 35 hours, but, to enjoy all the road has to offer, two to three weeks is recommended. Alternatively, some road-trippers break the route down into small stretches, exploring a few states over the course of a single week.

To plan a successful Route 66 road trip, you'll need to consider everything from which attractions you want to visit and what kind of distance you'll cover, right down to the specific details surrounding car insurance, gas stops, and accommodations (especially in rural locations). For safety, plan regular stops to avoid growing tired behind the wheel and check the weather in advance—some roads are hazardous in winter months. Since the highway spans multiple states, do remember that laws and speed limits vary between them.

## CHOOSING YOUR VEHICLE

If you have your own vehicle, there's little stopping you from heading out onto Route 66. If you don't, renting a car is generally a simple task, though companies often only rent to drivers over 21 years old, and most impose a daily surcharge on drivers under the age of 25. Major rental agencies along the route include Enterprise, Budget, Hertz, and Avis, and you'll find rental centers at airports, in cities, and even in mid-sized towns.

Driving an electric vehicle (EV) is a great way to minimize your road trip's environmental impact, but it does require a bit more planning. Though the route's EV infrastructure is improving, charging stations remain far less common than gas stations. PlugShare, ChargePoint, and Electrify America are all helpful apps for finding charging points.

## DOCUMENTS AND INSURANCE

International drivers will need a valid driver's license from their home country and an International Driving Permit. Both documents should be in your possession whenever you're in your vehicle. If driving your own car, keep your registration and insurance documents in the vehicle; if renting, do the same with all rental documentation.

It's important to buy the most comprehensive insurance in case you require roadside assistance. Overseas visitors planning to rent a vehicle can easily purchase car insurance from the rental agency. Should you get in an accident, dial 911 for emergency assistance.

Health care in the U.S. is good but expensive. Overseas visitors should secure comprehensive medical travel insurance before arrival in the U.S.

## RULES OF THE ROAD

The legal driving age varies by state, ranging from 16 to 18 years old. Speed limits can also vary by state but, broadly speaking, they range from 35 to 65 mph (56.3 to 104.6 km/h), with 55 mph (88.5 km/h) commonly enforced by U.S. police. Always pay attention to the posted limit and keep an eye out for tolls, which typically appear on Interstates and major highways. Stop signs should also be obeyed.

Using your cell phone while driving is banned in most states, so have your route planned before setting off. Rules also apply to drinking: the blood alcohol content limit in the U.S. is 0.08 percent. Under no circumstances should you drive under the influence of drink or drugs.

If your car breaks down or has a mechanical issue, move off the road or into the emergency lane, turn on your hazard lights, and call for roadside assistance.

## ROAD CONDITIONS

Around 85 percent of the original highway is still drivable, though signage has largely disappeared and GPS often doesn't recognize Route 66 as a continuous path. Plan your route in advance on a navigation system by selecting "avoid motorways" and entering in the attractions you want to visit.

It's not unusual to drive for an hour without coming across a gas station, so fill up whenever you can. Check road conditions online before heading out, and drive with care as many roads are potholed. Winter weather in mountainous areas, particularly in the likes of Arizona and New Mexico, can make travel difficult or impossible, and climate change is increasingly creating hazards like wildfires and flash floods. State department of transportation websites and social media feeds are reliable sources of information on road closures, accidents, and anything else that might impact your drive.

## USEFUL WEBSITES

**GasBuddy**
A must for Route 66 road-trippers, this app and website locates nearby gas stations and finds the best deals on gas.
*gasbuddy.com*

**what3words**
This locations app helps 911 teams find people in emergencies, especially those in rural areas.
*what3words.com*

**Route 66 Navigation**
Offers offline directions and real-time updates on road closures and detours.
*route66navigation.com*

**Route 66 Planner**
A planning tool for identifying driving times and distances, and locating hotels en route.
*theroute-66.com*

# INDEX

Page numbers in **bold** refer to main entries.


## A

Accidents, road 248, 249
Acoma Pueblo, NM 183
Adrian, TX 154–5
Affeldt, Allan 200
Albuquerque, NM 168, 172, **178–81**
Amarillo, TX 144–51, 152
Amboy, CA 227, 237
Americana *see* Oddities and Americana
American Giants Museum (Atlanta, IL) 29, **30–31**
Antelope Canyon, UT 194
Ant Farm 144
Arapaho people 107
Arcadia, OK 124–5
Arizona **188–219**
Arroyo Seco Parkway (Los Angeles, CA) 241
Ash Grove, MO 78–9
Asian District (Oklahoma City, OK) 129
Atchison, Topeka, and Santa Fe Railroad 179
Atlanta, IL 30–31
Auckerman, Chris 89
Autry, Gene 184, 200
Avery, Cyrus 6, 76, 81, 111, **114–15**, 172

## B

Baker, Joel **28–9**, 30
Barbed wire 142–3
Baxter, John 96
Baxter Springs, KS **96–7**
Becklund, Lisa 121
Berghoff's (Chicago, IL) **25**
Big Texan Steak Ranch and Motel (Amarillo, TX) **146–7**
Birthplace of Route 66 Festival (Springfield, MO) 77
Black Americans 6, 9, 40–41, 42–3, 45, 113, 123
Black Dog 96
Black Mountains, AZ 218
Blake, Brad and Kelly 218
Bland, Joe 73
Blue Hole (Santa Rosa, NM) **166–7**
Blue Swallow Hotel (Tucumcari, NM) **160–61**, 163
Blunt, General James 97
Bogart, Humphrey 184
Breakdowns 248
Buck and Stella Atom (Tulsa, OK) 112
Bunyan, Paul 16, 209

## C

Caddo people 106
Cadillac Ranch (Amarillo, TX) 144–5
Cahokia Mounds State Historic Site (Collinsville, IL) 50–51
California 220–47
  Dust Bowl migration to 153
California Route 66 Museum (Victorville, CA) 232–3
Camino Real de Tierra Adentro 172, 179
Camping, Mojave Desert, CA 227
Canyon Road (Santa Fe, NM) 174
Car rental 248
*Cars* 38, 84, 90, 141, 155, 214
Carson, Colonel Kit 194
Cars on the Route (Galena, KS) 90–91
Carthage, MO 82–3
Central Avenue (Albuquerque, NM) 179, 180–81
Chacon, Nanibah 181
Chelsea, OK 104–5
Cherokee people 106, 107, 112
Cheyenne people 107
Chhoker, Raj and Harpreet 134, 135
Chicago, IL 9, 22–5
Churches and chapels
  Loretto Chapel (Santa Fe, NM) 173
  Our Lady of Guadalupe Chapel (Flagstaff, AZ) 209–210
  San Felipe de Neri church (Albuquerque, NM) 181
  San Miguel Chapel (Santa Fe, NM) 173
Civil Rights Act (1964) 41
Civil War 70, 96–7
Clark, William 59
Coconino National Forests, AZ 209
Cole, Nat King 6, 16, 184
Collinsville, IL 48–51
Colter, Mary 200
Cook, Lt. Ralph 97
Coral Court Motel (St. Louis) 66–7
Cowboys 109, 112, 127–8, 146, 166, 218
Cozy Dog Drive In (Springfield, IL) 16, 36–7, 38
Creek people 106, 112
Crites, Lt. John 97
Cuba, MO 72–3
Cyrus Avery Route 66 Memorial Bridge (Tulsa, OK) 114

## D

Dalí, Salvador 175
Davis, Lowell 82
Dean, James 160
Delaware people 106
Delgadillo, Angel 214, **216–17**
Delgadillo, Juan 214
Delgadillo, Vilma 214
Depew, OK 120–21
Devil's Rope Museum (McLean, TX) **142–3**
Diamond, Neil 232
Dill, Lester 70
Diners and dining spots 14
  Apple Pan (Los Angeles, CA) 243
  Berghoff's (Chicago, IL) **25**
  Big Texan Steak Ranch and Motel (Amarillo, TX) **146–7**
  Clifton's Brookdale (Republic) (Los Angeles, CA) 41, 243
  Cozy Dog Drive In (Springfield, IL) 16, **36–7**, 38
  Delgadillo's Snow Cap Drive-In (Seligman, AZ) 214
  Dog House Drive In (Albuquerque, NM) 181
  Donut Drive-In (St. Louis) 60
  Galaxy Diner (Flagstaff, AZ) 210
  Galco's Soda Pop Stop (Los Angeles, CA) 242
  Ike's Chilli (Tulsa, OK) 111
  Living Kitchen Farm and Dairy (Depew, OK) **120–21**
  Lou Mitchell's (Chicago) **25**
  Midpoint Café and Gift Shop (Adrian, TX) **154–5**
Diners and dining spots (cont.)
  Mother Road Brewing Company (Flagstaff, AZ) 211
  M'tucci's Bar Roma (Albuquerque, NM) 181
  Pink Elephant Antique Mall (Livingston, IL) **46–7**
  Plaza Cafe (Santa Fe, NM) 171
  Pops 66 Soda Ranch (Arcadia, OK) **124–5**
  Rae's Restaurant (Los Angeles, CA) 243
  Roadkill Café (Seligman, AZ) 214
  Ted Drewes Frozen Custard (St. Louis) 60
  Truck Stop 40 (Sayre, OK) **134–5**
Donkeys (Oatman, AZ) 218–19
Donnegan, William 42
Douglas, Kirk 184
Driver's licenses 248
Drought 152–3
Dust Bowl 6, 17, **152–3**, 232

## E

Eagle-Picher Strike **92–3**
*Easy Rider* 144
Ed Galloway's Totem Pole Park (Foyil, OK) **104–5**, 107
Einstein, Albert 200
Electric vehicles 248
Elmer's Bottle Tree Ranch (Oro Grande, CA) **230–31**, 232
El Rancho Hotel (Gallup, NM) **184–5**
El Reno (OK) **130–31**
Emancipation Proclamation 35
Emergency assistance 248
*End of the Trail* (Fraser) 128
Eureka, MO 68

## F

Federal-Aid Highway Acts (1921/1956) 16
Federal Center (Chicago, IL) 25
Fields, William Jason 76
First Original McDonald's Museum (San Bernardino, CA) **234–5**, 237
Flagstaff, AZ 16, **208–211**

Food and drink *see* Diners and dining spots
Ford, Linda 121
Ford Model T. 232, 233
Fort Blair Historic Site, KS 97
*Founder, The* 234
Four Corners region 182
Foyil, OK 104–5
Franklin, Benjamin 239
Fraser, James Earle 128

## G

Gable, Clark 218
Galena, KS 88–93
Galloway, Ed 104
Gallup, David L. 186
Gallup, NM 184–7
Gary's Gay Parita (Ash Grove, MO) **78–9**
Gas stations 249
Gateway Arch (St. Louis, MO) 59, 65
Gemini Giant (Wilmington, IL) 26–7
George Galanis Multicultural Center (Gallup, NM) **186–7**
Ghost roads 66
Ghost towns 38, 66, 82, 227, 237
Global warming 131
Glorieta Pass, NM 168, 169
Grand Canyon, AZ 192, 200, 209
*Grapes of Wrath, The* (Steinbeck) 17, 153
Great Lakes Indigenous peoples 106, 107
Great Migration 42, 45
Great Plains 168
Greektown (Chicago) 25
Greenlease, Bobby 67
Green, Victor Hugo/Green Book **40–41**, 42, 243
Greenwood (Tulsa, OK) **113**
Greetings from Galena Mural (Galena, KS) **88–9**
Griffith, D.W. 184
Grundy, Stacy 42, **44–5**
Guthrie, Woody 113

## H

Hackberry, AZ 38
Hall, Carl 67
Hammit, Brenda 155
Hamons, Lucille **132–3**
Hannett, Arthur T. 180
Harvey, Fred 200
Heady, Bonnie 67
Heritage sites 13
  Baxter Springs, KS **96–7**
  Cahokia Mounds State Historic Site (Collinsville, IL) **50–51**
  Fort Blair Historic Site, KS 97
  Lincoln Home National Historic Site (Springfield, IL) **32–5**
  Red Oak II (Carthage, MO) **82–3**
  Route 66 State Park (Eureka, MO) **68–9**
  Santa Monica Pier, CA 241, 243, **244–5**
Highland Park (Los Angeles, CA) 241–2
Hispanic heritage, Albuquerque, NM 179, 180–81
History
  100 years of Route 66 16–17
  Birthplace of Route 66 **76–7**
  Eagle-Picher Strike **92–3**
  Green Book **40–41**
  Indigenous heritage **106–7**
  Navajo and Hopi Culture **194–5**
  New Mexico's Pueblos **182–3**
  Route 66 and the Dust Bowl **152–3**
  Route's changing course **64–5**
  *Twisters* and Tornados **130–31**
Holbrook, AZ 196–7, 199
Hollywood 184, 218, 241
Homolovi State Park (Winslow, AZ) **202–3**
Hopi culture **194–5**, 202–3, 206
Hopper, Edward 239
Hotels and motels 15
  Americana Motor Hotel (Flagstaff, AZ) 210
  Big Texan Steak Ranch and Motel (Amarillo, TX) **146–7**
  Blue Swallow Hotel (Tucumcari, NM) **160–61**, 163
  Chase Park Plaza Hotel (St. Louis, MO) 60
  Coral Court Motel (St. Louis, MO) **66–7**
  El Don Motel (Albuquerque, NM) 181
Hotels and motels (cont.)
  El Rancho Hotel (Gallup, NM) **184–5**
  El Rey Court (Santa Fe, NM) 41, 171–2
  El Vado (Albuquerque, NM) 181
  La Posada Hotel (Winslow, AZ) 41, **200–201**
  Monterey Motel (Albuquerque, NM) 181
  Westward Ho! Motel (Albuquerque, NM) 181
  Wigwam Motel (Holbrook, AZ) **196–7**
Houser, Fran 155
Huggins, W.A. 160
Huntington, Henry Edwards 239
Huntington, The (San Marino, CA) **238–9**

## I

Illinois **18–53**
Indigenous peoples/heritage 6, 9, 15, 50–51, **106–7**
  Albuquerque, NM 179, 181
  arts and crafts 173–4
  Blue Hole (Santa Rosa, NM) 166
  Cahokia Mounds State Historic Site (Collinsville, IL) **50–51**
  George Galanis Multicultural Center (Gallup, NM) **186–7**
  history and traditions **106–7**
  Homolovi State Park (Winslow, AZ) **202–3**
  Navajo and Hopi Culture **194–5**
  New Mexico's Pueblos **182–3**
  Oklahoma City, OK 128
  Pecos National Historical Park, NM **168–9**
  Topock Maze (Needles, CA) **224–5**
  Tulsa, OK 112
  Walnut Canyon National Monument, AZ **206–7**, 209
Insurance 248
International Driving Permit 248
Interstate Highway System 66, 67, 76

## J

Jack Sisemore RV Museum (Amarillo, TX) **150–51**
*Jazz Singer, The* 232
Jim Crow laws 40, 41
Johnson, Ike and Ivan 111
Joshua trees 227

## K

Kansas **84–99**
Kante, Joni and Ben 117
Keen, Louis 72–3
Kerouac, Jack 144
Kroc, Ray 234

## L

Landon, Alf 93
Land Rush (1889) 106, 113, 127
La Posada Hotel (Winslow, AZ) **200–201**
Lathan, Dr Gina 42, **44–5**
Lewis, Chester 196
Lewis, Meriwether 59
LGBTQ+ scene 9
  Oklahoma City, OK 129
  Santa Fe, NM 171
Lincoln, Abraham 33–5, 42
Lincoln, Mary Todd 33, 34
Lindsay, Vachel 35
Living Kitchen Farm and Dairy (Depew, OK) **120–21**
Livingston, IL 46–7
Lochapoka people 112
Lombard, Carole 218
Long, Elliott 231
Long, Elmer 231
Looff, Charles 244
Los Angeles, CA 9, **240–43**
Lou Mitchell's (Chicago, IL) **25**
Lowell Observatory and Astronomy Discovery (Flagstaff, AZ) 210–211
Lowell, Percival 210, 211

## M

MacArthur Bridge (St. Louis, MO) 64
McDonald, Maurice and Richard 234, 237
McKinley Bridge (St. Louis, MO) 64

McLean, TX 142–3
Mailer, Norman 22
Main Street America program 142
Maps
Arizona 190–91
California 222–3
Illinois 20–21
Kansas 86–7
Missouri 56–7
New Mexico 158–9
Oklahoma 102–3
Route 66 10–11
Texas 138–9
Marsh, Stanley 144
Martin, George R.R. 175
Mason, Fred 78
Meadow Gold Mack (Tulsa, OK) 112
Medwick, Joe 73
Meow Wolf 175
Meramec Bridge (MO) 66
Meramec Caverns (Sullivan, MO) **70–71**
Meramec River 66
Meteor Crater National Landmark, AZ **204–5**
Mexican–American War 172
Midpoint Café and Gift Shop (Adrian, TX) **154–5**
Mies van der Rohe, Ludwig 22
Military Park (Oklahoma City) 129
Milk Bottle Building (Oklahoma City, OK) 129
Mining 92–3, 218
Mion, Tina 200
Mississippian culture 50
Mississippi River 59, 65, 106
Missouri **54–83**
Mojave Desert, CA 224
Mojave National Preserve, CA **226–7**
Mojave Trails National Monument, CA 227
Monks Mound (Cahokia) 50, 51
Monroe, Eva Carroll 42
Monument Valley, AZ/UT 194
Morris, William 239
Motels *see* Hotels and motels
Muffler men 13, 26–7, 29, 30, 111, 112, 209
Murals 88–9, 129, 164–5, 181
Muscogee people 112
Museums and galleries 13
Abraham Lincoln Presidential Museum (Springfield, IL) 35
Affeldt Mion Museum (Winslow, AZ) 200
Amarillo Area Motorsports Hall of Fame (Amarillo, TX) 151
American Giants Museum (Atlanta, IL) 29, **30–31**
Baxter Springs Heritage Center & Museum (Baxter Springs, KS) 96
California Route 66 Museum (Victorville, CA) **232–3**
Cars on the Route (Galena, KS) **90–91**
DECOPOLIS (Tulsa, OK) 111
Devil's Rope Museum (McLean, TX) **142–3**
El Rancho de las Golondrinas (Santa Fe, NM) 172
First Americans Museum (Oklahoma City, OK) 128
First Original McDonald's Museum (San Bernardino, CA) **234–5**, 237
Galena Mining & Historical Museum (Galena, KS) 89, 93
Gary's Gay Parita (Ash Grove, MO) **78–9**
George Galanis Multicultural Center (Gallup, NM) **186–7**
Georgia O'Keefe Museum (Santa Fe, NM) 174–5
Greenwood Cultural Center (Tulsa, OK) 113
Greenwood Rising History Center (Tulsa, OK) 113
History Museum (Springfield, MO) 77
Homolovi Visitor Center, AZ 203
House of Eternal Return (Santa Fe, NM) 175
The Huntington (San Marino, CA) **238–9**
Indian Pueblo Cultural Center (Albuquerque, NM) 179
Jack Sisemore RV Museum (Amarillo, TX) **150–51**
Joliet Area Historical Museum (Wilmington, IL) 26
Museums and galleries (cont.)
Lowell Observatory and Astronomy Discovery (Flagstaff, AZ) 210–211
Meteor Crater National Landmark 204
Museum of Arizona (Flagstaff, AZ) 211
Museum of Contemporary Native Arts (Santa Fe, NM) 174
Museum of Indian Arts & Culture (Santa Fe, NM) 174
National Cowboy & Western Heritage Museum (Oklahoma City, OK) 127–8
National Hellenic Museum (Chicago, IL) 25
National Hispanic Cultural Center (Albuquerque, NM) 179
National Museum of Transportation (St. Louis, MO) **61**, 67
New Mexico History Museum (Santa Fe, NM) 172
New Mexico Museum of Art (Santa Fe, NM) 174
Route 66 Association of Illinois Hall of Fame and Museum (Pontiac, IL) 38
Route History Museum (Springfield, IL) **42–3**, 45
Sky City Cultural Center (Acoma Pueblo, NM) 183
Tower Station and U-Drop Inn (Shamrock, TX) **140–41**
Uranus Sideshow Museum (St. Robert, MO) 74
Will Rogers Memorial Museum (Claremore, OK) 109
Woody Guthrie Center (Tulsa, OK) 113
Music 11


## N


National Association for the Advancement of Colored People (NAACP) 42
National Museum of Transportation (St. Louis) **61**, 67
Natural wonders 15
Blue Hole (Santa Rosa, NM) **166–7**
Natural wonders (cont.)
Meramec Caverns (Sullivan, MO) **70–71**
Meteor Crater National Landmark, AZ **204–5**
Mojave National Preserve, CA **226–7**
Pecos National Historic Park **168–9**
Petrified Forest National Park, AZ **192–3**, 196
Navajo Code Talkers 187
Navajo culture **194–5**
Needles, CA 224–5
*Negro Motorist Green Book, The* **40–41**
Nelson, Scott 94
Nevin, Joy **198–9**
New Mexico **156–87**


## O


Oak Creek Canyon, AZ 209
Oatman, AZ **218–19**
Oddities and Americana 14
Cadillac Ranch (Amarillo, TX) **144–5**
Ed Galloway's Totem Pole Park (Chelsea/Foyil, OK) **104–5**, 107
Elmer's Bottle Tree Ranch (Oro Grande, CA) 132, **230–31**
Greetings from Galena Mural (Galena, KS) **88–9**
The Red Rocker (Cuba, MO) **72–3**
Tee Pee Drive-in (Sapulpa, OK) **118–19**
Uranus (St. Robert, MO) **74–5**
Oil industry 111
O'Keefe, Georgia 174–5
Oklahoma **100–135**
Oklahoma City, OK **126–9**
Okura, Albert 234, **236–7**
Old Chain of Rocks Bridge (IL/MO) 17, 52–3, 59, 65
Old Oraibi, AZ 195
Old Riverton Store (Riverton, KS) **94–5**
Old State Capitol (Springfield, IL) 35
Oro Grande, CA 230–31
Osage people 106, 112
Ottawa people 106
Ozark Trails 114

## P

Pacific Wheel (Santa Monica, CA) 244
Painted Desert, AZ 192
Palace of the Governors (Santa Fe, NM) 172
Parks and gardens
  Creek Nation Council Oak Park (Tulsa, OK) 112
  Ed Galloway's Totem Pole Park (Chelsea/Foyil, OK) **104–5**, 107
  Forest Park (St. Louis) 60, 61
  Homolovi State Park (Winslow, AZ) **202–3**
  The Huntington (San Marino, CA) 239
  Pacific Park (Santa Monica, CA) 244
  Pecos National Historical Park, NM **168–9**
  Petrified Forest National Park, AZ **192–3**, 196
  Route 66 State Park (Eureka, MO) **68–9**
Peck, Gregory 184
Pecos National Historic Park **168–9**
Pecos, NM 168–9
Petrified Forest National Park, AZ **192–3**, 196
Pink Elephant Antique Mall (Livingston, IL) **46–7**
Plains Apache 106
Plains Native Americans 107
Planning 248
Po'Pay 182
Pops 66 Soda Ranch (Arcadia, OK) **124–5**
Potawatomi people 106
Presley, Elvis 6, 141, 214
Puebloans, Ancestral 168, 169, 182, 192, 202
Pueblo Revolt 183
Pueblo tribes
  Arizona **194–5**, 206
  New Mexico 179, **182–3**

## Q

Quantrill, William 97
Quapaw people 107
Quarles, Doug and Sharon 164–5

## R

Ranft, Joe 90
Redman, Floyd 163
Redman, Lilian **162–3**
Red Oak II (Carthage, MO) **82–3**
Red Rocker, The (Cuba, MO) **72–3**
Retribution Road 180
Rio Grande Valley 168
Rittenhouse, Jack D. 65
Riverton, KS 94–5
Road conditions 249
Rogers, Will **108–9**, 111
Rookery, The (Chicago, IL) 25
Roosevelt, Franklin D. 200
Route 66
  100th anniversary 17
  100 years of Route 66 16–17
  birthplace **76–7**
  changing course 17, **64–5**
  decommissioned 17
  distance and drive time 10
  and the Dust Bowl **152–3**
  map 10–11
  *see also* History
Route 66 Corridor Preservation Program 17
Route 66 State Park **68–9**
"Route 66" (TV series) 16
Route History Museum (Springfield, IL) 42–3, 45
Rowe, Alfred 142
Rules of the road 249
RVs 150–51

## S

Saarinen, Eero 59
St. Louis, MO **58–61**, 64, 66–7
St. Robert, MO 74–5
Sanazaro, Dan 73
San Bernardino, CA 234–5
Sandburg, Carl 22
Sandia Pueblo, NM 179
San Francisco Peaks, AZ 209
Sangre de Cristo Mountains 168
San Marino, CA 238–9
Santa Domingo (Kewa) Pueblo, NM 183
Santa Fe, NM 168, 169, **170–75**, 179, 180, 183
Santa Fe Trail 168–9, 171
Santa Monica Boulevard (Los Angeles, CA) 241
Santa Monica, CA 143, 144–7
Santa Monica Pier, CA 241, 243, **244–5**
Santa Rosa, CA 172, 179
Santa Rosa, NM 166–7
Sant Fe Railway 200
Sapulpa, OK 118–19
Sat Nav 249
Sauk people 106, 107
Sayre, OK 134–5
Schuyler, Molly 146
Scuba diving 166
Seligman, AZ **214–15**, 217
Seminole people 106
Seneca people 106
Shamrock, TX 140–41
Shops and stores 14
  Baxter Flea Market (Baxter Springs, KS) 98–9
  Old Riverton Store (Riverton, KS) **94–5**
  Pink Elephant Antique Mall (Livingston, IL) **46–7**
  Route 66 Gift Shop (Seligman, AZ) 214, 217
  Rusty Bolt (Seligman, AZ) 214
  Santa Fe art market (NM) 173–4
Sinagua people 206
Sinkholes 166–7
Southern Pacific Railroad 224
Spanish colonists 168–9, 171, 172, 182–3
Springfield, IL 32–7, 42–3, 76
Springfield, MO 76–7
Springfield Race Riot (1908) 42
Springsteen, Bruce 144
Staffleback, Ma 89
Steinbeck, John 6, 17, 153
Strand, Don 36
Sullivan, MO 70
Sunset Crater, AZ 209
Suuronen, Matti 46

## T

Tee Pee Drive-in (Sapulpa, OK) **118–19**
Texas **136–55**
Threatt, Allen **122–3**
Threatt Service Station (Luther, OK) 123
Times Beach (MO) 66
Tombaugh, Clyde 210, 211
Topock Maze (Needles, CA) **224–5**
Tornado Alley 130
Tornadoes **130–31**
Totem poles 104–5
Tower Station and U-Drop Inn (Shamrock, TX) **140–41**
Tracy, Spencer 184
Troup, Bobby 16
Tucumcari, NM 160–65
Tulsa, OK **110–113**
Tulsa Race Massacre 113
Turner, Gary 78

## U

Underground Railroad 42, 70
Union Station (Los Angeles, CA) 242
Uranus (St. Robert, MO) **74–5**

## V

Victorville, CA 232–3

## W

Waldmire, Bob **38–9**, 89
Waldmire, Ed 16, 36
Wallis, Michael 90, 111
Walnut Canyon National Monument, AZ **206–7**, 209
Walter the Wonder Donkey 218
Warhol, Andy 239
Wayne, John 117, 184, 200
Websites 249
West Loop neighbourhood (Chicago, IL) 25
White, John 89
Wichita people 106
Wigwam Motel (Holbrook, AZ) 107, **196–7**
Williams, AZ 16
Williams, Leo and Lora 94
Willis Tower (Chicago, IL) 25
Wilmington, IL 26
Winslow, AZ 200–203
Woodruff, John T. 6, 76, **80–81**
World War II 187, 199, 218, 232
Wright, Frank Lloyd 25
Wupatki National Monument, AZ 209
Wyandot people 106

## Z

Zia Pueblo, NM 183

# ACKNOWLEDGMENTS


DK would like to thank the following people for their contributions to this book:

**Jacqui Agate** is a travel journalist specializing in the U.S. She is the North America Editor at *Wanderlust Magazine*, and regularly contributes US features to newspapers. Her travels have taken her from the wilds of Alaska and the cypress swamps of Florida to the music clubs of Louisiana and Mississippi.

**Zoey Goto** is a journalist covering travel and American culture. She writes for *National Geographic Traveller, Rolling Stone*, *Vogue*, *GQ*, and *Condé Nast Traveller.* Assignments have included staying in Elvis's teenage bedroom, sleeping on Dolly Parton's tour bus, and interviewing Priscilla Presley.

**Charles Usher** is an American writer and editor, born and raised in Wisconsin. He writes about travel and culture for many outlets, including DK, and specializes in the American Midwest and South Korea. He lives in Milwaukee with his wife and dog, Bono.

**Christian Northeast** has lived in Ontario, Canada, for a number of years with his family. An English-born digital collage artist with a totally distinctive approach, his art has appeared on book covers, billboards, and bottles of booze. He's worked with everyone from Nickelodeon to *The New York Times*.


**References for quotations**


**p6** line 25: Steinbeck, J. (1939). *The Grapes of Wrath*. 1st edition. London: Heinemann.

**p17** column 5, box 5, lines 2–3: Steinbeck, J. (1939). *The Grapes of Wrath*. 1st edition. London: Heinemann.

**p22** line 7: Mailer, N. (1968). *Miami and the Siege of Chicago*. 1st edition. New York: World Publishing.

**p22** line 11: Sandburg, C. (1914). "Chicago", *Poetry* (1914).

**p29** lines 12–13: Baker, J. "Rise of the Muffler Men," *Fifty Grande* (2024).

**p29** lines 19–21: Baker, J. "Rise of the Muffler Men," *Fifty Grande* (2024).

**p30** lines 14–16: Thomas, B. (2025). "Rise of the Muffler Men," *Fifty Grande* (2024).

**p35** lines 19–20: Lindsay, V. (1915) *The Congo and Other Poems*. 1st edition. New York: Macmillan Company.

**p45** lines 6–8: Provided by Dr. Stacy Grundy to DK (2025).

**p45** lines 15–19: Provided by Dr. Stacy Grundy to DK (2025).

**p65** column 4, lines 7–9: Rittenhouse, J. D. (1946). *A Guide Book to Highway 66*. 1st edition. Los Angeles: Jack D. Rittenhouse.

**p121** lines 3–4: "Livingkitchenfarm," Instagram (2024).

**p153** column 4, lines 2–7: Steinbeck, J. (1939). *The Grapes of Wrath*. 1st edition. London: Heinemann.

**p163** lines 16–17: "Blue Swallow Motel: A Historic Route 66 Legend," National Trust for Historic Preservation (2018)



The publisher would like to thank the following for their kind permission to reproduce their photographs:

(Key: a-above; b-below/bottom; c-centre; f-far; l-left; r-right; t-top)

**1221 Photography/ Zach Adams:** 44

**Alamy Stock Photo:** Media Drum World / Valentina Abinanti 130, Allen Creative / Steve Allen 107tl, Alpha Historica 187, AP Photo / The (Champaign) News-Gazette, Cindy Pringle 39, Associated Press 17bl, Todd Bannor 25, Peter Bennett / Citizen of the Planet 243, Alexandra Buxbaum 47br, Alexandra Buxbaun 43, Roger Coulam 146, Richard Cummins 232, Ian Dagnall 32, Danita Delimont 65tr, © Arnold Drapkin / ZUMAPRESS.com 175, E. Jason Wambsgans / Chicago Tribune / TNS / Alamy Live News 216, David A Eastley 90, 143b, Richard Ellis 226t, Callum Fraser 88, 105, Everett Collection Inc / Ron Harvey 107tr, David Jennings 15tl, 106, Madeleine Jettre 51, Inge Johnsson 145, Kim Karpeles 37, Betty LaRue 129cr, Giuseppe Masci 154, MJ Photography 75tl, NB / FEMA / Public domain 131cl, Niday Picture Library 65c, Parker Photography 147b, Nicola Patterson 72, 75tr, Chuck Place 183cl, T. W. Kines / NB / PR 65tl, RaksyBH 131c, Lee Rentz 104, 140br, Roberto E. Rosales / Albuquerque Journal via ZUMA Press Wire 179, James Schaedig 147tl, SilverScreen 17c, Stars and Stripes 205tr, TCD / Prod. DB / © Universal Pictures - Warner Bros. Pictures - Amblin Entertainment 131tr, Travelpix 47tl, 60bl, Jim West 113t, 128tr, Daniel Wilson 168, Eva Worobiec 155tl, ZUMA Press, Inc. 234, 235bl

**Arizona State Parks and Trails:** 202
**Shaun Astor:** 225

**AWL Images:** Walter Bibikow 128tl, Alan Copson 93cl, 164–165, Danita Delimont Stock 62–63, 147tr, 196, Christian Heeb 15bl, 77cl, 124, 197t, 208, Tom Mackie 238t, 238br, Stefano Politi Markovina 22, Mark Sykes 15r, Steve Vidler 212–213

**Bridgeman Images:** An Osage Warrior, c.1804 (colour litho), 107c, Prismatic Pictures 115

**Valerie Bromann:** 47bl

**Charles David Threatt, Threatt Filling Station Foundation:** 122

**Courtesy of El Rancho de Las Golondrinas:** Richard Gonzales 173

**Courtesy of El Rey Court Motel:** Zeb Wilson 172

**Courtesy of Hotel El Rancho:** 184

**Courtesy of Meramec Caverns:** 71

**Courtesy of Missouri State Parks:** 68b

**Courtesy of Mother Road Brewing Company:** 211

**Courtesy of Tee Pee Drive-In:** 118tl, 118tr, 118b

**Courtesy of the Americana Motor Hotel:** 210tr

**Courtesy of the Galena Mining & Historical Museum:** 92

**Courtesy of the Oklahoma Historical Society:** 132

**Courtesy of the Route History Museum:** 42

**Courtesy of the Wigwam Motel:** 197b

**Courtesy of the Will Rogers Memorial Museum:** 108

**Greg Disch:** 94

**Dreamstime.com:** Alexkane1977vi 244, 245, Raul Hernandez Balbuena 16br, Andrey Bayda 17cr, 17bc, Bdingman 148–149, Jon Bilous 13tr, 14bl, 93tl, 95t, 98–99, Natalia Bratslavsky 183tl, Clovercity 226br, Sandra Foyt 60tl, 77c, 144, 186, 201, Roberto Galan 131tl, Cynthia Hanevy 74, 75cr, Eric Laudonien 230, Miroslav Liska 235t, Mykola Lukash 205b, Minacarson 24, Raisa Nastukova 178, Sean Pavone 58, 126, 170, Photovs 176–177, Anne Richard 210tl, Pecci Roberto 219b, StockPhoto Astur 52–53, Vitalyedush 242bl, Wirestock 70, Wisconsinart 140bl

**Explore St. Louis:** Gregg Goldman 50, Cassidy Hintz 61, Mark Hermes 64,

**Steve Fitch:** 162

**Jerod Foster:** 143tl, 143tr

**Ben Geier:** 2, 7, 8, 9, 14tl, 30, 31, 36tl, 36bl, 46, 48, 78, 79, 82, 83, 91, 160, 161, 185, 228–229

**Georgia O'Keeffe Museum:** Interior. 2024. Santa Fe, New Mexico. © Georgia O'Keeffe Museum 174bl

**Getty Images:** Bettmann 40, 152, Buyenlarge 153tr, Cavan Images 12, Christopher Creese / Bloomberg 113b, Jack Delano / PhotoQuest 41c, FSA 153c, PhotoQuest 17tc, Arthur Rothstein / Library Of Congress / Stringer 93tr, Transcendental Graphics 153tl

**Getty Images / iStock:** Peter Blottman Photography 206, Jeff Goulden 203, 207, HABesen 192, Sanya Kushak 35br, Dee Liu 110, Robert Michaud 200, Miroslav_1 218, Kelly Murphy 219t, S. Greg Panosian 242br, Powerofforever 169, Sanfel 233, Boris Zec 13tl, 23, Zrfphoto 193

**Shellee Graham:** 66t

**© The Huntington:** 238bl

**Illinois Department of Transportation:** 17cl

**Historic American Buildings Survey (HABS), Historic American Engineering Record (HAER), Historic American Landscapes Survey (HALS) / Public domain:** 17tl

**Image courtesy of History Museum on the Square, Springfield, Missouri:** 80

**Image in the Public domain:** 77tl

**Joel Baker/ youtube.com/ user/AmericanGiant:** 28

**Kahn & Busk Real Estate Team:** 69

**Kansas Tourism:** 97b, Doug Stremel 95b

**Library of Congress, Washington, D.C.:** John Collier Jr. 1913–1992 17tr

**Rhys Martin/ Cloudless Lens Photography:** 17br

**Meow Wolf:** Kate Russell 174br

**New Mexico True:** 167, 180, 181

**Lauri Novak:** 140t

**NPS:** Image in the Public domain 16cl

**Oklahoma Tourism & Recreation Department:** Lori Duckworth 135t, 135bl, 135br, Saxon Smith 134cl

**Tyler Layne Photography:** 112t

**Photos courtesy of Lincoln Home National Historic Site:** 34l, 34r

**Pixels.com:** Steve Stuller 60tr, Susan Rissi Tregoning 27, 155tr

**researchroute66.org:** Image in the Public domain 16tr, 76

**Jim Ross:** 214

**Erich Schlegel:** 150

**Ryan Schude:** 235br, 236

**Shutterstock.com:** Courtney Jenckes 125, Kit Leong 205tl, Francisco Marques 77tr

**The Baxer Springs Historical Society /The Baxter Springs Heritage Center & Museum:** 96, 97t

**The Digital Research Library of Illinois History Journal:** 16c

**Unsplash:** Ryan Ancill 246–247, Jack Finnigan 243tr, Mick Haupt 112b, Joseph Menjivar 240, Devin Santiago 241, Priyanka Thakran 215, Derek Thomson 226bl, Steve Wrzeszczynski 14r

**uranusgeneralstore.com:** 13bl

**Visit OKC:** "Summer of 66" mural by © Nick Bayer 2021 / @createcostudios / www.createcostudios.com 129bl

**Visit Tulsa:** photo Henry Ninde 116–117

**Valerie Wei-Haas / Wei-Haas Creative:** 120, 121t, 121b

**Wikimedia Commons:** 1950sUnlimited, CC BY 2.0 41tl, 16cr, Ansel Adams, Public domain 182, Victor Hugo Green, Public domain 41tc, Los Angeles Illustrated Daily News staff, Public domain 153cl, Pat McDermott Public Relations, Public domain 16bl, National Archives at College Park, Public domain 183c, North Carolina State Highway Commission; North Carolina State Highway and Public Works Commission, No restrictions 16tc, William S. Soule, Public domain 107cl, Donovan Shortey from United States, CC BY 2.0 195cr, Unattributed, Public domain 35bl, Unknown Author, Public domain 16bc, 41tr, 66b, 93c, 183tr, 194, 195tl, 195tr, William S. Prettyman (18581932), Public domain 13br

**With kind permission of the Navajo County Historical Society:** 198

Maps contain data derived from OpenStreetMap, licensed under the Open Data Commons Open Database Licence by the OpenStreetMap Foundation.

**Senior Editor** Lucy Richards
**Senior Designer** Michael Curia
**Editors** Lucy Sara-Kelly, Tijana Todorinovic, Catrina Conway
**Designer** Hello Daly
**Proofreader** Ben Ffrancon Dowds
**Indexer** Helen Peters
**Picture Researcher** Claire Guest
**Senior Cartographic Editor** James Macdonald
**Publishing Assistant** Simona Velikova
**Jacket Designer and Illustrator** Christian Northeast
**Image Retoucher** Michelle Briers
**Senior Production Editor** Dave Almond
**Production Controller** Kariss Ainsworth
**Managing Art Editor** Gemma Doyle
**Editorial Director** Hollie Teague
**Art Director** Maxine Pedliham
**Publishing Director** Georgina Dee

First American edition, 2026
Published in the United States by DK Publishing,
a division of Penguin Random House LLC
1745 Broadway, 20th Floor, New York, NY 10019

First published in Great Britain in 2026 by
Dorling Kindersley Limited
20 Vauxhall Bridge Road,
London SW1V 2SA

The authorized representative in the EEA is
Dorling Kindersley Verlag GmbH. Arnulfstr. 124,
80636 Munich, Germany


26 27 28 10 9 8 7 6 5 4 3 2 1
001–355548–Feb/2026



A CIP catalog record for this book is available from the British Library.

ISBN: 978-0-2417-8474-7



Printed and bound in China
**www.dk.com**

**A note from the publisher**
Every effort has been made to ensure that this book is as accurate and up-to-date as possible at the time of going to press. Some details, however, such as the fastest tornado ever documented, are liable to change. The publishers cannot accept responsibility for any consequences arising from the use of this book, nor for any material on third-party websites. We value the views and suggestions of our readers very highly. If you notice we've got something wrong, we want to hear from you. Please get in touch at travelguides@dk.co.uk.

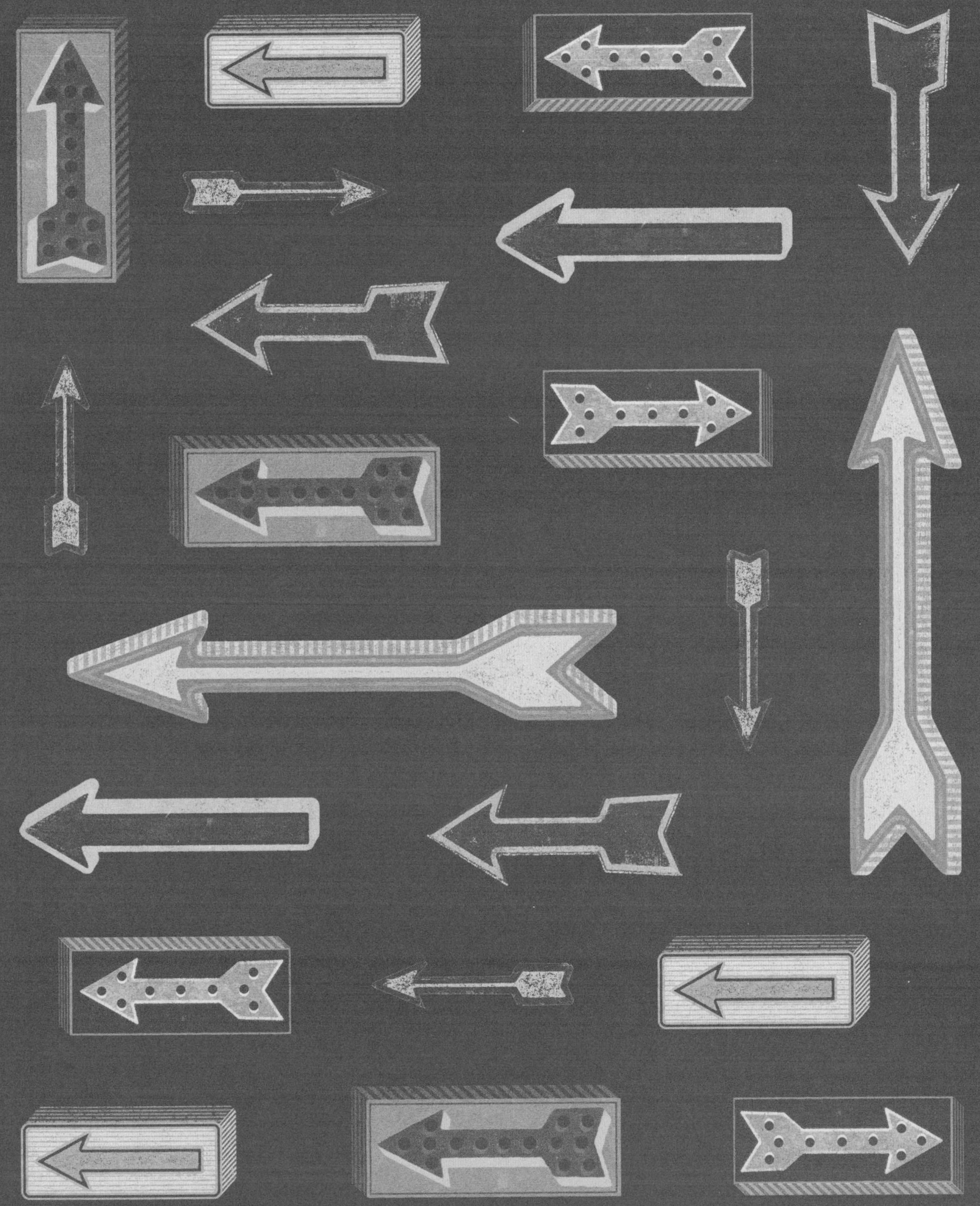

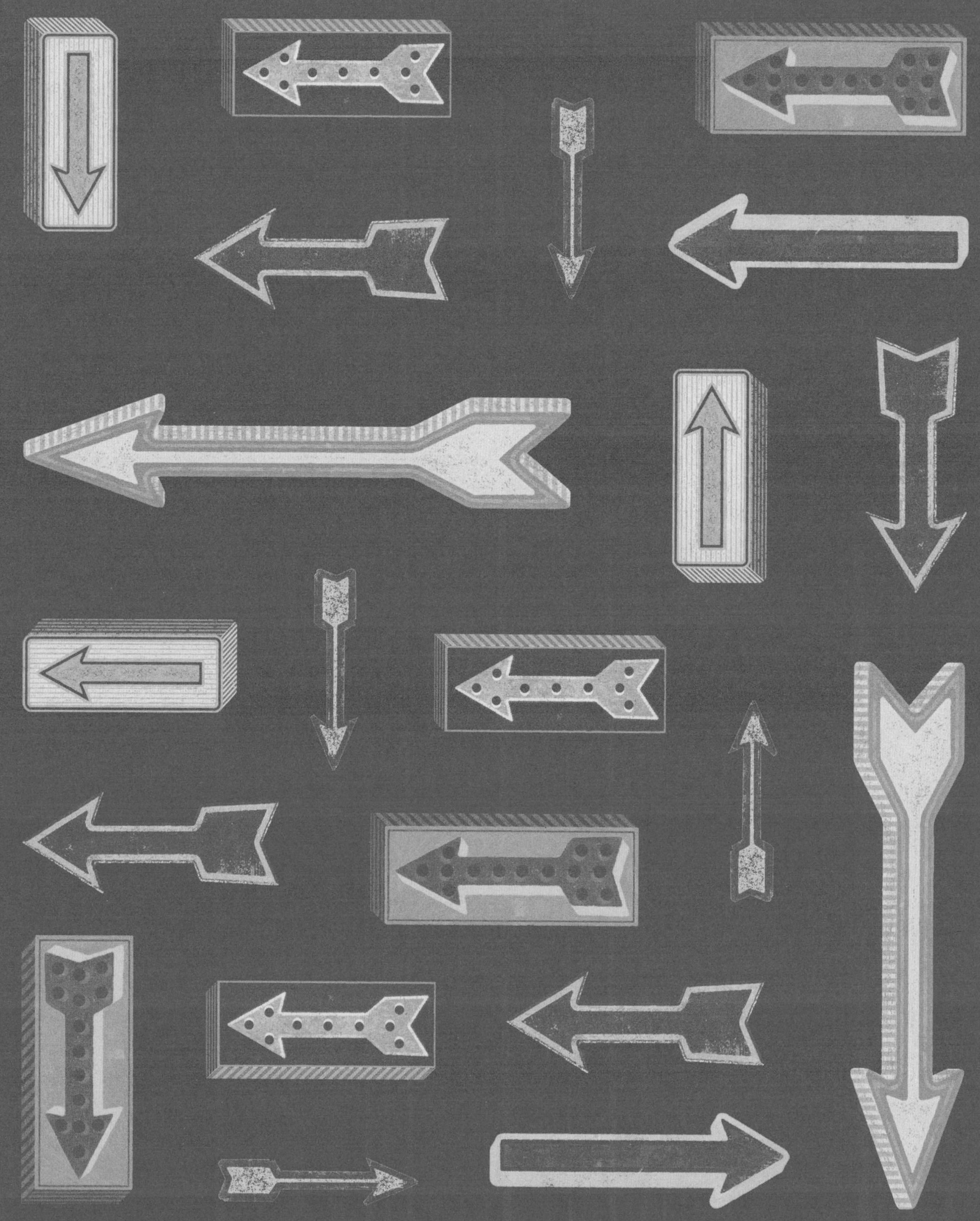